AN
IGNATIAN
SPIRITUALITY
READER

AN
IGNATIAN
SPIRITUALITY
READER

EDITED BY

GEORGE W. TRAUB, SJ

LOYOLAPRESS.
A JESUIT MINISTRY
Chicago

LOYOLA PRESS.
A JESUIT MINISTRY

3441 N. Ashland Avenue
Chicago, Illinois 60657
(800) 621-1008
www.loyolapress.com

Cover design by Judine O'Shea
Interior design by Think Design Group and Joan Bledig

Copyright acknowledgments appear on pages 275–77 and constitute a continuation of this copyright page.

Library of Congress Cataloging-in-Publication Data
An ignatian spirituality reader / edited by George W. Traub.
    p. cm.
  Includes bibliographical references and index.
  ISBN-13: 978-0-8294-2723-3
  ISBN-10: 0-8294-2723-6
1. Ignatius, of Loyola, Saint, 1491-1556. Exercitia spiritualia. 2. Spirituality—Catholic Church.
3. Catholic Church—Doctrines. 4. Spiritual exercises. I. Traub, George W.
  BX2179.L8149 2008
  248.3—dc22

                                                                            2008019602

Printed in the United States of America
08 09 10 11 12 13 Versa 10 9 8 7 6 5 4 3 2 1

For

William A. Barry, SJ
Howard J. Gray, SJ
John W. O'Malley, SJ

brothers of mine in the company
and scholars, teachers, practitioners
of Ignatian spirituality and Jesuit history

Contents

Prayer

The Spiritual Exercises

Discernment

Preface

Some years ago, my friend and colleague Leo Klein, SJ, longtime vice president for mission and ministry at Xavier University in Cincinnati, came back from a Lilly Fellows Program annual meeting with a copy of *The Lutheran Reader*. He showed it to me and said, "Maybe someday you'll do a Jesuit reader." Well, "someday" has finally arrived. When Xavier University granted me a sabbatical from directing its Ignatian Programs in the academic year 2003–2004, I began this project, and my partners in Ignatian Programs—Debra Mooney, Rebecca Schroer, and briefly Laura Keitel—carried most of the usual programming burden during the summer and fall of 2005 and the spring, summer, fall, and winter of 2006–07, while I completed it.

An Ignatian Spirituality Reader is designed first of all for those engaged in any kind of Jesuit ministry—from high schools and universities (faculty, staff, administrators, and trustees) to retreat houses, parishes, and social justice centers (staff and trustees/council), and the Jesuit Volunteer Corps, JVC International, and the Ignatian Lay Volunteer Corps. But those involved in other Catholic and Christian institutions as well as those not engaged in explicitly religious endeavors will also find valuable material here. The broader Ignatian family continues to grow.

This anthology seeks to make available from a wide variety of sources—some not readily accessible—the finest recent short essays (most of them ten to fifteen pages or fewer) on Ignatius of Loyola and Ignatian spirituality. Perhaps the most widespread and influential ministry to rise from Ignatian spirituality is the work of Jesuit education, and thus a companion volume, *A Jesuit Education Reader* (Loyola Press, 2008), is also available.

As with all anthologies, the selection process was not an easy one. Some of my favorite pieces ultimately had to be left out or just mentioned among this volume's "Further Reading" essays. In both volumes, I was guided by writings that have been particularly fruitful when used in our Ignatian Programs at Xavier University: "Manresa," the initial process of orientation for new faculty, staff, and administrators; "AFMIX," or Assuring the Future Mission and Identity of Xavier, an elective two-year process of further development that helps people carry out their particular work in a more mission-focused way; and the "Ignatian Mentoring Program," funded initially by a grant from the Lilly Fellows Program, which pairs second-year tenure-track faculty with senior faculty members who have been involved in AFMIX.

This anthology is not the sort of book you're likely to sit down and read from cover to cover. Whether you're an individual seeking further knowledge about a subject or the planner of an orientation, seminar, or other group program, I hope that the section headings will help you quickly find what you're looking for at any given time. Sometimes the placement of an essay within a section is obvious; at other times, I must admit, an essay might just as well fit under one or two other categories. So if you don't find what you seek at first glance, I encourage you to search around, use the index. Further, you may notice ideas or themes from earlier essays repeated in later sections. Because the goal is not merely to acquire information but also to assimilate it, such "Ignatian repetition" can facilitate a fuller personal appropriation of the material.

From the beginning, I have thought of this reader as a companion to my short glossary of Ignatian terms, *Do You Speak Ignatian?* At times in the anthology, I recommend reading or rereading one or more of the brief entries in *Do You Speak Ignatian?* as a prelude to a section or an individual essay, to enrich your understanding of key terms and concepts. For your convenience, that glossary is reprinted as an appendix to this volume.

A final note: for all my years as a Jesuit and my involvement with the Spiritual Exercises and Ignatian spirituality, my knowledge of resources has its limitations. And so I have been assisted in my selection for this reader by colleagues—mostly from Jesuit schools and other Jesuit ministries—who have drawn on their own expertise, experience, and practice. Needless to say, I am grateful to all the authors, editors, and publishers for making this reader possible. Publication has been aided by grants from presidents of U.S. Jesuit colleges and universities. Thanks to them and to Charles Currie, SJ, president of the Association of Jesuit Colleges and Universities, for their support.

Special thanks to George Lane, SJ, president of Loyola Press, for his support of this project from the beginning all the way through publication, and to my good editors at the press, Matthew Diener and Heidi Toboni.

May you find *An Ignatian Spirituality Reader* useful, enlightening, even inspiring!

George Traub, SJ
Xavier University
July 31, 2008
Feast of St. Ignatius of Loyola

Prologue

Introduction

Where to start a collection of readings on Ignatian spirituality? For many years now, when we welcome and orient new personnel at Xavier University as part of our Ignatian Programs/Division of Mission and Identity, we have relied on an article from *America* magazine by Ronald Modras, "The Spiritual Humanism of the Jesuits." In it, the author describes how, as a layperson teaching in a Jesuit university and trying to understand his role there, he began reading Jesuit history and asking Jesuits what made them different. Over time, he came to a conclusion: "It is precisely their spirituality, rooted in the Ignatian [Spiritual] Exercises, and their humanism, rooted in the Renaissance, that made and continue to make Jesuits distinctive."

Along the way, it became clear to Modras that Ignatian spiritual humanism was not just for Jesuits, not just for Catholics, not just for believers. For these Jesuits, these (originally) European "men for others," went out to other (non-Christian) cultures and fell in love with the people and their culture; and they dedicated themselves to the study and teaching not just of theology, but of every known academic subject and even of ones that were not known until Jesuits engaged in them, such as ethnology and cultural anthropology. Further, Modras writes about spirituality as awareness of experience; about Ignatian spirituality as engagement with the world rather than flight from it; about adaptation (today called "inculturation") as the way of Jesuit mission; about the use of pre-Christian literature, or the "classics," to educate and form students in virtue; and about Jesuit General Congregation 34, the gathering of representative Jesuits from countries and cultures around the world, which was just then taking place in 1995.

All these topics that Modras introduces—and more—have their place in this anthology. So read on.

Understanding the Terminology: Suggested Readings from *Do You Speak Ignatian?*

Before beginning the Modras article, you may want to refresh or enrich your appreciation of some fundamental concepts. Below are recommended readings of related entries in the glossary *Do You Speak Ignatian?*, which is reprinted for your convenience as an appendix to this volume.

- God
- Jesus
- Judeo-Christian Vision or Story
- Spiritual/Spirituality

Also, if you are new to St. Ignatius, Ignatian spirituality, and the Jesuits, you may also want to read the following entries:

- Laity
- Religious Order/Religious Life
- Society of Jesus
- Jesuit
- *Ratio Studiorum*
- Inculturation
- Vatican Council II

The Spiritual Humanism of the Jesuits

Ronald Modras

From *America*, 1995

This past August the U.S. Episcopal Church's house of bishops added to their liturgical calendar—of all people!—St. Ignatius Loyola. Though the action was reportedly taken without much debate, there were questions about appropriateness. Jesuits, after all, had been banned from Anglican England under penalty of death. And, along with the Council of Trent, what group more than the Society of Jesus had come to symbolize the Counter-Reformation, with its anti-Protestant, anti-Anglican defensiveness?

Bishop Frank Griswold of Chicago championed the inclusion of Ignatius in the Episcopal prayer book. He described himself as but one of many Anglicans nourished by Ignatian spirituality. The prayer authorized for the feast encapsulizes what he meant. It reads in part: "Almighty God . . . we thank thee for calling Ignatius of Loyola to the service of thy Divine Majesty and to find thee in all things."

Apparently Jesuit spirituality is not just for Roman Catholics any more. Maybe it never was. Back in 1954, Yale professor Louis Martz pointed out in his book *The Poetry of Meditation* that Ignatius's Spiritual Exercises had a marked influence both on the spirituality and popular culture of Elizabethan England. Ensuing seventeenth-century English verse bore a similar imprint. One finds it in the meditative poetry not only of Jesuit Robert Southwell but of such Anglicans as John Donne, George Herbert, and Richard Crashaw.

It seems that Jesuit treatises on meditation enjoyed the same widespread popularity in late-sixteenth-century England that they had on the continent. In England, however, the treatises had to be anonymous or falsely attributed. The Society of Jesus was outlawed, and its members were constrained to work underground. Given those undercover operations, it is not surprising that the *Oxford English Dictionary* gives as a secondary meaning to the word *Jesuit*: "a dissembling person; a prevaricator."

The Jesuits have come a long way from the connotations of *Jesuitical*, and not just because there are Anglo-Catholics who make Ignatian retreats. For some time now, Jesuit spirituality has not been just for Catholics or even just for Christians. In my fifteen years teaching theology alongside Jesuits at Saint Louis University, I have found my Jewish and Muslim students affected by it as well, not by becoming Catholic but by becoming more religious, more devoutly Jewish or Muslim.

That used to give me pause. Was this to be counted as a failure of our theology program or a success? Were the students in my classes receiving a "Jesuit education" from me, whatever that meant? And how could a non-Jesuit Roman Catholic like me help provide them a Jesuit education, not to speak of my colleagues in the theology department who are of Lutheran, Presbyterian, or Anglican traditions? I began reading about Jesuit education and found I was not the only one asking questions like these.

Suzanne Matson, a professor of English at Boston College, describes herself as an agnostic. In the fall 1994 issue of *Conversations*, a quarterly on Jesuit higher education, she writes about being compelled to confront the anomaly of her situation. Was it hypocrisy for someone like her, with more "questions than belief," to be part of a Catholic university community?

She tells about attending a Jesuit institute on faith and the academic vocation, where she and other lay faculty at Jesuit educational institutions were asked to consider how their intellectual and spiritual lives intersected. There she was introduced to some "generous and hospitable ideas" about sacramentality, community, and social justice, ideas that have since become part of the texture of her own thinking. Professor Matson describes herself as still having religious doubts, but now with fewer defenses, a new sense of identification with her Jesuit home university, and a lot of things to think about. Jesuit spirituality for self-described agnostics?

Origins and Identity

In that same issue of *Conversations*, Professor David J. O'Brien of Holy Cross looked at the issue of Catholic identity and higher education. He admitted in passing that conversations about Jesuit identity and higher education are friendlier and a "lot more civil" than those about Catholic identity. Jesuits enjoy enormous respect these days, Professor O'Brien wrote, without explaining why that is. The only reasons he suggested were that Jesuit academics are "extremely well educated" and his belief that "Jesuits have been working hard at being better known and liked." But what is there to know and like?

Professor O'Brien was writing on Catholic, not Jesuit, identity, so he could not be expected to come up with a more probing analysis of the distinction between the two. At one time, few would think there was one. Most non-Jesuits, like the dons who authored the *Oxford English Dictionary*, even most Catholics have tended to identify Jesuits as simply the vanguard of the Counter-Reformation. With the Second Vatican Council and the end of that reactive era, the Catholic Church changed and the Jesuits did too. That is all there was to them. Or so it might seem.

But the Jesuits were not founded to counteract Protestants, nor for that matter to become residential school teachers. St. Ignatius's original intention was that he and his companions would be missionaries among the Muslims in the Holy Land. While waiting in Venice for a ship to take them there, they used their time to work at a variety of ministries, among them working in a hospital for patients with syphilis. They washed dishes, scrubbed floors, and emptied slop pails.

When war made it clear that they would never set sail for Palestine, they accommodated. Ignatius and his companions put themselves at the disposal of the pope, requesting direction as to where he thought they could be most useful, eventually taking a fourth vow to work at whatever ministry the popes would ask of them. Outsiders do not ordinarily think of Jesuits as male nurses tending to victims of sexually transmitted disease, but long before they began teaching school, they were involved in any number of similar, supposedly non-Jesuit ministries—to criminals in prison, to homeless victims of famine, to women driven by poverty into prostitution.

Ignatius described himself and his companions as pilgrims constantly on the move. They were to accommodate to their situations and go wherever they could do the most good. He and the others of his company had received advanced degrees at the University of Paris, but their education was never intended for its own sake. It was so that they could do more and do it better. *More* (*magis* in Latin) was a favorite word for Ignatius, and he used it often in his writings about the Society of Jesus.

Ignatius founded the Jesuits to give glory to God by "helping souls," as he put it, doing whatever needed to be done. When asked to provide teachers for a boys' school, Ignatius acceded to the request. It was fourteen years after the first Jesuits had banded together and eight years after they had become a religious order. Teaching school was simply another opportunity to "help souls."

So what do these origins and this broad range of activity mean for non-Jesuits, like me, teaching at a Jesuit university? I found myself thinking about this after I experienced how much in the way of financial and human resources the administration at Saint Louis University was expending to communicate to the non-Jesuit faculty and staff what it meant to be part of an institution with a Jesuit identity. I was encountering attempts to describe Jesuit identity in terms of "dynamism," "adaptability," and the pursuit of "excellence." Such phrases may have been inspired by Ignatius's pilgrim metaphor and his proclivity for the word *magis*, but the translation sounded more like automobile advertising to me.

I began reading histories of the Jesuits and asking them how they understood themselves to be different. The conventional answers to my question tended to describe Jesuit identity along lines like "active contemplation," concern for social justice, and "solidarity with the poor." I had difficulties with those answers, however. Long before Ignatius and his companions came along, Benedictines were conjoining work and prayer, Dominicans were sharing the fruits of their contemplation, and Franciscans had pretty well tied up poverty as a hallmark. And social justice is a quite modern concept born of a quite modern social situation long after the Jesuits' origins.

So are they simply more (*magis*) of the same? Are Jesuits simply factotums who recapitulate or fine-tune the various traits and spiritualities of the religious orders that preceded them? Are they really more distinctive for what they do not do, like not staying put in a monastery and not praying in choir? There is some truth to all of the above, but there is something else too, something quite peculiar to Jesuits that has been there from the beginning and is, I would argue, far too little communicated.

It may be presumptuous of me as an outsider to suggest to so astute and articulate a group of men what stands out about them, but I believe it is what makes them congenial at once to Episcopal bishops and their fellow non-Jesuit, even agnostic, academics. It is what attracts readers to this periodical and makes it peculiarly Jesuit. As one proximate enough to observe Jesuits close up, yet distant enough to make out the forest for the trees, I am struck time and again at what, for lack of a better term, I can only call their *spiritual humanism*.

Jesuit Spirituality

There is no understanding Jesuits without some idea of Ignatius's Spiritual Exercises. Every Jesuit makes at least two thirty-day retreats based on them. First on his sickbed at Loyola and then for eleven months near the town of Manresa, Ignatius had profound experiences that changed not only his life but history. He had no doubt, as he later related in his *Autobiography*, that God was treating him as a child "whom he is teaching." And like a diligent student privileged to learn under such a teacher, Ignatius took notes. He began recording into a copybook his perceptions of what was going on deep inside him, in that core dimension of the personality that, for lack of a better word, we metaphorically call the human spirit.

Those copybook notes Ignatius made matured over the years into the *Spiritual Exercises*, unquestionably one of the most influential books ever written. It has been published some 4,500 times, an average of once a month for four hundred years. The number of copies printed has been estimated to be some 4.5 million—despite the fact that the book is about as dry and uninspiring as a teacher's manual. For that is what the *Spiritual Exercises* are, a how-to handbook with a set of directions on how to discern and decide: amid the cacophony of conflicting voices, how to hear the voice of a God who speaks in the deeper stillness of the heart; and amid the many options regarding what to do with one's life, how to respond.

While a student himself at the University of Paris, Ignatius began guiding a group of his fellow students in prayer along the lines laid down in the *Spiritual Exercises*. And what began as a fraternity of college friends eventually became the Society of Jesus. Ever since those beginnings, Jesuits have been about spirituality, which is to say, about experience and awareness. As a former courtier and soldier born at the end of the Middle Ages, Ignatius used the metaphors of warring kingdoms, battlefields, and banners. And where Jewish mystical tradition speaks of the presence of God that accompanied Israel even into exile (the Shekinah), where mystics in other religious traditions speak of ineffable intimacy and oneness, Ignatius used the Trinitarian language of Catholicism, which assumes strong interior guidance by the Holy Spirit. The Spirit of God that gave the Ten Commandments, the Spirit of Christ that guides and governs the church, that self-same Spirit speaks to us. We need only to learn how to pay more attention. The experience of God is not only for a selected few mystics but for anyone who would listen.

From the time of his sickbed conversion and then repeatedly for the rest of his life, Ignatius had intense mystical experiences. He could have them anytime, anywhere—not only at prayer or in churches but in classrooms and on street corners. The sight of a flower or a piece of fruit could bring him to tears or send his spirit soaring. There were times, he later confessed, when he would have to brush these ecstasies aside so he could study or get some sleep.

As a corollary of these experiences, Ignatius came to see God as present and busily at work in all creation. God's spiritual presence so infuses the universe that nothing is merely secular or profane. Hence the Ignatian ideal of "finding God in all things," first canonized in the Jesuit *Constitutions* and now echoed in the liturgy of the U.S. Episcopal Church. For Jesuits there was never anything like a flight from the world, nothing like the medieval idea of Thomas à Kempis (*Imitation of Christ*), that leaving the monastery meant coming back less a monk. As one early Jesuit (Jerome Nadal) put it: The whole world is our home.

That became true, not only literally, for the missionaries of the Society, but figuratively, for its scholars. It allowed Jesuit spirituality to become at once worldly and humanistic, seeing God as deeply immersed in all creation and in all human endeavor. It could take for its own the words of Terence, the pre-Christian (do we still say *pagan?*) poet—*Nil humanum alienum a me puto* ("Nothing human is foreign to me")—because nothing human is merely human. And no enterprise, no matter how secular, is merely secular. We live in a universe of grace. From the Jesuit perspective, therefore, it followed that holiness and humanism require each other.

Renaissance Humanism

Thirty years ago, the Lutheran theologian Paul Tillich suggested that the word *spiritual* had been so misused and misunderstood that, even within the church, it was no longer usable. Time proved Tillich wrong. Not only for Christian writers but for anyone thinking seriously about the human condition and the contemporary search for meaning, the concept of spirituality has proven to be indispensable. Just as indispensable for understanding Jesuits, I believe, is their humanism, a term equally problematic and, within most Christian circles at least, as much in need of rescue.

The words *humanist* and *humanism* have an old and distinguished heritage that long allowed them to be applied to such worthies as Petrarch and Erasmus, St. Thomas More and Jacques Maritain. More recent usage, however, at least in the United States, has narrowed the meaning of humanism *tout court* [simply] to its non-theist variety. The American Humanist Association and its periodical *The Humanist* have been allowed to appropriate the terms for themselves. The religious right wing aided and abetted the co-option, happy to identify humanism with a rejection of God and to hold it up as the demon responsible for all that is wrong with pop culture, the public school system, and the world.

In its widest sense, humanism describes those attitudes and beliefs that attach central importance to the human person and human values. Originally it designated the Renaissance emphasis upon classical studies in education, going back to Petrarch and his enthusiasm for the classics of Latin antiquity ("the humanities"). Even today, the definition of humanism as human-centeredness has the firmer claim to correctness over non-theistic secularism.

The fifteenth-century *umanisti* were not only engaged in but devoted to the *studia humanitatis*, in which *humanitas* entailed the development of human virtue in all its forms and to its fullest extent, not only insight and understanding but eloquence and action. For the humanists, the study of the classics led to an active, not sedentary or reclusive, life. Insight without action was barren, and action without insight was barbaric. Holding up *humanitas* as an ideal meant striving to strike a balance between action and contemplation. It was a balance born of complementarity.

Clearly the Jesuits were born of the Renaissance. Before they became engaged in the Counter-Reformation, Ignatius and his companions were contemporaries of Michelangelo and Da Vinci. They spoke and read classical Latin and as students breathed the air of humanism at the University of Paris. The "contemplation in action" they aspired to was not of medieval provenance but drawn from the ideals of their humanist contemporaries.

The Renaissance rediscovered the pre-Christian classics and sought to imitate their eloquence. Like the other *umanisti*, Ignatius believed that there was much in the classics that was useful for leading a devout and fully human life. This fit in with the Ignatian view of a God actively engaged in the world, speaking everywhere, even in and through "pagan" authors. Jesuit education would come to emphasize good literature as beneficial to good morals, and eloquence as an objective. Even the Jesuit habit of accommodation had its origins in Renaissance rules for rhetoric. To have an impact on people, an effective Jesuit missionary or spiritual director, no less than an effective speaker, had to know when and how to adapt to circumstances.

Spiritual Humanism

It is precisely their spirituality, rooted in the Ignatian Exercises, and their humanism, rooted in the Renaissance, that made and continue to make Jesuits distinctive. It carried through their history, winning them both friends and critics. Working in India, Jesuit missionary Roberto de Nobili took up the lifestyle of a Hindu holy man. He wore the same clothes, ate the same food, fasted and prayed with the same ascetic rigor as the Brahmins.

Similarly in China, Matteo Ricci and Adam Schall assumed the garb and lifestyle of Chinese mandarins. They and their Jesuit successors mastered the languages and literature of China. Not only did they translate Confucius; they called him *Shang*, the Chinese word for *venerable*, but close enough to *saint* to alarm less-accommodating Catholics in high places. That got those early Jesuit missionaries into trouble with the Vatican, but they had come not only to respect but to love the cultures of India and China, not as something alien but as something human and hence not without God's spiritual presence.

These Jesuit missionaries could affirm non-Christian cultures in India and China because back home their confreres were teaching the pre-Christian classics of Greece and Rome. Cicero and Virgil, even Horace and Ovid (without the racy sections), were all part of the detailed course of studies prescribed for all Jesuit schools and eventually codified in the *Ratio Studiorum*.

Within twenty-five years of their approval as an order, Jesuits were staffing schools from Portugal to Poland, teaching not only Catholic doctrine but grammar, philosophy, and the humanities. As John O'Malley, SJ, writes in *The First Jesuits*, the Jesuits "glided" into school work without initially taking much account of it. Education of youth was only one of several Jesuit ministries at first, but it soon became the dominant one, once again because of their humanism.

Because of their Renaissance culture and upbringing, Ignatius and the early Jesuits believed in the power of education, or "good letters" as they put it. Ever since Petrarch, it had been a commonplace assumption of the humanists that good literature led to virtue. Cicero provided not only a model for eloquence but religious and moral inspiration. Studying the so-called pagan classics made one a better person.

When the Jesuits opened their first school, it was to teach "all the disciplines" except law and medicine. Soon enough that led to Jesuits' teaching not only the humanities but mathematics and the natural sciences as well. When Pope Gregory XIII needed advice on how to revise the Julian calendar back in 1582, he turned to the Jesuit mathematician Christopher Clavius. Clavius came up with a formula that required the suppression of ten days. Protestants proclaimed the whole idea a "Jesuit plot," but the formula worked, and the Gregorian calendar has come into general use virtually everywhere. Clavius enjoys little celebrity these days, except for the honor of having a crater on the moon named after him. It is a distinction, however, that he enjoys with some thirty other Jesuit scientists and mathematicians.

Engagement with the secular sciences eventually became a hallmark of the Jesuits, so that even missionaries saw themselves as having a cultural as well as religious calling. George Kamel, a Czech Jesuit, worked as both a missionary and a pharmacist in the Philippines. He would send specimens of plants peculiar to the Orient back to Europe so they could be studied and compared. His contributions won him the honor of having a plant named after him. But who outside of a few Jesuits knows that the camellia was named after George Kamel? Or that the bark of the cinchona tree, sent back by missionaries for its remarkable ability to bring down fever, was once known as "Jesuit bark." We just call it "quinine."

It is also fair to say that, were it not for the research and writing of early Jesuit missionaries, geography and ethnography would not have become serious branches of study as early as they did. Jesuits were the first explorers with higher educations, the first Europeans altogether to venture into the interiors of Mexico, Mongolia, and the Amazon. Jesuits were the first Europeans to study Sanskrit in India and to write grammars in Chinese. They did the same with the native languages of Brazil. In fact, Jesuits have been credited with doing the foundational work for the grammars and dictionaries of ninety-five languages.

I could go on about Jesuits and the Baroque ("Jesuit architecture," the Italians called it). Or Jesuits and theater. (The school pageant is one of their more dubious though lasting contributions to modern civilization.) Would you believe that a Jesuit wrote the first serious treatise on ballet? My intention, however, is not to write a paean but to argue a point. Jesuits have been from their very beginnings at the center of the dialogue between science and religion, at the inter-section of secular culture with faith. They found themselves there because of their spiritual humanism. It put them at a boundary that allowed them to speak in a worldly way about piety and piously about the world.

Jesuits obviously could not and did not always live up to the ideals of their origins, but they did it often enough to find themselves in the middle of any number of cross fires. Their less accommodating Catholic critics viewed Jesuit affirmation of non-Christian cultures as toleration of idolatry and a betrayal of the Christian heritage. For anticlerical humanists like Diderot and Voltaire, the Jesuits were too spiritual. Because of their humanism, Blaise Pascal and Jansenists found them too lax.

But the Jesuits have a knack of outliving their enemies, so that even the word *Jesuitical* has virtually died out of the English language. Thanks to the Second Vatican Council and Jesuit theologians like Karl Rahner, Jesuit spirituality has become mainstream Catholic thinking. Rahner's concept of the "anonymous Christian" was, as he himself admitted, a less than felicitous phrase, but it sought to express the Ignatian conviction that the world is infused with God's presence. Similarly, the council described the church as symbolizing a grace that extends far beyond its visible confines. It implied that non-Catholics, non-Christians, even nonbelievers, conceptual agnostics, and atheists can be living in the divine presence and serving as instruments of grace. Reaching out for and being touched by sacred mystery does not require having correct ideas about God.

For only the thirty-fourth time in their more than 450-year history, Jesuit delegates from all over the world are now gathered in Rome for a general congregation. It is only the eighth time a congregation was called not just to elect a new superior general but to consider other substantial matters, in this instance, how the Society of Jesuits plans to meet the challenges it faces as it enters the third millennium. According to one of those delegates, Vincent T. O'Keefe, SJ, writing in *Company* (Winter, 1994), one of the "crucial" topics to be addressed at the congregation is to define how Jesuits can enter into fuller, more formal collaboration with the laity and their non-Jesuit colleagues in their ministries.

I hope the *patres congregati* think to include in their deliberations not just Roman Catholic laity and Episcopal bishops but Protestants, Jews, and even agnostics. Their spiritual humanism is more attractive than they may realize. It is not just for (Roman) Catholics anymore.

Further Reading

After writing the preceding article, Ronald Modras went on to be the principal scriptwriter for the St. Louis University three-part video series *Shared Vision: Jesuit Spirit in Education* (available from the Institute of Jesuit Sources). In addition, he expanded his *America* article into the book *Ignatian Humanism: A Dynamic Spirituality for the 21st Century* (Loyola Press, 2004). There, after initial chapters on Ignatian spirituality and Renaissance humanism, he offers biographical essays on five Jesuits to show how their lives and work exemplify Ignatian humanism. The five are Matteo Ricci (1552–1610), the first Jesuit to enter forbidden China, who adopted Chinese language and culture and wrote two of the great masterpieces of Chinese (Mandarin) literature; Friedrich Spee von Langenfeld (1595–1635), who risked his life and used every gift of intellect and rhetoric to expose the scapegoating of women as "witches" and to prevent their execution (burning at the stake); Pierre Teilhard de Chardin (1881–1955), longtime exile in China, paleontologist, philosopher, poet, mystic, and precursor of today's environmentalists in their respect and love for the earth; Karl Rahner (1904–1984), whose presence behind the scenes at Vatican II had a profound impact on most of the council's major documents, and who when asked late in life about the greatest influence on his teaching and writing answered "the Ignatian Spiritual Exercises"; and Pedro Arrupe (1907–1991), missionary to Japan, superior general of the Jesuits for nearly twenty years, and founder of the modern, post-Vatican II Society of Jesus. I cannot recommend *Ignatian Humanism* too highly.

Another important resource for information on aspects of Ignatian spirituality is the recently completed, comprehensive, two-volume *Dictionary of Ignatian Spirituality*. Seven years in preparation, this work of 157 scholars from 25 countries comes to 383 entries and 1,816 pages. So far (early 2008) it is available only in a Spanish edition (*Diccionario de Espritualidad Ignaciana*: salterrae@salterrae.es), but it is expected to be available in English in the near future.

The Cambridge Companion to the Jesuits, edited by Thomas Worcester, SJ (Cambridge University Press, 2008), "combines both breadth and depth of scholarship. . . . The chapters range from Jesuit spirituality to geography to architecture, from history and biography to the arts to politics, from theology to education to science," says John W. Padberg, SJ, director of the Institute of Jesuit Sources.

Ignatius: His Life

Introduction

The place to start a study of Ignatian spirituality is the life of Ignatius of Loyola. It may seem trite to say so—where else would you start the study of any spiritual tradition except with the life of its founder? With Ignatian spirituality, however, this starting point is preeminently right, because it so clearly grew out of Ignatius's reflection on his own life experience.

We begin this section with a very short but superb vignette, "St. Ignatius of Loyola (1491–1556)," by Michael Paul Gallagher, SJ, dean of the Faculty of Theology at the Gregorian University in Rome. The piece was part of a year-long series Spiritual Stars of the [Second] Millennium, in the British lay Catholic weekly *The Tablet*. The essay speaks for itself; so much of Ignatius is captured in just a few words.

The section's main feature is perhaps the finest contemporary biographical essay on Ignatius, "The Pilgrim," by Ron Hansen, novelist and Gerard Manley Hopkins, SJ, Professor in the Arts and Humanities at Santa Clara University. With the perspective of an outsider (who still has strong Jesuit connections) and with a novelist's eye for the right detail, Hansen provides a compelling portrait.

Understanding the Terminology:
Suggested Readings from *Do You Speak Ignatian?*

- Ignatius of Loyola

St. Ignatius of Loyola (1491–1556)

Michael Paul Gallagher, SJ

From *The Tablet*, 2000

There have been various proposals to make a film about St. Ignatius of Loyola. I would suggest beginning the picture in 1550, a Jubilee year, with a panorama of the Roman skyline just after sunset. We would see the outline of the new St. Peter's, without its dome, but with Michelangelo's "drum" under construction. Gradually the camera zooms in on a lighted window in a small building. Gazing at the sky is a bald man in his late fifties; as the camera moves closer, we realize that he is weeping quietly, and if the actor were good enough, we would know that these are tears of joy. Looking at the stars, Ignatius is overwhelmed by the glory of God. Behind him one can glimpse papers covered with elegant handwriting, his first draft of the *Constitutions* for his ten-year-old order, the Society of Jesus. Beside them is the first edition of his *Spiritual Exercises*, published in 1548.

In 1521, when he had his leg broken in battle, and then his dramatic conversion during convalescence at Loyola, he never imagined spending long years in Rome. Ignatius came from the Basque country [of northeastern Spain], and spent his youth as a courtier and only as a part-time soldier. After his conversion he thought of himself as a poor "pilgrim," a layman living on alms and offering spiritual advice to anyone who would listen. But he got into trouble with the Spanish

Inquisition on account of his lack of theology, so at the age of thirty-three went back to study ("to help souls"), learning Latin with small boys.

His studies continued until he was forty-four. By that stage he had gathered several companions around him at the University of Paris, having led them personally through a month of guided prayer. They planned to go to Jerusalem together, but when that proved impossible they offered their services to Pope Paul III in Rome (eventually taking a special fourth vow of obedience to the pope for missions). Thus the Jesuits were born through a series of outer accidents, and through the inner vision of this courtier turned contemplative, whose apostolic energy drove him to work both with princes and prostitutes.

Starting the film in that way would be an attempt to go beyond the misleading image of Ignatius as a severe soldier who founds an order of "shock troops" to combat the Reformation. His diary reveals another side altogether, symbolized by his weeping (which happened so often during Mass as to endanger his eyesight). The elegant writing sums up a man of courtly reverence, a quality that marked his relationship with God as Trinity. The *Constitutions*, over which he prayed for years, are unique in their emphasis on flexibility, giving priority to frontier ministries of different kinds. They embodied a non-monastic approach to religious life and, as such, had a crucial influence on later "apostolic" religious congregations. The novelty of this approach no doubt gave Jesuits a more individualistic stamp than older religious families.

The greatest legacy of Ignatius, however, lies in his *Spiritual Exercises*, which are more a set of instructions for a retreat director than a text to be read. I remember my disappointment, as a lay university student, when I borrowed the little book from a library, only to find it seemingly as ineloquent as a driving manual. But, as for many others through the centuries, it came alive years later when I "did" the thirty-day retreat. Ignatius drew on his own spiritual adventure to offer contemplative scaffolding for a succession of graces—trust, contrition, discipleship, freedom for the service of Christ. In this way, the Exercises guide a retreatant through a pedagogy of prayer into "interior knowledge of the Lord."

Even though it was often interpreted in rigid ways, authentic Ignatian spirituality is marked by his typical preference for flexibility. His is a spirituality of discernment of choices, both everyday and lifelong. His advice is to find "whatever is most helpful and fruitful," and he tells the retreat director to get out of the way of God so as to allow the Creator, in his surprising words, "to deal immediately with the creature." There is a fundamental trust here that the "movements" of the Spirit are recognizable in everyone's experience.

Secular historians often speak of Jesuit colleges as another major inheritance from Ignatius. They were not part of his original plan of a highly mobile ministry. But after 1548, when he was convinced of the importance of educational work, the schools mushroomed and evolved new ways of humanistic formation, encouraging, for instance, the writing of poetry and the staging of elaborate theatricals. Historians also stress the creative character of Jesuit missions, ranging from India to Paraguay—an outreach that started under Ignatius. But they should also mention times when Jesuits lost their roots and became inflexible and elitist.

What are the better hallmarks of the Ignatian tradition? Depth and practicality together. Order and adaptability. Contemplation and creativity. Remembering the mystic on the balcony, I think of Ignatius as outwardly controlled, inwardly emotional, and humanly a welcoming courtier. He welcomed history at a time of huge change—the outset of modernity—and he embraced change as the theater of the Spirit.

The Pilgrim:
Saint Ignatius of Loyola

Ron Hansen

From *A Stay Against Confusion: Essays on Faith and Fiction*, 2001 ("The Pilgrim" originally appeared in 1994)

More than two hundred miracles were attributed to Ignatius of Loyola when the judges for the cause of his canonization, the Rota, assembled their sixteen hundred witness statements in 1622. A surgeon held a signature of Ignatius to his head and his headaches and sight problems ended. A Franciscan nun's broken femur was healed when a Spanish priest applied a patch of Ignatius's clothing to her thigh. A Spanish woman held a picture of Ignatius to her hugely swollen stomach and was soon cured of dropsy. Juana Clar, of Manresa, was gradually losing her sight until she got down on her knees and permitted a fragment of Ignatius's bones to be touched to her eyelids. She felt at once such pleasure that it was as if, she said, she'd seen fresh roses. Within a day her pain went away and her vision was perfectly restored. And so on.

Even though I presume those stories are true, I find myself oddly unaffected by them; it's as if I heard that Saint Ignatius, like Cool Hand Luke, could eat fifty eggs. I have read every major biography and book about Ignatius, I have held his shoes in my hands, I have walked through his freshly restored rooms in the house next to what is now the Church of the Gesù, and I have next to me as I write this a nail that was in one of the walls. Supernatural prodigies have nothing to do with my rapt and consuming interest in him. I have simply been trying to figure out how to live my life magnificently, as Ignatius did, who sought in all his works and activities the greater glory of God.

Iñigo López de Loyola was born in the Loyola castle in 1491, the last son of thirteen children born of a wealthy and highly esteemed family in Azpeitia in the Basque province of Guipúzcoa. His father, Beltrán de Loyola, died in 1507, but we do not know when his mother, Marina Sánchez de Licona, died, only that she predeceased her husband; it's highly probable she died in the child's infancy, for Iñigo was nursed by María de Garín, a neighboring blacksmith's wife, who later taught him his prayers and with whose children he played.

Guipúzcoa means "to terrify the enemy," and there was a huge, legendary emphasis on fearlessness and aggressiveness among the region's men. Juan Pérez, the oldest of Iñigo's brothers, joined a ship's escort for Christopher Columbus and finally died heroically in the Spanish conquest of Naples, and another brother, Hernando, gave up his inheritance in order to go to the Americas, where he disappeared in 1510. In fact, of Iñigo's seven older brothers, only one was not a conquistador or fighting man. That brother, Pero López, took holy orders and became rector of the Church of San Sebastián at Azpeitia; and his father may have sought holy orders for Iñigo as well, for he was enrolled in pre-seminary studies in the arts of reading and writing before he was sent, at the age of thirteen and probably at his own behest, to acquire the skills and manners of a courtier in the household of his father's friend, the chief treasurer of King Ferdinand of Castile.

His fantasies became those of intrigue and gallantry and knightly romance. Of him in his twenties it was written: "He is in the habit of going round in cuirass and coat of mail, wears his hair long to the shoulder, and walks about in a two-colored, slashed doublet with a bright cap." We have evidence that he was cited in court for brawling, and he himself confessed that "he was a man given over to the vanities of the world; with a great and vain desire to win fame, he delighted especially in the exercise of arms." We have no evidence from him of his affairs of the heart beyond his furtive confession that he was "fairly free in the love of women" and, later, that he often spent hours "fancying what he would have to do in the service of a certain lady, of the means he would take to reach the country where she was living, of the verses, the promises he would make to her, the deeds of gallantry he would do in her service. He was so enamored with all this that he did not see how impossible it would all be, because the lady was of no ordinary rank"; indeed, she seems to have been Doña Catalina, the glamorous sister of Emperor Charles V and future queen of John III of Portugal.

When his employer, the king's treasurer-general, died in 1517, the twenty-six-year old Iñigo found another friend and benefactor in the viceroy of Navarre, who hired him as his "gentleman," a kind of factotum or righthand man. Iñigo de Loyola was a finished hidalgo by then, a haughty Lothario and swashbuckler, famous for his flair and charm and machismo, his fastidiousness and fondness for clothes, his highly educated politeness and chivalry and hot temper, his ferocity of will, his fortitude and loyalty—his Basqueness, as the Spanish would say—and also his acuity and craft in negotiations, his penetrating stare, his photographic memory, his fine penmanship, his reticence and precaution in speech, his love of singing and dancing. Like his Spanish friends, he was religiously naive, and Catholicism seems to have been rather perfunctory for him—high-table rituals without flourish or kisses. "Although very much attached to the faith," a friend and biographer wrote, "he did not live in keeping with his belief, or guard himself from sin: he was particularly careless about gambling, affairs with women, and duelling."

Iñigo was not a professional soldier then, as he'd fancied he'd be, but a public administrator, "a man of great ingenuity and prudence in worldly affairs and very skillful in the handling of men, especially in composing difficulties and discord." But in May 1521, his skillfulness in the handling of men put Iñigo alongside the magistrate of Pamplona in Navarre, defending its fortress in the midst of a huge French offensive on the region along the Pyrenees that the Spanish king had annexed five years earlier. We have no idea how many citizens were with Iñigo, but there could not have been more than a handful holding out against a highly trained French force of three hundred. Late in the nine-hour siege of the fortress, an artillery shot crashed between Iñigo's legs, shattering the right and harming the other. After he fell, the fortress surrendered, and the French made it a point of chivalry to treat Iñigo with such exemplary kindness it may have seemed a form of sarcasm. Their finest physicians operated on him and graciously hospitalized him for a fortnight in his own Pamplona residence before hauling him forty miles northwest to Azpeitia on a litter.

In his family's castle Iñigo's fever and illness grew worse, and village surgeons decided the skewed bones of his leg would have to be broken again and reset—without anesthetic. Even thirty years later he would describe that agony as "butchery," but he was fiercely determined to give no "sign of pain other than to clench his fists." When finally his right leg healed, Iñigo realized that it was foreshortened and that the fibula had knitted jaggedly so that an ugly jutting was just under his knee. Still thinking of finding fame in royal courts and of striding forth in fashionably tight leggings and knee-high boots, he made himself "a martyr to his own pleasure" and underwent the horrific ordeal of having the offending bone chiseled and shaved away.

And then a change began to occur in him. While lying about and suffering further treatments that failed to lengthen his brutalized leg, he sought books of medieval chivalry to read. Surprisingly, the only books available in the Loyola mansion were a four-volume *Vita Jesu Christi* by Ludolph of Saxony and a kind of dictionary of saints called *Flos Sanctorum* by Jacopo da Varazze. With a sigh he read even those. A confidant later overstated the situation by writing of Iñigo that "he had no thought then either of religion or of piety," but it can be fairly said that his simple, unreflective, folk Christianity had not forced him to take his life here seriously nor to compare himself to the holy men of the past, whom Ludolph of Saxony called knightly followers of Christ—*caballeros imitadores*. Speaking of himself in the third person in his autobiography, Ignatius put it this way:

> As he read [the books] over many times, he became rather fond of
> what he found written there. Putting his reading aside, he sometimes
> stopped to think about the things he had read and at other times about

the things of the world that he used to think about before. . . . Our Lord assisted him, causing other thoughts that arose from the things he read to follow these. While reading the life of Our Lord and of the saints, he stopped to think, reasoning within himself, "What if I should do what St. Francis did, what St. Dominic did?" So he pondered over many things that he found to be good, always proposing to himself what was difficult and serious, and as he proposed them, they seemed to him easy to accomplish.

We are challenged by Ignatius in much the same way that he was challenged by Francis and Dominic. And that may be the best purpose for books of saints: to have our complacency and mediocrity goaded, and to highlight our lame urge to go forward with the familiar rather than the difficult and serious. We often find tension and unease with the holy lives we read about because there is always an implicit criticism of our habits and weaknesses in greatness and achievement. We know God wants us to be happy, but what is happiness? What is enough? What is the difference between that which is hard to do and that which ought not be done by me? Women are often put off or mystified by this highly masculine saint, but I find so many points of intersection with Iñigo's life that I feel compelled to ask, What if I should do what Ignatius did? And it does not seem to me easy to accomplish.

Iñigo was thirty years old, which was far older then than now, and yet he found himself wrought up by questions about his purpose on earth that his friends had put a halt to as teenagers. But he was helped in his religious crisis by his discovery of affective patterns to his inner experience, a discovery that would later form the basis for the "Rules for Discernment of Spirits" in his *Spiritual Exercises*.

When he was thinking about the things of the world, he took much delight in them, but afterwards, when he was tired and put them aside, he found that he was dry and discontented. But when he thought of going to Jerusalem, barefoot and eating nothing but herbs and undergoing all the other rigors that he saw the saints had endured, not only was he consoled when he had these thoughts, but even after putting them aside, he remained content and happy. . . . Little by little he came to recognize the difference between the spirits that agitated him, one from the demon, the other from God.

Concluding that he ought to change radically, Iñigo chose to give up his former interests and pursuits, and, on a pilgrimage to Jerusalem, undergo the hard penances for his sins that "a generous soul, inflamed by God, usually wants to do." Confirmation of that choice came one August night in his sickroom when he was graced with a clear and tremendously consoling image of Our Lady with the Infant Jesus, "and he was left with such loathing for his whole past life and especially for the things of the flesh, that it seemed that all the fantasies he had previously pictured in his mind were driven from it." Even his family noted the difference in him and, far from thinking him crazy, seemed inspired by his faith and good example. Seeing that Iñigo wanted to go even farther in his religious life, however, Martín García de Loyola took his limping brother from room to room in the grand old house, pointing out the jasper and furnishings and fine tapestries, and appealing to him to "consider what hopes had been placed in him and what he should become . . . all with the purpose of dissuading him from his good intention."

But Iñigo was not budged. He filled three hundred pages of a blank account book with extracts from the Gospels and his readings, found a picture of Our Lady of Sorrows and a book of hours of Our Lady, fitted himself out like a knight-errant, and finally left the Loyola house in late February 1522. Offering farewells to his sister Magdalena at Anzuola and to his former employer, the viceroy of Navarre, in Navarrete, he went eastward on his mule another two hundred miles to the Benedictine monastery of Montserrat in Catalonia. After a full, general confession of his past life in writing, which took three days, Iñigo gave up his fine clothes to a tramp, put on a penitential sackcloth tunic and rope-soled sandals, and on the eve of the Annunciation of Our Lady observed a knightly vigil-at-arms at the feet of the Black Madonna, where he vowed perpetual chastity and left his flashing sword and dagger in the shrine. Effectively, his former life was over.

Barcelona was the port of embarkation for Rome where, through agreement with the Turks, pilgrims were given permission to go to the Holy Land by the pope himself at Easter. But Adrian of Utrecht, the new pope-elect, was himself in Spain and on his slow way to the port, and Iñigo was at pains to avoid his old friends in the Navarrese nobility, whom he rightly presumed would be part of Adrian's retinue. So he went from Montserrat to Manresa, a few miles north, with the intention of staying perhaps three days, but the affective experience of God he felt there was so powerful that Iñigo stayed in Manresa almost a year, a period he later thought of as "my primitive Church."

To vanquish his vanity there, Iñigo let his nails go untrimmed and his hair and beard grow full and wild as nests, and as he tilted from door to door for food and alms in his prickly tunic, he found joy and sweetness in the jeering of children who called him *El hombre saco*—Old Man Sack. He helped with the poor and sick in the hospital of Santa Lucia, finding no task offensive, and primarily resided in a Dominican friary, though he often withdrew to a hermit's cave in the hillsides above the river Cardoner. Eating no meat and drinking no wine, fasting until he was little more than skin and skeleton, ill and sleepless much of the time, flagellating himself for his sins, Iñigo was nevertheless an Olympian at prayer, attending Matins with the Dominicans, and Mass, Vespers, and Compline in the cathedral, where the canons regular chanted the office in Latin, of which he knew not a word. Exhausting as that regimen might have been, he gave a full seven hours more to kneeling at prayer and, if he found a peseta of free time, read to the point of memorization *The Imitation of Christ* by Thomas à Kempis, a book he would later call "the partridge among spiritual books." And yet, as he says in his autobiography,

> Sometimes he found himself so disagreeable that he took no joy in prayer or in hearing mass or in any other prayer he said. At other times exactly the opposite of this came over him so suddenly that he seemed to have thrown off sadness and desolation just as one snatches a cape from another's shoulders. Here he began to be astounded by these changes that he had never experienced before, and he said to himself, "What new life is this that we are now beginning?"

Compared to his former life as a grand hidalgo, it seemed to have no purpose, and he was so further anguished by his infirmities, fasts, mortifications, and scruples that he found it hard to imagine going on as he had and was assailed with the urge to kill himself, fear of offending God being the one thing that held him back. But gradually Iñigo figured out—possibly with the help of his Benedictine confessor—that he'd simply gone too far, and he gently tempered his penances in obedience, he thought, to the promptings of a Holy Being who was treating him, as he said, "just as a schoolmaster treats a child whom he is teaching."

Enlightenment came to him on the foremost aspects of Catholic orthodoxy, of the Holy Trinity functioning like three harmonious keys in a musical chord, of how God created the world from white-hot nothing, of how Christ was really present in the Eucharist; and frequently over the next few years he saw the humanity of Christ and Our Lady, giving him "such strength in his faith that he often thought to himself: if there were no Scriptures to teach us these matters of the faith, he would be resolved to die for them, only because of what he had seen." And one famous day on the banks of the Cardoner, the pilgrim, as he habitually called himself, was graced with an illumination of such great clarity and insight about "spiritual things and matters of faith and of learning" that "he seemed to himself to be another person and had an intellect other than he had before." Testimony to the great learning Iñigo seemed to have acquired, as he said, *de arriba*, from above, was provided later by Martial Mazurier, a professor of theology at the Sorbonne, who asserted "that never had he heard any man speak of theological matters with such mastery and power."

Because he often referred to his Cardoner illumination as the foundation of all that he would later do, it has been argued that Iñigo was given foreknowledge then and there of the Society of Jesus that would be formally instituted in 1540, but far more likely was it the origin of Iñigo's shift from a worried, isolated, flesh-despising penitent to a far more tranquil and outgoing man who was less concerned with harsh penances than he was with Christ-like service to others.

Essential elements of his *Spiritual Exercises*—finally published in 1548—were probably composed in Manresa about this time.

Influenced in part by Ludolph of Saxony's *Vita Jesu Christi*, the abbot of Montserrat's *Ejercitatorio de la vida espiritual*, and *Meditationes vitae Christi* by a fourteenth-century Franciscan, the *Spiritual Exercises* fashioned for the first time what is now popularly known as a retreat. The handbook offered spiritual directors a practical and systematic method of having retreatants meditate, in silence and solitude over an intensive four-week span, on God's plan in the creation of human beings, humanity's fall from grace through sin, the gifts of humility and poverty, and the glory of the life, passion, and resurrection of Jesus. Each psychologically astute meditation gently guided a retreatant to choose a fuller Christian life and, as the author himself had done, "to overcome oneself, and to order one's life, without reaching a decision through some disordered affection."

Early in the *Spiritual Exercises* practitioners are told to reflect on themselves and ask, "What have I done for Christ? What am I doing for Christ? What ought I to do for Christ?" Iñigo's own reply to that final question was to complete his long-delayed pilgrimage to Jerusalem. *El hombre saco* was by then affectionately being called *El hombre sancto*, the Holy Man, and when in the hard winter he forsook his tunic and sandals for a family's gift of shoes and beret and two brown doublets, the family preserved his sackcloth as a holy relic. Refusing alms that were offered from friends—possibly because they themselves were in such great want—Iñigo left Manresa on foot in late February 1523 and stayed in Barcelona twenty days, going from door to door to beg for food and provisions for his journey and so impressing Isabel Roser with his talk of God and religion that she paid for his sea passage to Rome and remained his principal benefactor throughout his life.

Whoever met him seems to have liked him; he found no trouble getting an apostolic blessing for his pilgrimage in Rome from Adrian VI, the former Spanish prime minister, nor finding free passage on ships in Venice and Cyprus, and on September 4, Iñigo walked into the Holy City in the midst of a huge procession of Christians and Egyptian Jews. He hoped to never leave.

Palestine was then fiercely held by Turkish Muslims, whose Christian go-betweens were Franciscan friars. After following a highly regulated program of pilgrimages to the Holy Sepulcher,

Bethany, Bethlehem, and the Jordan, Iñigo's fervor was such that he approached a friar and told him of his plan to stay on in the city where Jesus had walked, continually venerating the holy sites and helping souls. But he was forbidden that option by the friar's superior, who feared the Spanish crusader would be killed by the Turks. In fact, five hundred Turkish cavalrymen freshly arrived from Damascus were truculently prowling the city and the panicked governor of Jerusalem was urging the pilgrims to leave. After hurried last looks at Christ's footprints on the Mount of Olives, for which he paid the Turkish guards a penknife and scissors, Iñigo obediently left with the other pilgrims for Europe, hoping to find his way to Jerusalem again, but preferring, for the time being, to immerse himself in philosophical and theological studies.

To do that he would need Latin. Hence he withstood the hazards of four months of shipboard travel to go back to Spain, where Isabel Roser furnished the little that Iñigo needed while he was taught, gratis, by a professor of Latin grammar at the University of Barcelona. His life there was full of self-imposed hardships: he slept on the plank floor of a friend's garret room, walked about in shoes that had no soles, and begged food for the poor while subsisting himself on plain bread and water.

I feel farthest from Iñigo when he seems to ignore his needs and inflict miseries upon himself. A healthy discipline, chastity, and solidarity with the poor are all honorable desires, of course, but so often Iñigo seems to go over the top, to hate and scourge what is wholly natural and, in essence, pure gift. God finds us where we are, however, and God found Iñigo with one foot in the Middle Ages, believing, as the faithful did then, that the flesh and spirit were at war and fearing that pleasure was a kind of death to the holy. There was little integration of flesh and spirit then, only rivalry and argument. We have not completely shaken those notions to this day.

After two years in Barcelona, his Latin tutor gave Iñigo permission to go to the University of Alcalá, just east of Madrid, where he studied the physics of Albertus Magnus, the logic of Domingo de Soto, and Peter Lombard's twelfth-century theological treatise *Four Books of Sentences*. And in his free time, he said, "he was busy giving spiritual exercises and teaching Christian doctrine and in so doing brought forth fruit for the glory of God."

In so doing he also brought forth the fruit of the Spanish Inquisition, as officials accused Iñigo and his followers of being heretical *Alumbrados,* or Illuminists, because they wore ankle-length cassocks of cheap *pardillo* that looked like religious habits and because Iñigo was giving high-tension religious instruction whose affect often produced fainting and weeping in his audiences. In Holy Week of the year 1527, Iñigo was jailed and held in a cell for forty-two days, but he frustrated officials with his frankness and serenity, and depositions from his female admirers only proved how orthodox were his principles: "Weekly confession and Communion, examination of conscience twice a day, the practice of meditation according to the three powers of the soul," that is, memory, intellect, and will. When Iñigo was finally released in June, he was given as a kind of peace offering a free black cassock and biretta, the fashion for students then, and was forbidden to teach on faith and morals until he completed four years of theology.

For that he went to the prestigious University of Salamanca, but within a fortnight he was dining with Dominican friars who heard hints of the Dutch humanism of Desiderius Erasmus in his talk and held him in their chapel until an inquisitor from Toledo could get there. Iñigo was again jailed. After twenty-two days of being shackled to a post in a foul upper room, he was interrogated by four judges, who found no great error in his teaching and ruled that he could catechize again, but only insofar as he did not try to define what were mortal and what were venial sins. Ethical distinctions in conscience and conduct were so at the heart of his public talks that Iñigo may have felt that they'd told him to teach geometry without azimuths. Hamstrung by that sentence, he thought it was high time to get out of Spain.

After hiking seven hundred miles north, he arrived in Paris on February 2, 1528, and went to the Sorbonne, a consortium of fifty colleges that was the greatest international center of learning in Europe. Even in peculiar times, he was a peculiar student, a frail mystic who knew no French, was less than fluent in Latin, and was then in his thirty-seventh year. Because his hasty studies at Barcelona and Alcalá had left him deficient in fundamentals, Iñigo enrolled in humanities at the Collège de Montaigu and studied Latin with boys of nine and ten. Habitually heedless of money, he asked a Spanish friend at Montaigu to hold for safekeeping the princely sum he had been given for his education, but the friend frittered it away on wild living, and by Easter Iñigo was forced to find horrible lodging far away at the hospice of Saint-Jacques and to go begging again, first among the wealthy Spanish merchants in Bruges and Antwerp in Flanders, and finally in England, garnering enough that he himself was able to be a magnanimous almsgiver back in France.

In the fall of 1529, Iñigo transferred to the Collège de Sainte Barbe, home mainly to the Portuguese at the University of Paris, and shared housing with his professor and with two highly regarded scholars whose lives he was to significantly change. The first was Pierre Favre of Savoy, a gentle, intelligent, psychologically intuitive twenty-three-year-old whose intent was the Catholic priesthood and who'd recently passed examinations for the licentiate in philosophy. Francisco de Javier—or Francis Xavier, as we know him—was also twenty-three, and a handsome, jubilant, outgoing grandee and fellow Basque from Navarre who wanted to be a famous professor or counselor to princes, as his father had been, and was already a regent in philosophy in the Collège de Beauvais. Each finally succumbed to Iñigo's imprecations and agreed to go through a full month of his Spiritual Exercises. Upon finishing them, Favre and Xavier were inflamed "friends in the Lord" with Iñigo, filling their hours with theological studies, religious practices, and conversations, and in thinking about a future that still had no firm goal. Allied with them were the Portuguese student Simão Rodrigues, who was at Sainte Barbe on a royal burse from King John III; Diego Laínez and Alfonso Salmerón, both Spaniards and former students at Alcalá; and Nicolás de Bobadilla, a philosopher at Alcalá and theologian at Valladolid before becoming a regent in the Collège de Calvi.

Ignatius de Loyola was given the title Master of Arts at Easter ceremonies in 1534. We have no certainty about his change of name. It may be that he thought of the familiar name Ignacio as a[n] easier variant of Iñigo, but it's also possible that in the age of reformation he was inspired by the Syrian prelate, Ignatius of Antioch, who faced the persecutions and theological disputes of second-century Christianity and whom Emperor Trajan threw to the lions in Rome.

We do know that Ignatius was seeking priesthood by Easter of 1534, and in preparation for holy orders he was studying the *Summa Theologica* of Thomas Aquinas with the highly esteemed Dominican faculty of the Collège de Saint-Jacques. But Pierre Favre was the first companion ordained, and on August 15, 1534, the feast of the Assumption of Mary, he celebrated Mass for his friends on the heights of Montmartre in the shrine of the martyrdom of Saint Denis and his companions. At Communion, Ignatius, Xavier, Rodrigues, Laínez, Salmerón, and Bobadilla professed vows to a life of poverty and to undertake a pilgrimage to Jerusalem or, failing that, to offer themselves to the Vicar of Christ, the pope, for whatever mission he wished. Chastity was not vowed but presumed, for they all intended to receive holy orders. Even Ignatius seems not to have thought that their profession was the origin of a new religious order, but in hindsight it was.

Within a year, Claude Le Jay, a Savoyard friend of Pierre Favre, had completed the Spiritual Exercises and made the same vows, and a year after that, again on August 15, the group was increased by Paschase Broet of Picardy and Jean Codure of Dauphiné. Ignatius missed those ceremonies. Chronic stomach pains that were prompted by gallstones forced him in 1535 to go on horseback to Azpeitia for the familiar weather and air of home that was thought then to heal a host of ills. After some health-restoring time in Spain, he went ahead of his "friends in the Lord" to Venice, where they all hoped to find a ship to the Holy Land. While waiting for them to get there, Ignatius studied theology, taught catechism, and helped a Spanish priest named Diego Hoces through the Spiritual Exercises and later welcomed him as another companion. And, it would seem, Ignatius was thinking a good deal about how a religious foundation ought to be organized, for he wrote a chiding letter to Gian Pietro Caraffa, a founder of the first order of clerks regular, called the Theatines:

When a man of rank and exalted dignity wears a habit more ornate and lives in a room better furnished than the other religious of his order, I am neither scandalized nor disedified. However, it would do well to consider how the saints have conducted themselves, St. Dominic and St. Francis, for example; and it would be good to have recourse to light from on high; for, after all, a thing may be licit without being expedient.

Of the Theatines in Venice, who shut themselves in their houses of prayer and passively filled their needs with gifts from the faithful, Ignatius wrote that people "will say that they do not see the purpose of this order; and that the saints, without failing in confidence in God, acted otherwise."

Caraffa, the Italian bishop of Chieti, was a good but impatient and tempestuous Neapolitan who in December would be created a cardinal, and he did not take kindly to faultfinding from a Spaniard, an unfinished theologian, and a forty-five-year-old mendicant who was not yet even a priest. We have lost his reply to Ignatius, but we know the hostility of Caraffa was such that when the companions from the Sorbonne finally got to Italy in 1537, Ignatius sent them on to Rome without him so that Cardinal Caraffa would have no punitive reason to foil their Easter presentation to Pope Paul III.

At that papal audience in Castel Sant' Angelo, the humble but impressive companions told the pope of their project to go to Jerusalem and begin an apostolate to the infidel there, and of their further wish to receive holy orders. Knowing the Turkish fleet was belligerently plying the Mediterranean, Paul III quietly put it that, "I do not think you will reach Jerusalem." And yet their requests were not only granted by the pontiff, but they were given close to three hundred escudos for the voyage.

In Venice on the feast of Saint John the Baptist, June 24, 1537, Vincenzo Nigusanti, bishop of Arbe, ordained Ignatius, Bobadilla, Codure, Xavier, Laínez, and Rodrigues under the title of poverty, *ad titulum paupertatis*. Bishop Nigusanti would later frequently repeat that he'd never gotten such pure consolation from an ordination. In humility, Ignatius put off presiding at his first Mass for a year and a half, so he would be the last of the ten to have that honor, and so he could perhaps celebrate it at a shrine in Bethlehem. When that proved impossible, he chose to celebrate his first Mass in Rome on Christmas 1538 at the Church of Santa Maria Maggiore, which Christians believed held the true crib of the child Jesus—a worthy substitute, he thought, for Christ's birthplace.

While waiting for a ship to Palestine in the fall of 1537, the new priests preached in the streets and performed works of mercy in hospitals throughout the Republic of Venice, but for the first time in nearly forty years however, hot rumors of war and piracy kept any ship from sailing to the East. Gathering together again in Vicenza that winter, the priests chose to be patient in their hopes of sea passage and to concentrate their preaching in cities with universities, where they might find high-minded students to join them. If anyone asked who they were, they agreed, "it seemed to them most fitting that they should take the name of him whom they had as their head, by calling themselves the 'company of Jesus.'"

Acknowledging at last that their hoped-for pilgrimage to Jerusalem was improbable, Ignatius, Favre, and Laínez walked two hundred fifty miles south to Rome in order to offer their services to the pope in fulfillment of the vow they had professed on Montmartre. Stopping in the outskirts of Rome, at a place called La Storta, Ignatius and Laínez went into a chapel, where Ignatius prayed that Mary hold him in her heart as she did her son. Then he felt a change in his soul, and later told Laínez that he beheld "Christ with the cross on his shoulder, and next to Him the eternal Father, who said to Him: 'I want you to take this man as your servant,' and Jesus thus took him and said: 'I want you to serve us.'" Ignatius also told Laínez "that it seemed to him as if God the Father had imprinted the following words in his heart: *Ego ero vobis Romae propitius.*" I will be favorable to you in Rome.

Uplifted by the La Storta illumination, Ignatius and his friends went into the city in late November 1537 and were again graciously received by the pontiff. Hearing their offer of service, Paul III gladly assigned Diego Laínez to teach scholastic theology at La Sapienza, a palace that housed the University of Rome. Pierre Favre was to fill an office in positive theology there, giving commentaries on Sacred

Scripture. With those surprising first papal assignments, the Italian Compagnia di Gesù ever so gradually became a company of teachers, but Ignatius sought to forgo the classroom in favor of giving the Spiritual Exercises in Rome, first to the ambassador of Emperor Charles V, then to the president of the pontifical commission for reform of the Church, to the ambassador of Siena, to a Spanish physician, and to Francesco de Estrada, a Spanish priest who'd worked for the formidable Cardinal Caraffa in Rome and been fired. Upon completion of the Exercises, Estrada too joined the Company of Jesus, and late in life would be named the Jesuit provincial of Aragón in Spain.

Rome became Ignatius's and the companions' Jerusalem. After Easter 1538, all of them gathered there and, through the skills of Pietro Codacio, a papal chamberlain and the first Italian companion, got title to the Church of Santa Maria della Strada, Our Lady of the Wayside, chosen by Ignatius because it was on a high-traffic piazza that was handily near the papal court, government offices, a significant Jewish community, palaces of the upper class, houses of prostitutes, and the hovels of the poor. Santa Maria della Strada was the first foundation in the Eternal City for a host of what Ignatius called "works of piety": homes for children that were supported by the Confraternity of Saint Mary of the Visitation of Orphans; the Catechumens, a house for the religious instruction of new Jewish converts; the Casa Santa Marta, a house of refuge for former prostitutes; and the Conservatorio delle Vergini Miserabili, a house for girls who might be attracted to prostitution. Significant to their primary ministry later was their work at the Collegio Romano, a high school in grammar, humanities, and Christian doctrine that was free for boys in Rome. Costs of education were defrayed by a magnificent gift from Francisco Borgia, the duke of Gandía in Spain, the great-grandson of Pope Alexander VI and King Ferdinand V, a father of eight, and, after the death of his wife, a Jesuit priest and the third superior general.

But the foundation of the greatest importance was, of course, that of the Society of Jesus—*societas* being the Latin for company—which was confirmed by Paul III in the papal bull *Regimini Militantis Ecclesiae* on September 27, 1540. Ignatius sketched the "formula" for the institute in five brief chapters that he introduced in this way:

Whoever desires to serve as a soldier of God beneath the banner of the cross in our Society, which we desire to be designated by the name of Jesus, and in it to serve the Lord alone and his vicar on earth, should, after a solemn vow of chastity, keep what follows in mind. He is a member of a community founded chiefly to strive for the progress of souls in Christian life and doctrine, and for the propagation of the faith by means of the ministry of the word, the Spiritual Exercises, and works of charity . . .

Upon hearing the "formula" read to him, the aged Paul III had orally given his approval and added, "*Digitus Dei est hic*," "The finger of God is here." Ignatius and Jean Codure later expanded "A First Sketch of the Institute of the Society of Jesus" into *Constitutions* of forty-nine points regulating frugality, governance, admission and formation of novices, and housing and other practical matters, but generally offering Jesuits flexibility in their ways of proceeding in order to give room to, as Ignatius put it, "the internal guidance of the Holy Spirit."

In fulfillment of their rules on governance, on April 8, 1541, Ignatius was elected the first superior general of the Society of Jesus, the only ballot against him being his own. Xavier's ballot was probably typical of the others; he voted for "our old leader and true father, Don Ignacio, who, since he brought us together with no little effort, will also with similar effort know how to preserve, govern, and help us advance from good to better."

Ignatius was then fifty and far different from the man he'd fantasized he'd be when he was a page to Spanish royalty, or a pilgrim to the Holy Land, or a philosopher at the Sorbonne. Ever seeking the greater glory of God and the good of souls, Ignatius surely imagined a grander fate than that of fifteen years of grinding office and managerial work in the house for forty professed fathers that he built on Via Aracoeli, or that of having as one of his prime contributions to history his hand-cramping composition of more than seven thousand letters to his scattered Jesuit sons—twelve full volumes in the *Monumenta Historica Societatis Iesu*. We hear no regret in his letters, however, no aching to be elsewhere, only geniality and hunger for news as he writes to the Jesuit *periti* at the Council of Trent; gentle hints as to how a homosexual scholastic could preserve his chastity; tenderness for the many Spanish women for whom he was a spiritual director; sympathy for a priest in Sicily afflicted by scruples, as he had been; fatherly reproof as he orders a house in Portugal to curb their hard penances; affection to his dearest friend Xavier in Japan: "We have rejoiced in the Lord that you have arrived with health and that doors have opened to have the Gospel preached in that region."

His holiness was unmistakable; he practiced self-mastery until there seemed to be no difference between God's will and his own. "Eres en tu casa," was his wide-armed greeting to anyone who visited him—"You are at home"—and all who talked with him left with the impression that he was kindliness itself: Michelangelo was so affected by Ignatius that he offered to build the Church of the Gesù for nothing. Ever a mystic, at times the saint was in the midst of an official transaction when his thoughts would lift up to God and hang there, and his witnesses would shyly shuffle their shoes until he got back to his papers again. But there were also stories of him surprising a melancholic with a jig in order to cheer him up, and his happiness was such that he said he could no longer apply his own rules for discernment of spirits because he was finding consolation in all things—he once said he saw the Holy Trinity in the leaf of an orange tree. Although children threw apples at him when he first preached in the streets of Rome—probably because of his horrid Italian—he soon was as genuinely beloved as the pope. In fact, he was so highly thought of by prelates that in the 1550 conclave at which Julius III was elected pontiff, Ignatius de Loyola received five votes. And we can get a feeling for the high esteem in which he was held by his fellow Jesuits when we read letters such as this from a Frans de Costere, SJ, of Cologne:

> The day before yesterday I saw for the first time, with indescribable joy and eagerness, Reverend Father Ignatius. I could not see enough of him. For his countenance is such that one cannot look upon it long enough. The old man was walking in the garden, leaning on a cane. His face shone with godliness. He is mild, friendly, and amiable so that he speaks with the learned and the unlearned, with important people

and little people, all in the same way: a man worthy of all praise and
reverence. No one can deny that a great reward is prepared for him in
heaven. . . .

But Gian Pietro Caraffa, whom Ignatius insulted in his frank letter
about the Theatines, thought of him as a tyrant and a false idol. In
fact, the friction between Caraffa and Ignatius was such that when,
in 1555, Ignatius heard that Caraffa had been elected pontiff, as Paul
IV, Ignatius's face went white, and he falteringly limped into a chapel
to pray. But after a while he appeared again and happily said the new
Pope Paul IV would be good to them, which he was, but only to a
degree, for after Ignatius died he tried to merge his Theatines with
the Jesuits and briefly forced them to sing the Divine Office in choir
and to limit the superior general's term to three years.

Even some of his first companions had difficulties with Ignatius,
though: Nicolás de Bobadilla angrily called him "a rascally sophist and
a Basque spoiled by flattery" and Simão Rodrigues, whose contrari-
ness prompted Ignatius to recall him from Portugal, claimed that the
superior general did so out of passion and hate, and with slight regard
for his reputation. Juan de Polanco was supposed to have made do
with hardly one compliment during his nine years as Ignatius's secretary; Jerónimo Nadal was often so harshly criticized that he couldn't
hold back his tears; and Diego Laínez, a favorite of his, once objected,
"What have I done against the Society that this saint treats me this
way?"

An affectionate man who was wary of his *affectus*, Ignatius was
probably hard on his friends in accordance with his fundamental
principle of *agere contra*, that is, to go against or contradict one's own
inclinations if they are not for the honor and glory of God or for the
good of others. We see hints of this in the sixteenth annotation to his
Spiritual Exercises, in which Ignatius wrote: "If by chance the exercitant
feels an affection or inclination to something in a disordered way, it
is profitable for that person to strive with all possible effort to come
over to the opposite of that to which he or she is wrongly attached."

He was harder on himself than on his friends, punishing himself
for his sins, getting to bed late and waking up at half past four, hardly

ever going outside the house or strolling in the gardens, which he insisted on for his "sons," dining on food that he called a penance, holding his gaze on the ground when he did walk in Rome, loving plainchant but forbidding choir for the order.

All of that took its toll. By 1556 his health was failing to such an extent that to his chronic stomach pains were added a hardening of the liver, high fevers, and general exhaustion. He was rarely seen outside his room and ate little more than fish scraps and broths and lettuce prepared with oil. Spells of illness had troubled him so frequently in the past, however, and he'd shown such resilience in healing, that no one was especially upset by his confinement, and physicians often failed even to visit him as they ministered to others in the house who were thought to be far worse off, among them his friend Diego Laínez. But Ignatius knew how far he'd sunk, and on the afternoon of July 30, he thought it would be fitting if Juan de Polanco, the secretary of the Society, would go and inform Paul IV that Ignatius "was near the end and almost without hope of temporal life, and that he humbly begged from His Holiness his blessing for himself and for Master Laínez, who was also in danger." Misprizing his superior's condition, Polanco asked if he could put off the walk, because he was trying to finish some letters for Spain before a ship sailed. Ignatius told him, "The sooner you go, the more satisfied I shall be: however, do as you wish."

Brother Tommaso Cannicari, the infirmarian, slept in a cell next to the superior general's quarters, and off and on heard Ignatius praying until, after midnight, he heard only, over and over again, the Spanish sigh, "*Ay, Dios!*" At sunrise the fathers in the house saw that Ignatius was dying, and Cannicari hurried to find the superior general's confessor while Polanco hurried to the papal residence to request the Holy Father's blessing. But it was too late. Two hours after sunrise on Friday morning, July 31, 1556, Ignatius of Loyola died, without having received the quite unnecessary graces of extreme unction or viaticum or papal blessing.

In the first week of the *Spiritual Exercises*, Ignatius had offered this as the "Principle and Foundation" for all the meditations that would follow:

Human beings are created to praise, reverence, and serve God our Lord, and by means of doing this to save their souls.

The other things on the face of the earth are created for the human beings, to help them in the pursuit of the end for which they are created.

From this it follows that we ought to use these things to the extent that they help us toward our end, and free ourselves from them to the extent that they hinder us from it.

To attain this it is necessary to make ourselves indifferent to all created things, in regard to everything which is left to our free will and is not forbidden. Consequently, on our own part we ought not to seek health rather than sickness, wealth rather than poverty, honor rather than dishonor, a long life rather than a short one, and so on in all other matters.

Rather, we ought to desire and choose only that which is more conducive to the end for which we are created.

Saint Irenaeus said that the glory of God is a human being fully alive. But what is it to be fully alive? We are apt to look at Ignatius's life as one of harsh discipline and privation, and find only loss in his giving up of family, inheritance, financial security, prestige, luxury, sexual pleasure. But he looked at his life as an offering to the God he called *liberalidad*, freedom, and God blessed that gift a hundredfold in the Society of Jesus. The house of Loyola ended when Doña Magdalena de Loyola y Borgia died childless in 1626, but in that same year there were 15,535 Jesuits in 36 provinces, with 56 seminaries, 44 novitiates, 254 houses, and 443 colleges in Europe and the Baltic States, Japan, India, Macao, the Philippines, and the Americas.

Further Reading

There are several translations available of Ignatius's *Autobiography*. My Xavier colleagues and I have found the one by Joseph Tylenda, SJ—with its running commentary at the bottom of each page—most helpful (*A Pilgrim's Journey: The Autobiography of Ignatius of Loyola* [Wilmington, DE: Michael Glazier, 1985]). Also very good is the translation by Indian Jesuit Parmananda Divarkar, especially as it appears in *Ignatius of Loyola: Spiritual Exercises and Selected Works* (Mahwah, NJ: Paulist Press, 1991), with explanatory endnotes by editor George Ganss, SJ. Another compendium, *St. Ignatius of Loyola: Personal Writings* (New York: Penguin Putnam, 1996), contains a translation by British Jesuit Philip Endean. And the translation by Joseph F. O'Callaghan, SJ, which opens with an important introduction by historian of Catholic reform John Olin (New York: Harper & Row, 1974), is long out of print but continues to be used by scholars.

The standard critical biography of Ignatius, accurate to the last detail, is *Ignatius of Loyola, Founder of the Jesuits: His Life and Work*, by Candido de Dalmases, SJ, translated by Jerome Aixala (St. Louis: Institute of Jesuit Sources, 1985). Easier and more inviting to read are *Ignatius of Loyola: The Pilgrim Saint* by Ignacio Tellechea Idígoras (Chicago: Loyola Press, 1994) and *Ignatius Loyola: A Biography of the Founder of the Jesuits* by Philip Caraman, SJ (San Francisco: Harper & Row, 1990). A delight for the eyes as well as the mind is *St. Ignatius of Loyola: A Pictorial Biography* (Chicago: Henry Regnery, 1956), with stunning black-and-white photos by Leonard von Matt and excellent accompanying text by Hugo Rahner, SJ; though long out of print, it is available in many a Jesuit university library. Finally, an indication that the study of Ignatius has come a long way since the early works of hagiography (saints' lives noted more for piety than accuracy), we have the study by Freudian psychoanalyst W. W. Meissner, SJ, MD,

The Psychology of a Saint: Ignatius of Loyola (New Haven, CT: Yale University Press, 1992).

Addressing what Ignatius means for us today, Karl Rahner, SJ (1904–1984), the great German Catholic theologian, put into the mouth of Ignatius what the saint might have said to him and to us in: "Ignatius of Loyola Speaks to a Modern Jesuit" (*Ignatius of Loyola, with an Historical Introduction by Paul Imhof, SJ, Colour Photographs by Helmut Nils Loose*, translated by Rosaleen Ockenden [London: Collins, 1979])—a fascinating essay, though hampered in this translation by nearly unrecognizable references to Jesuitica (for example, "regulations of the ecclesiastical mind" for "Rules for Thinking with the Church").

Finding God
in All Things

Introduction

"'Finding God in all things'—Ignatian spirituality is summed up in this phrase," as the corresponding entry in *Do You Speak Ignatian?* begins. "It invites a person to search for and find God in every circumstance of life, not just in explicitly religious situations or activities." The vision expressed by this spirituality was revolutionary in the sixteenth century, with its departure from monastic withdrawal and an invitation to embrace the world in all its ambiguity through action that is service to others.

But how does one grow in this ability to find God everywhere? Howard Gray, SJ, internationally known interpreter of Ignatius and Ignatian spirituality, has mined Ignatius's *Constitutions* and come up with a model of what spiritual growth and development meant for the Jesuit leader. It turns out to be as applicable and feasible for laypeople as it is for Jesuits. Stated simply, the model says:

(1) *be attentive* to reality;
(2) *reverence* (that is, appreciate) what you see and hear and feel in all its particulars;
(3) and "then you will *find Devotion* [what Ignatius also called "consolation"], the singularly moving way in which God works in that situation."

The phrase "Finding God in all things" also becomes a title for scholars to write synthetically about Ignatian spirituality. The late Monika Hellwig, longtime professor of theology at Georgetown and subsequently head of the Association of Catholic Colleges and Universities (ACCU), writes in "Finding God in All Things: A Spirituality for Today" about five features of Ignatian spirituality that make it particularly apt for our time. The other essay in this section, Howard Gray's

"Ignatian Spirituality," is the pivotal essay of this entire volume. Gray's treatment looks back to an earlier section of this reader—Ignatius's sense of his life as a pilgrimage—and looks ahead to the coming sections, Prayer, the Spiritual Exercises, and Discernment.

Understanding the Terminology:
Suggested Readings from *Do You Speak Ignatian?*

- Finding God in All Things
- Ignatian/Jesuit Vision

Finding God in All Things:
A Spirituality for Today

Monika K. Hellwig

Excerpted from *Sojourners*, 1991

Ignatius of Loyola, founder of the largest Catholic religious order, the Jesuits, has been attracting widespread attention this year, the five hundredth anniversary of his birth. Ignatius's legacy goes far beyond the founding of the Jesuits—he launched a distinctive style and tradition of spirituality that is particularly apt for our time. . . .

The Spiritual Legacy of Ignatius

In their basic form, the Spiritual Exercises [of Ignatius] consist of a silent retreat of about thirty days in which four or more hours are given each day to certain prescribed meditations. In an alternate form, the Exercises are spread over a much longer period of time and are done while a person follows his or her ordinary occupations, making time each day for one period of meditation.

For young people trying to discern their particular vocations in life, for people at a crucial juncture in their lives who can make themselves free for thirty days, and for those training to direct others, complete withdrawal from everyday life to some quiet retreat house seems to be a suitable plan.

But there are many people who can derive great profit from the experience who could never get away like that. For such people, the extended part-time retreat has special advantages of its own. Resolutions and conversions made in withdrawal from one's ordinary life may look very different when regular activities and contacts are resumed, while those made in the everyday context of life are likely to be more realistic and therefore firmer.

When Ignatius set out the pattern of meditations for the *Exercises*, he took the content from the basic structure of Christian beliefs as rooted in the Bible, especially in the gospels, often concretized in imagery drawn from the traditions of his childhood. The material is divided into four sections called "weeks." The first week is focused on the theme of creation, including reflections on the nature and consequences of various disruptions of the harmony of creation and the focus and balance of human life by sin.

The second week consists of meditations on the hidden life and public ministry of Jesus, including some very colorful and dramatic meditations geared to recognizing and adjusting one's own stance of discipleship. The third week consists of meditations on the passion and death of Jesus, and the fourth week is given to the events of the resurrection.

Besides offering the subject matter in brief comments and sending the retreatant back to the texts of scripture, Ignatius describes different ways of praying and has the exercitant explore ways of prayer most suited to that individual.

But perhaps most characteristic of all, the whole process is geared to consciousness raising of the individual (though that term does not occur in the text) to be alert to one's own motivations and inclinations, and to learn to discern what is the voice of the Holy Spirit of God and what is the voice of a spirit that is counter to God's Spirit, a spirit of destruction and disorientation. For this, Ignatius thought, it was necessary to be sensitive to the light of the Holy Spirit in prayer so as to make appropriate discernments in uncharted situations.

These *Exercises* have been at the foundation of the training of Jesuits. They have shaped the way this congregation of vowed, celibate men (most of whom are priests) has run its many schools, has carried on a practice of spiritual direction of laity, has carried out missions and pastored local churches, and has engaged in social justice issues in far-reaching and radical ways.

In a similar way, the *Exercises* have been basic in the formation and spirituality of a number of congregations of religious women. Through the Jesuit schools, they have shaped many generations of young boys, and through Jesuit colleges and universities, generations of intellectuals, male and female. In their schools and in their parishes, Jesuits have invited laypeople into groups called "Sodalities" (now known as Christian Life Communities) for spiritual formation, support, and apostolic outreach, and have served as spiritual directors.

In his early apostolic outreach, Ignatius would direct several people in a town through the Spiritual Exercises. He would then expect some of them to direct several others each so as to spread the influence as far as possible. In the course of generations and centuries, more tradition has built up and more training and experience are expected of directors. A living tradition has been created for which the text is just a rough guideline. Each generation shares in the cumulative wisdom garnered from the prayer, reflection, and life experience of all the foregoing participants.

Out of this living process comes a vigorous, optimistic, world-affirming spirituality, committed to service but critical at all times of what is or is not really service for the reign of God in the world.

Grounded in Gratitude and Reverence

Because it is based in the *Spiritual Exercises*, Ignatian spirituality is grounded in intense gratitude and reverence. It begins with and continually reverts to the awareness of the presence and power and care of God everywhere, for everyone, and at all times.

This sense of a wholly integrated universe, society, and personal life is one that certainly still existed in the Spain of Ignatius's youth, but was rapidly disintegrating for most people in his mature years. In his youth he lived in a culture in which intimacy with God, and a sense of belonging and being protected, could still be taken for granted, requiring no special effort or attention on the part of the individual.

By the time Ignatius was guiding other people through the Exercises, the culture did not automatically convey such a sense of intimacy with God, so that the individual had to make a deliberate effort to cultivate it. That, of course, is very much the case in our own culture, in which people can live most of their lives without ever being confronted with the question of the ultimate meaning and purpose of their lives.

There are two primary types of prayer and relation to the divine in Christian tradition. The first, known as *via negativa*, tries to encounter God by leaving senses, imagination, and intellect behind to meet God in the darkness and silence of pure presence without content. The second, known as *via positiva*, tries to encounter God through the appreciation of what God does in creation.

Ignatian spirituality emphatically chooses the latter as the predominant and ordinary type intended for most people. In that choice lies a directive to cultivate visual and other sensory imagination in prayer—contemplating scenes from the gospels by entering into them in imagination to play a role and to come to a relationship of warm affection with Jesus and his family, friends, and followers.

The process seeks to bring about a sense of the attitudes and responses that Jesus would take in situations that do not actually arise in the gospel narratives but do arise in our lives. Nothing is more central in Ignatian spirituality than this sense of intimate companionship with Jesus, and the total service that follows from such intimacy as a matter of both gratitude and family loyalty.

A Cultivation of Critical Awareness

A second significant factor in Ignatian spirituality is the cultivation of critical awareness of what is right and wrong in one's own life and attitudes, one's society and culture, and in specific situations. To many people of our own time, no matter how well disposed in Christian faith, the idea of repeated meditations on sin, day after day, is repugnant. The idea so pervasive in our culture that one should always look on the positive side, and that guilt is a manifestation of neurosis, can easily make Christians uncomfortable with the very idea of sin.

Yet what happens in the first-week meditations on sin is the subtle but effective cultivation of imagination and consciousness. To reflect on the classic stories of the sin of the fallen angels, the sin of Adam, and catastrophic destructive acts in history is not only to experience horror and grief, but also to know the disappointment over what might have been and has not been realized. Combined with the conviction of the unfailing power and loving care of God, and leading into reflection on the meaning and impact of the events in the life of Jesus, these meditations on sin are also an invitation to imagine the world and one's own life becoming quite different.

What is rediscovered in the Ignatian approach to spirituality is that the traditional Christian doctrine about the sin of Adam, also called original sin, is not a message of doom but one of hope. It declares that the world as we have it is not the best we can hope for, nor the world that God intends, but a badly broken and distorted one which can be restored and can be immeasurably better and happier than it now is.

Empowerment to Responsibility

Ignatian spirituality contains within it a strong sense of empowerment to accept and exercise responsibility in the work of redemption that is still going on in the world. There is much emphasis on the surrender of the will and all the faculties to God—not in a passive sense but rather on the model of an *hidalgo* such as the young Ignatius, dedicating (and in that sense surrendering) his freedom, strength, skills, and faculties to the service of his Lord. It implies, therefore, maximum ingenuity, diligence, and creativity—all at the single-minded service of the Lord's cause.

The *Exercises* are geared, among other things, to the experience and recognition of grace in one's own life. They have an implied understanding of grace not as divine action alongside of human freedom and action, but rather as divine action empowering human action, divine freedom liberating human freedom. In Ignatian spirituality individuals are taught to expect and to recognize their own empowerment by grace.

The pattern of this is very much like that which we find in testimonies of the Christians of the first and second centuries. These Christians wrote that Christ had done two things for them: He had illumined them and he had empowered them. The empowerment had to do with the clarity with which they now saw everything because of the illumination by Christ.

In our own times of introspective and psychological awareness, it is easy to recognize this process happening. The more clearly we see ourselves in the light of creation, sin, and redemption, the more encouraged and empowered we are to act in consort with Christ in the transformation and salvation of the world.

A Commitment to Action

Directly connected with this is the fourth characteristic of Ignatian spirituality: the focus and insistence on action. This appears as a theme with many variations. Loyalty is expressed in service. Love is appropriately manifested in actions rather than in words. Repentance means action for change. Serious conversion to Christ means commitment of all one's resources—material and personal—expenditure of all one's energies, steady focus of one's attention.

One very important consequence of this is the gradual elimination of the profane margins of one's life. But in Ignatian spirituality this does not mean that one no longer engages in worldly responsibilities or in social, economic, and political affairs. What it does mean is that engagement in such affairs ceases to be profane, which means outside the range of the religious commitment. All the secular activities of life are brought into the faith commitment and are therefore brought under scrutiny and evaluation in the light of what is revealed in Christ about the meaning and purpose and true orientation of all creation.

This approach applies not only to the immediate contacts of one's life, but also to social structures and policies at all levels of human society. This commitment to the integration of all aspects of life, therefore, does not allow a separation of politics and economics from religious values and judgments.

Redemptive action for justice and peace in the public affairs of the human race threatens the disproportionate privilege of many who call themselves Christians, probably in good faith, but think that this pertains only to their individual private lives. While the vigorous opposition to social justice and peace activities in the public realm may be in good faith, it is not disinterested.

The commitment to action and to public responsibilities often meets an objection of another kind. This is the view that contemplation is at the heart of religious faith, and that contemplation and action are incompatible with one another. Contemplation is certainly at the heart of faith, because contemplation means an attitude of receptivity, attention, and awareness of divine presence and guidance. This is beyond question.

However, Ignatian spirituality refuses to see contemplation as being in opposition to action or incompatible with it. It was said of Ignatius himself in his mature years that he seemed to be contemplative in action. What is seen as incompatible with contemplation is greed, possessiveness, acquisitiveness, cruelty, indifference to the needs of others, pride, self-assertiveness, and preoccupation with oneself and one's public image. But hard work, preoccupation with serving the needs of others, and so forth, are seen as opportunities to be contemplative in action.

A Revolutionary Spirituality

All of the foregoing leads to the final characteristic of Ignatian spirituality as countercultural and revolutionary in a nonviolent way. Much of the reflection in the *Exercises* is geared to an effort to share the vision of Jesus and understand what he was and is trying to do in the world and its history.

The meditations are very clear in their implication that the task that Jesus received from God is not to save souls out of the world, but to save the world, to refocus and reintegrate all creation by drawing the human race back into its proper relationship with God—and therefore proper relationships within the human race and all the created universe.

Such a perspective judges everything in terms of what we can know of the divinely intended outcomes. Such a vision leads to radical judgments about the way we are conducting the affairs of human society now. Such a vision certainly does not allow one to take for granted wars; poverty; famines; injustices; margination of ethnic, racial, linguistic, or economic groups; or other unnecessary sufferings or deprivations.

One cannot simply say that this is how it is and how it will always be because the world is like that—in the context of the *Exercises*, that is plainly untrue. It is untrue because God does not intend that kind of arrangement of human society in which so many are excluded. These sufferings are not divinely made but humanly made. God has not abandoned creation but reaches out at all times and to all peoples with possibilities and grace for redemption—not, according to the gospels, a redemption confined to life beyond death, but redemption of all aspects of human life in this world which we help to shape for good or for ill.

By these insights and criteria, radical change is not only possible but necessary, not only to be wished for but to be worked for in practical ways, not only an option for the remote future but a challenge in our present. These attitudes are formed in the meditations on the passion and death of Christ and those on the resurrection.

Meditation on the passion and death of Christ has often been proposed as an invitation to accept the way things are. But what is implicit in the Ignatian approach is contrary to this, because it invites attention not only to what Jesus suffered physically, but to the discernment process that Jesus went through and the action to which it led—which in turn provoked bitter persecution. This leads to an appreciation of the radical nature of the positions Jesus took in his own times and to the real impact of his teaching on political and social structures in the long run.

Readiness and confidence for personal discernment is a key element of Ignatian spirituality, and it is one that is particularly important in our times. It implies training, as well as constant attention in prayer in evaluating actions by the guidance of the Holy Spirit, working for an attitude of detachment from self-interest in making decisions, and trying at all times to enter into the mind and intentions of Jesus.

When someone does this and gains confidence, tempered by humility, that person has a basis for countercultural decisions, creative initiatives, and difficult undertakings. But unless an individual has the focus and the confidence for discernment in uncharted situations, that person is likely to be a passive obeyer of codes and commandments, not responding to the most important commandments of all: to love God with heart and soul and to love one's neighbors as oneself.

Ignatian Spirituality

Howard Gray, SJ

From *As Leaven in the World: Catholic Perspectives on Faith, Vocation, and the Intellectual Life*, 2001

Ignatius Loyola,[1] founder of the Society of Jesus,[2] described his spirituality as a journey towards God.[3] He envisioned most everything in life as part of that journey—as created realities that facilitated the journey or impeded its progress. Therefore, Ignatius also promoted the need for men and women—pilgrims all—to become people of discernment.[4] Moreover, in that discerning journey, Ignatius believed that there were three guides: Jesus Christ, the mission he gave to his Church, and human experience. Ignatian spirituality is at heart a discerning *pilgrimage* to God[5] guided by three important elements: the reality of *Christ*, the *mission entrusted to his Church*, and *human experience*.

The Pilgrimage

Ignatius did not intend to become a saint. He focused his sixteenth-century ambitions on the life of a courtier. However, battle wounds necessitated his convalescence at his family castle of Loyola. During his recuperation, Iñigo, as he was then called, asked for copies of popular romances to lighten his boredom. None was to be found in

Castle Loyola so, reluctantly, Iñigo read what was available: a life of Christ and a collection of the lives of the saints.[6] This reading ignited in Iñigo a desire to serve God alone, a desire that would have been unthinkable to him and all who knew him a few months earlier. Gradually, he determined to turn away from court ambition, to embark on a pilgrimage that was to last years and took him, finally, to studies for the priesthood at the University of Paris, where he gathered a group of disciples who, in turn, presented themselves to the pope as a new religious order.

What was pivotal in this process was Ignatius's—as he now called himself—self-designation as "the pilgrim."[7] He meant the title literally because after Loyola he traveled from Montserrat to Manresa, to Barcelona, to Rome, to Venice, to Jerusalem, to a series of Spanish university towns, and then to Paris. From city to city, from university to university, Ignatius learned how to discern the movements within his own soul. Out of this inner and outer pilgrimage, Ignatius was also refining the notes of his *Spiritual Exercises*,[8] a guidebook to help other men and women move into Christian discipleship. He himself described this process in these poignant words:

> God treated him at this time just as a schoolmaster treats a child whom he is teaching. Whether this was because of his lack of education and of brains, or because he had no one to teach him, or because of the strong desire God himself had given him to serve him, he believed without a doubt and has always believed that God treated him in this way. Indeed if he were to doubt this, he would think he offended his Divine Majesty.[9]

The *Exercises* represent a kind of spiritual journey, as they invite the one who makes them to consider the foundational truths of Christian life: creation as an act of love, human stewardship of creation, sin and forgiveness, the life and work of Jesus as a paradigm of discipleship, Christ's suffering, death, and resurrection and, finally, the surrender of all human life into the hands of a loving God. The Ignatian take on the Christian journey is to insist that it is a movement, an active progress towards a radical decision to live one's life in harmony with

Christ's vision and values. The movement towards Christ is both inward and outward, horizontal and vertical, contemplative and active.

The *Exercises* present an intense interiority, a call to spend time noting what in a person's life has been leading to life or to death, to love or to enmity. In that sense, then, the *Exercises* represent the introspective dimension of Ignatian spirituality. The prayer form that captures best this self-awareness before God is the examen of consciousness.[10] In the examen of consciousness the aim is not recrimination but rather a developing alertness to what really motivates a person, to a person's pattern of choices that gradually reveal the character and personality of a woman or man before God. For example, if one notes that all his or her choices are made primarily out of a desire to succeed, then questions confront that man or woman: What do I think a successful life really is? How do I imagine happiness, contentment, fulfillment? This introspective inventory of the soul's desire, especially when conducted in the companionship of an experienced guide, reveals much about the values, ambitions, dreams, and desires of a person.

But the *Exercises* are not only oriented towards self-scrutiny; they also orient the one who makes them towards self-donation. A rhythm of prayerful reflection on the direction of one's life in comparison to the direction of Christ's life constitutes another dynamic within the experience of the *Exercises*.[11] The life of Christ moves from one act of self-donation to another until the climatic self-offering of his death on the cross. The Risen Christ does not exist in some eternal sabbatical, but continues to work through his Spirit—inspiring, challenging, healing, leading. The Ignatian pilgrimage leads towards the mission of this Risen Christ, inviting men and women involved in the Exercises to look outward, beyond themselves, to the mission of the kingdom.

The kingdom for Ignatius is a gift "from above,"[12] from the eternal design of the fatherhood of God who calls all people to be saved. This vertical movement—the descent of God into human minds and hearts and into human structures in order to make all creation a reflection of peace, justice, and love—constitutes another type of prayer in the *Exercises*. Contemplation of the life of Christ as portrayed in the four

Gospels leads to discipleship, to a commitment to the Kingdom of God. God reveals in the incidents of Jesus' life the way God wishes to be known, to be loved, to be served.

The service of God, exemplified in Jesus, is also a horizontal movement. This movement reaches out to all other men and women, to all creation, to cultures and nations, to Christians and to people of other faiths. Service to God meant for Ignatius a service that "helps other people." As Ignatius moved through the early stages of his own pilgrimage, he found himself withdrawing from a lifestyle that had been dominated by isolation, penance, and asceticism to a growing solidarity with other people. He could understand this movement towards others only as a desire "to help people." "To help people" became a mantra for Ignatius, and later, for all the other early Jesuits. It was a phrase that epitomized all that gave them energy for their ministries and direction within their works.[13]

This desire to help people guides the discernment of the *Exercises*. The so-called "election"[14] of the *Exercises* is the peaceful resolution of a complex set of movements. Where, finally, does God call you to serve him through helping other people? Ignatian prayer leads to a practical choice about how to live in the world, how to make the gospel credible and vital, how to incarnate within oneself the values of the kingdom. Significantly, the climactic prayer of the *Exercises*, the suscipe, incorporates these movements into a summary of a contemplative who acts within the world:

> Take, Lord, and receive all my liberty, my memory, my understanding, and all my will—all that I have and possess. You, Lord, have given all to me. I now give it back to you, O Lord. All of it is yours. Dispose of it according to your will. Give me love of yourself along with your grace, for that is enough for me."[15]

In his reflection on the life of Ignatius, the novelist Ron Hansen says, "I have simply been trying to figure out how to live my life magnificently, as Ignatius did, who sought in all his works and activities the greater glory of God."[16] The spirituality Ignatius presented does lay claim to magnificent ambitions and ideals. But the initial process that led to his greatness of vision and spiritual ambition was that of the pilgrimage of God. It was a sustaining metaphor that implied traveling light, with the essential baggage being those values preached by Christ. The pilgrimage metaphor also meant a patient willingness to find God through the journeying. It also meant a willingness to risk a process of trial and error, of successes and failures, of some triumphs but also many humiliating defeats. The pilgrimage, finally, meant taking the journey to God by working for the kingdom in the midst of the world, not secluded from it.

Because every pilgrimage involves the willingness to be transformed along the way, Ignatius demands two conditions for every traveler through the *Exercises*. First, the one who makes them must be free enough to discern how God calls him or her, to give time and space for the endeavor.[17] Second, the one who makes them must be generous enough to embrace what God extends to him or her.[18] Thus, contemplative reflection and the generous implementation of what prayer reveals characterize Ignatian spirituality. It is an invitation to become a contemplative who acts.

Centrality of Jesus Christ

The *Exercises* present two dimensions of Christ. First, Christ is the gospel figure whose words and actions symbolize how God would live human life. Therefore, Christ is to be imitated—not in the physical details of his life but in the values, ideals, priorities, lifestyle he reveals.[19] To know Christ, Ignatius insists, is to love him, and to love him is to want to serve him. And the service Jesus models is to preach, to teach, to labor, to make God's kingdom available to all people.

Second, Christ is the Crucified and Risen Lord who lives in the glory of the Father but who, through his Spirit, lives in his followers and in the world he loved and saved. This Risen Christ summons every man and woman to read the gospel narratives as invitations to a fuller life and a more liberating love. The gospel narrative does not simply inspire but it has an animating, spiritual power that reaches into the history, psychology, and ambitions of men and women who make the *Exercises*.[20] This communication of the Risen Christ through his gospel stories contributes the principal prayer of the *Exercises*: Ignatian gospel contemplation.[21]

How does Ignatius present this gospel communication, this transforming, religious narrative? There are two features of Ignatian gospel contemplation. The first involves the way one learns how to integrate the gospel story into his or her consciousness. The second involves how one comes to focus on the unique way Christ calls him or her through the narrative.

To understand the method of prayerful integration that Ignatius teaches, we have to look at another source of Ignatian spirituality, the Jesuit *Constitutions*.[22] The *Constitutions* represent the major work of Ignatius's generalship of the Society of Jesus. The *Constitutions* are themselves a kind of pilgrimage that lays out the developmental stages of Jesuit formation, incorporation, mission, and life. In an especially rich section of ascetical and mystical advice, Ignatius proposes the way a young Jesuit can become contemplatively engaged with his world, finding in the world God's activity, design, and direction. What Ignatius proposes we may term *attention, reverence*, and *devotion*.[23] While the immediate context for this Ignatian wisdom is Jesuit formation, the process that he proposes constitutes what he also means by gospel contemplation within the context of the *Exercises*.

By *attention*[24] Ignatius means allowing the reality of the other to be present to you in all its integrity. To be attentive is to be focused, i.e., gently alert to what has been revealed. In our context, it is the gospel narrative in whole or in part. To sustain such a focus demands time, energy, and generosity. Consequently, Ignatius demands these as preconditions for making the *Exercises*. It is difficult, if not impossible, for one to make the *Exercises* without taking time to listen, to see, to be present to what God may reveal.

Let us use an example of gospel attentiveness. In Luke 15, Jesus offers the lovely but challenging parable of a prodigal son.[25] A superficial reading tempts someone to go immediately to the core moment, the elaborate welcome and restoration of the younger son extended to him by his ever-patient father. The point of the narrative is that God forgives us. But attention slows this process down. The narrative is a chapter in Luke's Gospel. It is the third in a series of parables in Luke 15. The context is an exchange between Jesus and the religious leader of his time. The issue is Jesus' intimacy with public outcasts—sinners and tax collectors. These are the people religious authority has judged unclean, to be shunned, but Jesus treats them as his friends, his table companions. Therefore, in the eyes of the righteous, either Jesus is himself sinner or ignorant or defiant of the prevalent ethico-religious social code. In any case, Jesus has pitted himself against the system. The parable is Jesus' answer to such accusations. His accusers have chosen to stand not with the father who forgives but the self-righteous older brother who condemns. Attention takes the time and energy needed to let the density of the episode become my story too. It is the difference between being merely a spectator or an active participant.

Once engaged by the reality of the gospel narrative, Ignatius then asks that the attentive viewer or hearer treat all that he or she has discovered with *reverence*. Reverence for Ignatius is not an artificial piety or a superstitious solicitude. *Reverence* means what one has been attentive to must now be accepted as it is, in its own terms.[26] Reverence is the exclusion of exclusion; e.g., my biases and prejudices, my fears and hesitancies. If attention symbolizes "letting in," then reverence is "embracing what I have let in." For example, I reverence the narrative of Luke 15 when I accept the universality of God's forgiveness as revealed in Christ: "I tell you, there will be rejoicing among the angels of the Lord over one sinner who repents" (cf. Luke 15:10). Or I reverence Luke 15 when I accept the extravagant generosity of the father in the parable as a hint of the free vulnerability of God before a sinner who returns to God. Or I reverence Luke 15 when I accept the profound significance of the words, "to them he addressed this parable" (cf. Luke 15:3). For this means that I accept the self-disclosure of Jesus himself, that this is the kind of God he represents and that these publicans, tax collectors, and sinners, are, indeed, the people he chooses to serve. Reverence helps the one involved in Ignatian gospel contemplation to see sacredness in all aspects of Jesus' teaching.

Out of attention and reverence the one making the Exercises pro-gresses to *devotion*, a term rich in significance for Ignatius:

> [F]or Ignatius, devotion was the actualization of the virtue of religion by means of an affection for God which is prompt, compliant, warmly loving, and impelled by charity. Its goal is the worship of God which is accomplished in all things and actions of oneself and one's fellow men [and women], since it gives worship to God by finding and serving God in all things. In the Ignatian vocabulary 'devotion' is intimately linked to other key phrases . . . such as union with God, consolation, famil-iarity with God, charity, discreet charity, . . . love, fervor, finding God in all things, and the like.[27]

Within the context of the *Exercises*, devotion connotes those specific parts of a gospel episode that speak most tellingly, most personally to an individual. Such moments can be characterized as peace or as a strengthened sense of being called or of a renewed insight into the personality of Jesus. For example, as someone engages more and more with the parable of the prodigal son, he or she may be drawn to the seemingly limitless mercy of the father of the parable. And in this process of attraction, the one making the Exercises understands personally, in ways never experienced before, how profoundly Jesus is the Son of just this kind of Father. Devotion represents a privileged moment of personal revelation. It is also a moment when the heart is touched, drawing the person to greater love or deeper faith or surer trust or to a more courageous willingness to follow Jesus. Such moments and such movements are called "consolations," movements towards God.[28]

Sometimes the experience of devotion may not be as gentle. There may be reverent attention that draws a person towards a harsh honesty where one experiences the discrepancy between his or her opera-tional values and God's revelation. For example, I may find myself far more at home with the self-righteousness of the elder brother of the parable. I may recognize painfully that I do not want to live with the kind of generosity and forgiveness that the father of the parable dra-matizes. I realize that in the deepest part of my heart I am not where

God is. Such realizations can shock a person; and its significance can even sadden him or her. But these movements of honest confrontation are also consolations, if they lead to a deeper yearning to be converted into the likeness of Jesus or into a deeper harmony with his discipleship or into a freer acceptance that God's extravagant mercy extends to everyone.

However, if such insights tempt me to discouragement, to cynicism, or to trivialize the entire gospel event so that I move away from its truth or reject it as too idealistic, then I would be moving toward desolation, away from God.[29]

Gospel contemplation centers on persons, especially on the person of Jesus. The aim of such contemplation is to integrate the mind and heart of the person making the Exercises with the values and affections portrayed by Jesus. Gospel contemplation works towards union. As a prayer of union, gospel contemplation is both human disponability [willingness to be led] and divine grace. I bring a focused attention and reverence to the gospel narrative. God draws me through moments of devotion to dwell on a particular facet of the gospel event. This process gradually reveals how I am being drawn to follow Jesus. The question that emerges is: How does someone engaged in the contemplative prayer of the *Exercises* know how God calls him or her here and now, in this concrete situation? The response to this question involves the second feature of gospel contemplation.

The discipline of Ignatian gospel contemplation originates from the structure of the day spent in the Exercises.[30] Each day of the full Ignatian retreat has five distinct prayer periods. Each day centers on two gospel narratives, e.g., the Incarnation and the Nativity—the announcement of the birth of Jesus to Mary (Luke 1:26–38) and the birth of Jesus (Luke 2:1–26). These two periods of prayer are followed by two other prayer periods called "repetitions" and a fifth called "the application of senses." This daily structure and rhythm represents important characteristics and principles of Ignatian spirituality. It is crucial to unpack their significance.

First, repetition is not remedial prayer work nor is it a kind of stress instruction. That is, the idea behind the Ignatian repetitions is not that of doing a prayer until you get it right. Neither is it a crude effort to dictate how a person should find grace or God's leadership. Rather, the repetitions are efforts to engage mystery, to center on the depth of riches within revelation, and to discover how God specifically invites this particular man or woman to find the meaning of a gospel event for him or her. In other words, the aim of Ignatian repetition is to personalize prayer. For example, a person hears Mary's *yes* in Luke 1:38. In the initial encounter with this scene, the *yes* of Mary may have been admirable, challenging, and vaguely inviting. In the course of the prayers of repetition, the man or woman making the Exercises may begin to feel drawn to pronounce his or her own *yes*, to recognize a developing attraction to stand with Mary in personal solidarity with her kind of discipleship. Such a movement will lead in time to a willingness to stand with Mary beneath the cross of her son.

Third, the process of increasingly intense personal engagement with the meaning of the gospel is a gift, a grace. Ignatian prayer is never a performance; it is an encounter. Ignatius insists that this encounter involves two freedoms, human and divine. So delicate is the moment of revelatory encounter that Ignatius insists one of the principal tasks of the guide of the *Exercises* (Ignatius himself avoided the term *director*) is to guarantee that there be no engineering of this encounter. In fact, in a document that guides the interview with candidates to the Society of Jesus, Ignatius instructs the interviewer to halt the process if the candidate indicates anyone had influenced his decision to apply for the Jesuits. The candidate is to be advised to rethink the attraction, to take time to make sure that he is totally free in his decision.[31] From his own experience Ignatius learned the essential importance of spiritual freedom. One can claim grace as genuinely and uniquely *his* or *hers* only if the conditions for a free encounter be sustained. Perhaps an even more crucial reason lies within the Ignatian understanding of discernment and its relationship to Christ. For Ignatius, Christ symbolized the privileged moment of human and divine encounter both within Jesus' own consciousness and in his relationship to Abba, the beloved Father.[32]

Discernment is not so much technique as it is an awareness of how God moves within one's life and within the events that surround a person. Discernment for Jesus was whatever in him and in his mission—his work—led to life and to love, not to death and enmity. Consequently, Jesus' choices, even his willingness to die faithful to his mission to reveal a loving Father, were expressions based on the affirmation of life and love over death and enmity. For this reason, in the act of discerning love, Ignatius saw the epitome of the Christian imitation of Christ.

The Jesuit poet, Gerard Manley Hopkins, has significantly caught the Ignatian purchase on Christ's significance in these words:

> Mark Christ our King. He knows war, served this soldiering through;
> He of all can reave a rope best. There he bides in bliss.
> Now, and seeing somewhere some man do all must man can do,
> For love he leans forth, needs his neck must fall on, Kiss,
> and cry "O Christ—done deed!" So God made flesh does too:
> Were I come o'er again cries Christ "it would be this."[33]

For Ignatius, then, Christ was the exemplar both of God's self-donation to the human and of the human person's self-donation to God. The *magis*—the greater good—was embedded within a harmony of two seemingly contradictory virtues, humility and magnanimity [great-heartedness].[34] The following of Christ meant for Ignatius the freedom of humility and the willingness to risk all for the kingdom of magnanimity. Only in humility and magnanimity can one truly love God and the neighbor and journey confidently as a pilgrim in the spiritual life.

Of course, the question that demands some adequate response concerns this centrality of Jesus Christ in the *Exercises* and in Ignatian spirituality. Does this insistence on the centrality of Jesus effectively restrict this spirituality to believing Christians? One of the great early Jesuit confidants of Ignatius, Jerome Nadal, asserted that the *Exercises* were for anyone who sought peace with God and help in discovering his or her own path to God.[35] The reason Nadal could say this, I believe, was the Ignatian teaching on pastoral adaptation within the *Exercises*. An introductory directive to the one giving the *Exercises* advised the guide to fit them to the faith, education, and experiences of the one who made them. If the experience of the entire *Exercises* was not fruitful for a person, then give only part of them. If a person were capable of making the *Exercises* in their entirety but simply did not have time for thirty-day solitude and prayer away from family or work, then give them over a period of time and in a modified prayer form, e.g., one hour a day.[36] What was indispensable for the *Exercises* were the willingness to commit to them, a singleness of heart before God, a generosity of spirit, and the desire to deepen one's relationship to God in prayer and in everyday life. These dispositions know no creedal restrictions and are open to all men and women of goodwill. Moreover, the values that Christ lived, preached, and taught are founded on Jewish religious experience and have much in common with other religious traditions. In an age of inter-religious dialogue and increasing cooperation among people of goodwill, in professional environments that presume a diversity of beliefs and convictions, we have to live in mutual openness and honest dialogue. Much of the *Exercises* can help anyone. Christ's example can be adapted. What challenges Ignatian spirituality in an ecumenical and pluralistic culture is developing the imagination to make them available to others who are not Christian but who are genuinely seekers of deeper relationships with God.

The Mission of the Church

We have to be up front that as a man necessarily culturally conditioned, Ignatius could not be anything other than a Catholic Christian.[37] Catholicism was a birthright, a hermeneutic for interpreting the meaning of life, and the matrix for his religious and ethical world. What his conversion at Loyola had done was to transform him from a cultural Catholic to a dedicated man of gospel discipleship. We cannot discuss here the complex features of Ignatius's understanding of the Church. Despite what some commentators facilely assert, neither the *Exercises* nor the Society of Jesus were intended to be instruments of the Catholic response to the Protestant

Reformation.[38] Rather Ignatius and his spirituality stand within the tradition of *Christianitas*, an effort to make Christian faith alive within a culture and to liberate whatever inhibited the gospel of Christ from informing society, especially in the case of the poor and socially and economically marginated.[39] *Christianitas* was an impulse towards helping people in every way, in soul, certainly, but also in mind, heart, and body. Ignatian spirituality was an effort to animate this mission of the Church. Consequently, Ignatius made an effort to tie the Society of Jesus to the saving mission of the Church and to avoid its politics and its controversies.[40] This particular purchase on church service, to animate its mission, does not neglect the development of Christian values within the believing community: prayer, sacramental life, union among the members, especially the hierarchy and the body of the community of the Church. But Ignatian spirituality is biased towards a Church that is a continuation of the itinerant ministry of Christ, particularly the mission of preaching, teaching, and incorporating the word of God into the lives of people. The model of such mission for Ignatius was Christ as the itinerant preacher, his disciples on their journeys, and Paul in his missionary work. Ignatius Loyola is more a saint of the book than of the altar, although his personal eucharistic devotion was intense and mystical. Ignatius forged a spirituality for the frontiers of faith, that land where belief and unbelief, where the churched and unchurched, where indifference to the lot of the poor and uneducated and profound human pain and need met.[41] Moreover, especially with the founding of the schools,[42] Ignatian spirituality engaged the cultures of the world, its learning, arts, and professions. In this engagement with the secular culture of its time, Ignatian spirituality found an even more profound application of its conviction that contemplation and action can fuse into a harmonious act of virtual prayer. The schools deepened what it meant to be a contemplative in action.

The fourth vow of the Jesuits is pronounced at the time of final profession and made in addition to the three traditional vows which designate a man or woman as a member of a recognized religious-life community in the Church.[43] The three traditional vows are chastity, poverty, and obedience. The fourth vow needs to be understood correctly:

> As by now should be clear, no treatment of "mission and the early Jesuits" would be complete without some comment on the "Fourth Vow." The formula, as given in the *Constitutions*, runs as follows:
>
> > I, [name], make profession, and I promise to Almighty God . . . poverty, chastity, and obedience; . . . I further promise a special obedience to the sovereign pontiff in regard to missions, according to the same apostolic letters and the Constitutions.
>
> Seldom in the history of religious life has something as central to an order's identity been so badly misunderstood. The vow is often referred to as the Jesuits' "vow to the pope." This elliptical manner of speaking is misleading in the extreme for it seems to indicate that the vow is made not to God but to a human being. "Vow to obey the pope" is in that regard an improvement, but in every other way misses the point by misconstruing what the vow is all about. The vow does not concern the pope: it concerns "missions," as the formula clearly states. The pope of course figures in the vow, but, as these "missions" were interpreted in the Jesuit *Constitutions*, the superior general of the Society also had a similar authority "to send" members.[44]

What this fourth vow dramatizes is the way Ignatian spirituality describes its special relationship to the Church, i.e., as part of the pastoral mission of the Church. To be in the Church of Christ is to be with Christ on mission. While the historical Jesus no longer walks this earth, his Spirit continues to animate his followers to continue the entire gamut of his ministry: preaching, teaching, reconciling, healing. But it also means a willingness to do this everywhere and in all areas of human life. And it is this dimension of being sent to carry the Gospel message everywhere that especially drives the action within Ignatian spirituality. To be on apostolic pilgrimage, adapting the values of the gospel to business, politics, academic life, social action, art and theater, science and technology, is integral to the way Ignatian spirituality expresses itself.

But to be on the mission of Christ through the pastoral presence of his Church means even more. The early Jesuits spoke about their "way of proceeding,"[45] which indicated their particular style of life and service. One aspect of this "way of proceeding" is an overriding determination to work for reconciliation rather than confrontation. Reconciliation is not facile tolerance or a phony ecumenism—a blurring of honest differences or a muting of essential belief or ethical commitments. For the early Jesuits, reconciliation meant the willingness to emphasize where God dwelt in seeming differences. The best Jesuit missionaries asked not, "Can we bring God to you?" but rather, "Where in your culture, in your profession, in your occupation, in your religious experience, in your life, does God already exist and act?" Reconciliation is an a priori desire to find how God dwells even in adversaries and to seek to make them friends or, at least, mutually respectful members of a dialogue.

Ignatian spirituality, then, risks leaving the security of domestic faith to find in apostolic pilgrimage new ways to explain the action of God and the significance of the gospel. The early Jesuits exhibited a trust in the generosity of God's presence so that between the culture of Europe and those ancient, but newly discovered, cultures of Asia, Africa, and Latin America there could be communication and mutual benefit. This instinct for pastoral mediation was for them an expression of the deeper wisdom of the Church, a wisdom that understood God as at once embedded in a culture and yet greater and more generous than any one culture. Today we would say that from its beginnings Ignatian spirituality included a concern for inculturation as part of its mission in the service of the Church.[46]

As a consequence of this developing missiology, Ignatian spirituality also served the Church by confronting the narrow sectarianism that inhibited the Church from finding God in all things. Of course, some Jesuits failed in this ideal and proved to be as narrow and rigid as any other culturally myopic European. But when a Jesuit truly grasped his own spirituality and what service to the Church through the gospel really meant, he entered generously and, frequently imaginatively, into new pastoral and cultural situations.

Ignatian spirituality today retains its loyalty to the pastoral identity of the Church. It is only one movement among many others in the contemporary Church. But it remains a spirituality reconciling culture and faith, the world and the Spirit, learning and social concern, the human and the divine. Today Ignatian spirituality continues to work for "the greater glory of God" by proclaiming a Church that is a religious event, an epiphany of God's truth and goodness unafraid to reach out to today's world.[47]

As a consequence, Ignatian spirituality sees a Church in the world, and discerning, challenging, confronting, yes, but also in dialogue and, therefore, also learning, growing in self-knowledge through interaction with the world. Is such a spirituality within the Church a risk? Of course, but two realities make this a "holy risk."[48]

First, this is the process whereby the Church came into its consciousness as a world church, moving beyond the world of Jerusalem.[49] Second, it is a way that demands discernment, gospel judgments about how to be the Church here and now. The risk of being genuinely a Church on mission leads us to the third, and final, guide to the Ignatian journey to God: human experience.

Human Experience

Both Christ and the Church invite response. Out of the gospel narratives Christ continues to challenge and to confront, to call people to wisdom and to compassion, to define what God's kingdom is. The Church in all its historical reality and existential presence today continues to engage either the loyalty or the hostility of contemporary men and women. Both Christ and Church are relational realities. By this I mean both have the power to engage the human mind and heart. Engagement assumes relationship of some sort. For example, we say that we believe in Christ or that we belong to the Church. Or we say that we do not believe in Christ or that we do not belong to the Church. For Ignatius there were two aspects of relationships: Do these relationships belong to you? *or* Do you belong to these relationships? To say that something belonged to you meant that you freely chose to let someone else or something else become a part of your life but not to own your life. You remain free, capable of choosing your career, lifestyle, or human partner in the journey of life. True, once you let another reality into your life, you care for that reality, respond to it, and, somehow or other, put this reality into your set of personal priorities. Ignatius called this kind of response "ordered,"[50] meaning such relationships lead—again those words—to life and to love. For example, every human person needs food, drink, affection, knowledge, if she or he is to develop into an integrated human being. But all these realities, and the people who make them possible for us, are meant to help a man and woman to express themselves, to become bearers of ethico-religious realities that most characterize their moral and spiritual selfhood. In other words, I become my choices.

Consequently, if someone were to be so captivated by food, drink, affection, or knowledge that any one of these realities claimed ownership over that man or woman, Ignatius would see this as a kind of slavery, what he would term "disorder."[51] Thus, for Ignatius the foundational human experience was freedom: freedom from all created reality and freedom for God's ownership over a person's life. This kind of spiritual balance—i.e., freedom from and freedom for—he called "indifference."[52] Ignatian indifference does not mean an absence of feeling, affection, pleasure, or care. It does mean that nothing ultimately owns me except God. Therefore, those moments in which I find God, the private solitude of soul that mark my spirituality, lead to God's possession of me. This is not a possession of domination but of love, a blessed companionship, an experience of discipleship intimacy.

Such freedom from and freedom for—this Ignatian indifference—founds the ability to pray peacefully, to discern honestly, and to choose wisely. This is the reason that indifference is an essential element in Ignatian spirituality.

In this environment of freedom, Ignatius believed that one could find both union with God and with all other creation. Ignatius saw human experience not as a bundle of sensations or passing affections but as "memory, understanding, and will."[53] By *memory* Ignatius meant more than simple recall. For him memory was that personal history which constitutes identity, reveals a person's talents, strengths, and weaknesses, and, ultimately, orients a person's deep affections and desires.

By *understanding* Ignatius meant the ability to integrate one's past with his or her present: to see how my childhood was the seed for my adulthood, how every love bestowed prepared one to love, how every moment of grief or joy molded my heart into its humanity.

By *will* Ignatius meant the power to make my ambitions, my desires, my values, my personal priorities come into life so that these personal, treasured realities become the basis for companionship, competency, and service.

This understanding of human experience as freedom expressed in self-possession and in self-donation constituted the only way for Ignatius in which a man or woman could be fully human. Prayer would be both those formal moments in which one encountered God but also those informal, daily moments when a person encountered life and discovered God in the midst of action. The spiritual life became the animating force for both private development and public service.

For Ignatius the greatest human gesture was in those moments when human experience became free self-donation to the God of self-donation. Ignatius called this exchange *liberality,* "the embodiment of that interchange which concretizes and constitutes mutual love."[54]

The structure of personal love involves two critical and developing insights in the *Spiritual Exercises,* insights that Ignatius frames as a preface [to] the "Contemplation for Attaining Love," but that govern the understanding of love throughout the entire work. First, there is of necessity an integrity between love and life, an integrity in which love manifests itself through its objectification in deeds or in historical events much more than in words or declaration. Secondly, though the closeness of this sequence is not often recognized, the deeds in which love is manifested are mutual liberality. This is a giving and sharing that is termed "*communicación de las dos partes*," a mutual communion: "Love consists in a mutual communion on both sides, i.e., the lover gives and shares with the beloved that which one has or can attain and also the beloved with the lover." Liberality in Ignatius is neither (as is sometimes preached) a *noblesse oblige* nor simply the love of gratitude; it is the donation and sharing of one's freedom with God as "He himself has given himself to me to the very limits of his power according to his divine ordinances." The liberality of the person is then the response to the divine liberality, because this interchange consists of love. Liberality is the conjunction of grace and human freedom, and it is the direction given to the manifold possibilities that a person is.[55]

Liberality celebrates the great virtue of Ignatian spirituality— magnanimous love.

Conclusion

Ignatian spirituality draws heavily on the personal religious experiences of Ignatius Loyola and the first Jesuits as well as on his *Spiritual Exercises*, the *Constitutions of the Society of Jesus*, his letters, and his dictated memoir of his conversion, which is sometimes simply called *The Autobiography*[56] or *A Pilgrim's Testimony*[57] or *A Pilgrim's Journey*.[58] But it is also a spirituality that has been illumined by centuries of study, research, and pastoral practice.[59] Sometimes a distinction has been made between Ignatian spirituality and Jesuit spirituality, with the former representing the experiences of the early Jesuits and the latter expressing developments and interpretations after the death of Ignatius in 1556. In this reflection I have emphasized the Ignatian experience but highlighted the interpretations that have characterized modern readings of Ignatian spirituality.

What I hope has emerged from this reflection is a spirituality highly dependent on experience, tested in the crucible of pastoral ministry, developed through a variety of apostolic demands, notably those of the schools, and practical in nature. Ignatian spirituality is theologically rich but focused primarily on helping people to pray and to discern.

Another dimension I hope comes through these reflections is the flexibility and accommodating character of this spirituality. Of course, the vocabulary and the symbols of Ignatius, particularly in the *Exercises*, reflect his sixteenth-century culture. He saw Christ as the ideal King.[60] He read the Gospels as history.[61] His psychological insights were limited.[62] But when you dig beneath the vocabulary and live closely with his symbols, the wisdom of Ignatius comes through. He understood the human heart, grasped the dynamics of the gospel challenge, saw the mission of the Church afresh, and welcomed the continuous need to adapt principles of Christian spirituality to the concrete reality of persons and cultures.

In short, Ignatian spirituality is a spirituality of pedagogy, teaching ways to make the gospel tradition, Church tradition, and humanist tradition available to people. It is no wonder, then, that the Jesuits found their development of a school system totally compatible with their "way of proceeding." For them education was a spirituality, a way to teach future generations how to find God in all things.

I hope that two other Ignatian realities have emerged in these reflections. First, Ignatius came to trust his own experiences, believing that God dealt directly with him. Second, Ignatius also saw in that process how much God trusted him and all human reality. God revealed God's very self to people. God placed his message of salvation and holiness within the fragile reality of human minds, hearts, and imagination. And if God trusts what was human to bear the divine, so would Ignatius. Trust is the glue that holds Ignatian spirituality together—trust of God, trust of the process of the *Exercises*, trust in fellow Jesuits, trust in people's own experience of God, trust in God's presence in cultures, in learning, in art, in music, in technology. The litany of the objects of Ignatius's trust goes on and on. Ultimately, Ignatian spirituality trusts the world as a place where God dwells and labors and gathers all to himself in an act of forgiveness where that is needed and in an act of blessing where that is prayed for.

Such a spirituality breathes a plurality that is not a ploy but simply a result of its own integrity. It is a spirituality that rejoices in the multiplicity of Christ's presence in the world of his Father's making:

> . . . For Christ plays in ten thousand places,
> Lovely in limbs, and lovely in eyes not his
> to the father through the features of men's faces.[63]

Ignatian spirituality is, then, the Christian experience, faithful to its foundation in the gospel, eager for the translation of that gospel in and through the times we live.

NOTES

1. Two helpful and available introductory volumes on Ignatius and his major works are: *Ignatius of Loyola, Spiritual Exercises and Selected Works*, ed. George E. Ganss, SJ (New York: Paulist Press, 1991) and *Saint Ignatius of Loyola, Personal Writings*, trans. Joseph A. Munitz and Philip Endean (London: Penguin Books, 1996). A solid, readable biography is that of José Ignacio Tellechea Idígoras, *Ignatius of Loyola, The Pilgrim Saint*, trans. Cornelius Michael Buckley, SJ (Chicago: Loyola University Press, 1994).

2. The best English introduction to the Society of Jesus and it foundations is John W. O'Malley, SJ, *The First Jesuits* (Cambridge, MA: Harvard University Press, 1993).

3. The phrase is also translated "a pathway to God." It is found in *The Formula of the Institute* which incorporates the document the first companions and Ignatius presented to Pope Paul III in 1539, describing their proposal for a new religious order; cf. *The Constitutions of the Society of Jesus*, trans. George E. Ganss, SJ (St. Louis: Institute of Jesuit Sources, 1970) [3], 67.

4. The literature on Ignatian discernment is extensive. The most thorough treatments in English are Jules Toner, SJ, *A Commentary on St. Ignatius' Rules for the Discernment of Spirits* (St. Louis: Institute of Jesuit Sources, 1982), and *Discerning God's Will: Ignatius Loyola's Teaching on Christian Decision Making* (St. Louis: Institute of Jesuit Sources, 1990). A briefer popular summary is his "Discernment in the Spiritual Exercises," in *A New Introduction to the Spiritual*

Exercises of St. Ignatius, ed. John E. Dister, SJ (Collegeville, MN: Liturgical Press, 1993), 63–72.

5. John C. Olin, "The Idea of Pilgrimage in the Experience of Ignatius Loyola," *Church History* 48 (1979): 387–97; Howard J. Gray, SJ, "What Kind of Document," *The Way Supplement* 61 (Spring 1988): 24–25.

6. Cf. Tellechea Idígoras, *Ignatius*, 119–21.

7. *A Pilgrim's Journey: The Autobiography of Ignatius of Loyola*, trans. Joseph N. Tylenda, SJ (Wilmington, DE: Glazier, 1985), 23, no. 15. Cf. Tylenda's note on 15–16, 22.

8. A succinct but authoritative narrative of the composition of the *Exercises* can be found in *The Spiritual Exercises of Saint Ignatius*, trans. George E. Ganss, SJ (St. Louis: Institute of Jesuit Sources, 1992), the Introduction, 2–4. It is this translation of the Exercises that I shall use in this essay.

9. This translation is from *A Pilgrim's Testament: The Memoirs of Saint Ignatius of Loyola*, trans. Parmananda R. Divarkar (St. Louis: Institute of Jesuit Sources, 1995), 39, no. 27.

10. For a thorough and helpful exposition of this prayer, cf. George A. Aschenbrenner, SJ, "Consciousness Examen," in *Notes on the Spiritual Exercises of St. Ignatius Loyola*, ed. David L. Fleming, SJ (St. Louis: Review for Religious, 1981), 175–85.

11. An excellent analysis of this kind of prayer, Ignatian gospel contemplation, is that of Brendan Byrne, SJ, "'To See with the Eyes of the Imagination . . .' Scripture in the Exercises and Recent Interpretation," in *The Way Supplement* 72 (Autumn 1991), 3–19.

12. I.e., *de arriba*; cf. the comments in Ganss, *Ignatius of Loyola: Spiritual Exercises and Selected Works,* 474. The classic exposition of the term and its significance is in Hugo Rahner, *Ignatius the Theologian* (New York: Herder and Herder, 1968), 1–31.

13. O'Malley, *First Jesuits*, 18–19.

14. *Exercises*, cf. nos. 135–89, 64–80. An extended treatment on the meaning of the Ignatian election can be found in Michael Ivens, SJ, *Understanding the Spiritual Exercises* (Trowbridge, UK: Cromwell Press, 1998), 128–45.

15. *Exercises*, no. 234.

16. Ron Hansen, "The Pilgrim," in *A Tremor of Bliss, Contemporary Writers on the Saints*, ed. Paul Elie (New York: Riverhead Books/Berkeley, 1995), 112. [This essay appears earlier in this volume.—Editor]

17. *Exercises*, nos. 5, 16, 18–20.

18. Ibid., nos. 15, 16, 19–20.

19. Ivens puts this well in his *Understanding the Spiritual Exercises*: "The 'imitation of Christ' is a total quality of life, a quality consisting not in external mimicry, but in a transformation of one's inner experience by the assimilation of Christ's own experience. Here one seeks to be taken into this experience in prayer, and hence to promote the further development of it in one's life. Such a prayer consists in contemplating the Christ of the Gospels as in the *Exercises* themselves, seeking the grace 'to feel with the Incarnate Word, as he reveals himself, looking and hearing, touching and tasting, in the gospel word'" (185).

20. It is the same process outlined by Luke Timothy Johnson in "The Process of Learning Jesus," in *Living Jesus, Learning the Heart of the Gospel* (San Francisco: Harper, 1999), 57–75.

21. Cf. note 11 above.

22. Cf. note 3 above.

23. *Constitutions*, no. 250.

24. An important discussion of *attention* can be found in Pierre Hadot, *Philosophy as a Way of Life*, trans. Michael Chase (Oxford: Blackwell, 1995), 126–44.

25. My reading and application of the parable relies on John R. Donahue, SJ, *The Gospel Parable: Metaphor, Narrative, and the Theology of the Synoptic Gospels* (Philadelphia: Fortress Press, 1988), 151–62; *The Gospel According to Luke*, trans. Joseph A. Fitzmyer, SJ (Garden City, NY: Doubleday, 1985), 2, 1082–94; *The Gospel of Luke,* commentary by Luke Timothy Johnson (Collegeville, MN: Liturgical Press, 1991), 234–42.

26. Charles O'Neill, SJ, *Acatamiento: Ignatian Reverence*, in *Studies in the Spirituality of Jesuits* 8, no. 1 (January 1976).

27. *Constitutions*, 155–56, no. 5.

28. Michael Ivens's comments in *Understanding the Spiritual Exercises* are a helpful addendum to my remarks:

> "It must be noted, first, that both consolation and desolation are defined as *spiritual*, the relation to the spiritual being positive in the case of consolation, negative in the case of the 'anti-spiritual' movement of desolation. To recognize these spiritual movements, one needs to be generally sensitive to the whole fluid and elusive

realm of one's feelings and reactions: but not every kind of positive or negative mood or stirring recognizable by a self-aware person is to be equated with 'consolation' and 'desolation' as understood in the *Exercises*. In the last analysis, consolation 'consoles' because whatever its form, whether unambiguous or implicit and discreet, it is a felt experience of God's love building up the Christ-life in us. And what characterizes every form of spiritual desolation is a felt sense of dissonance which is the echo in consciousness of an influence tending of its nature to undermine the Christ-life, and hence in the case of a person who remains fundamentally Christ-oriented to contradict their most deep-seated inclinations" (206).

29. Ibid. See also Michael J. Buckley, SJ, "The Structure of the Rules for Discernment of Spirits," *The Way Supplement* 20 (Autumn 1973), 19–37.

30. *Exercises*, nos. 45–72, gives the paradigm of a day of the retreat.

31. *The General Examen*, c. 3, no. 51 in the Ganss edition of the *Constitutions*:

Does he have a deliberate determination to live or die in the Lord with and in this Society of Jesus our Creator and Lord? And since when? Where and through whom was he first moved to this?

If he says that he was not moved by any member of the Society, the examiner should proceed. If the candidate says that he was so moved (and it is granted that one could licitly and meritoriously move him thus), it would seem to be more conducive to his spiritual progress to give him a period of some time, in order that, by reflecting on this matter, he may commend himself completely to his Creator and Lord as if no member of the Society had moved him so that he may be able to proceed with greater spiritual energies toward greater service and glory of the Divine Majesty.

32. Harvey D. Egan, SJ, "A Christ-Centered Mysticism," in *Ignatius Loyola the Mystic* (Wilmington, DE: Glazier, 1987), 86–118.

33. Gerard Manley Hopkins, *A Critical Edition of the Major Works*, ed. Catherine Phillips (Oxford: Oxford University Press, 1986), 168.

34. Ivens, *Understanding the Spiritual Exercises*, 75.

35. O'Malley, *The First Jesuits*, 38–39.

36. *Exercises*, nos. 18 and 19.

37. The historical reality of Ignatius is increasingly emphasized by scholars; e.g., Ganss's general introduction in *Ignatius of Loyola: Spiritual Exercises and Selected Works*, 10–26.

38. John W. O'Malley, SJ, "The Historiography of the Society of Jesus: Where Does It Stand Today?" in *The Jesuits: Cultures, Sciences and the Arts, 1540–1773*, ed. John W. O'Malley, SJ, Gauvin Alexander Bailey, Steven J. Harns, and T. Frank Kennedy, SJ (Toronto: University of Toronto Press, 1999), 3–37.

39. O'Malley, *The First Jesuits*, 87–88, 327.

40. Ibid., chap. 8, "The Jesuits and the Church at Large," 284–328.

41. John W. O'Malley, SJ, "Mission and the Early Jesuits," in *The Way Supplement* 79 (Spring 1994), 3–10.

42. Ibid., 6–7; O'Malley, *The First Jesuits*, 239–42. Indeed, the entire volume, *The Jesuits: Cultures, Sciences, and the Arts,* illustrates this.

43. John W. O'Malley, SJ, "The Fourth Vow in Its Historical Context: A Historical Study," *Studies in the Spirituality of Jesuits* 15 (January 1983).

44. O'Malley, "Mission," 7.

45. This phrase is rich in connotation. In many ways, O'Malley's *The First Jesuits* is all about their "ways of proceeding"; cf. 370–75. In the recently published volume cited above in nos. 38 and 42, its contributors emphasize the same pervasiveness.

46. Again, a recurring theme in *The Jesuits: Cultures, Sciences and the Arts*; on Ricci and Valignano, see 342–49.

47. I am thinking of General Congregation 34 of the Jesuits, held in Rome from January 5 to March 22, 1995. Its pivotal decrees on mission, justice, culture, and interreligious dialogue illustrate the commitment; *Documents of the Thirty-Fourth General Congregation of the Society of Jesus*, ed. John L. McCarthy (St. Louis: Institute of Jesuit Sources, 1995).

48. Cf. Decree, "On Having a Proper Attitude of Service in the Church," General Congregation 34.

49. "Universality," in *The Acts of the Apostles*, ed. Luke Timothy Johnson (Collegeville, MN: Liturgical Press, 1992), 16–18.

50. *Exercises*, nos. 2, 21, 97.

51. Ibid.

52. Ibid., no. 23.

53. Ibid., no. 50.

54. Michael J. Buckley, SJ, "Freedom, Election, and Self-Transcendence: Some Reflections upon the Ignatian Development of a Life of Ministry," in *Ignatian Spirituality in a Secular Age*, ed. George P. Schner, SJ (Waterloo, ON: Wilfrid Laurier University Press, 1984), 72.

55. Ibid.

56. Ganss, *Ignatius of Loyola*, 66–67.

57. Divarkar, *A Pilgrim's Testament*, vii.

58. Tylenda, *A Pilgrim's Journey*, ix.

59. Cf. O'Malley, "Historiography," footnote 38 above.

60. E.g., Hans Wolter, "Elements of Crusade Spirituality in St. Ignatius," in *Ignatius Loyola, His Personality and Spiritual Heritage, 1556–1956*, ed. Friedrich Wulf, SJ (St. Louis: Institute of Jesuit Sources, 1977), 97–134.

61. Ganss, *Exercises*, 163, note 63.

62. W. W. Meissner, SJ, M.D.*Ignatius of Loyola: The Psychology of a Saint* (New Haven, CT: Yale University Press, 1992).

63. Hopkins, "As kingfishers catch fire," in *Gerard Manley Hopkins, Critical Edition*, ll. 12b–14, 129.

Further Reading

Let me recommend six essays that, in one way or another, summarize Ignatian spirituality. All but the first two (which are fairly recent) come from the middle of last century and, by today's expectations, leave something to be desired in matters of style (e.g., inclusive language). They are classics, however, and their content will never go out of date:

John W. Padberg, SJ, "The Jesuit question," *The Tablet* (22 September 1990), 1189–91.

Joseph A. Bracken, SJ, "Jesuit Spirituality from a Process Perspective," *Studies in the Spirituality of Jesuits* (March 1990).

Jean Danielou, SJ, "The Ignatian Vision of the Universe and of Man," *Cross Currents* 4 (1954), 357–366.

Maurice Giuliani, S.J., "Finding God in All Things," in *Finding God in All Things: Essays in Ignatian Spirituality Selected from Christus* [French Jesuit journal], trans. William J. Young, S.J. (Chicago: Regnery, 1958), 3–24.

Karl Rahner, SJ, "The Ignatian Mysticism of Joy in the World," *Theological Investigations* 3, 281–93. This is a difficult essay; the main theme has been presented in easier form by Avery Dulles, SJ, "The Ignatian Experience as Reflected in the Spiritual Theology of Karl Rahner," *Philippine Studies* 13 (1965), 471–91.

To pursue these, you may need to visit a Jesuit or other Catholic university library.

Prayer

Introduction

Ignatius has nothing in his teaching like our first reading in this section, "Contemplation: A long loving look at the real," by the late Jesuit theologian-preacher Walter Burghardt. Ignatius could have taken for granted what Burghardt labors to present. What accounts for this shift in perspective and awareness? The Enlightenment (eighteenth century) and everything in the West that flows from it: critical intelligence applied to ever-narrower data, so as to control and exploit reality—and the consequent atrophy of a disinterested (nonproductive) appreciation of reality in all its splendor and terror and wonder.

The second selection—"Prayer as Conscious [Personal] Relationship," by psychologist and author-practitioner of Ignatian spirituality William A. Barry, SJ—builds on one of Ignatius's key directives in the initial part of the *Spiritual Exercises*—the "colloquy" or intimate personal conversation between the person who prays and God, "as one friend speaks to another" (no. 54).

Finally, we have a method of prayer that Ignatius taught and that he considered the most important a person could do each day—the so-called *examen*. As presented by Dennis Hamm, SJ, in "Rummaging for God: Praying Backwards through Your Day," we have a modern adaptation of Ignatius first popularized by George Aschenbrenner, SJ, in a 1971 article that broadens the traditional terminology "Examination of *Conscience*" into the "Examination of *Consciousness*."

Contemplation: A Long Loving Look at the Real

Walter J. Burghardt, SJ

From *Church*, 1989

This adventure in contemplation has three stages. First, some introductory remarks about obstacles to contemplation. Then, the more substantive issue: What is contemplation? Finally, practical suggestions on how to realize your capacity for contemplation.

The primary villain is a twentieth-century law, a law that hounds us without our knowing it, has a strong ring of virtue, seems self-evident for responsible living. Almost three decades ago, Walter Kerr framed that law as follows: "Only useful activity is valuable, meaningful, moral. Activity that is not clearly, concretely useful to oneself or to others is worthless, meaningless, immoral."[1]

By that law most Americans live. That is why they feel guilty if they have nothing to "do." That is why many are reluctant to confess they took yesterday off, "did" nothing, just enjoyed. That is why so many must justify a vacation: it will help them work better when they get back. That is why the introductory ploy at a cocktail party is not "Who are you?" but "What do you do?" That is why young coronary patients are characteristically restless during leisure hours and feel guilty when they should relax.

How did we come to this unpretty pass? Through a philosophy. Not that utilitarianism conquered our culture at one master stroke.

As Kerr phrased it, "Ideas that are powerful enough to dictate the conduct of whole generations . . . enter the blood and marrow of a people as spirochetes do—unnamed, invisible—quite a long time after a lonely thinker has set them loose in the silence of his study."[2]

You have to go back to Jeremy Bentham (d. 1832), identifying happiness with utility, pleasure with profit. Back to James Mill (d. 1836), rigid utilitarian educating his small son on a philosophy of rigid utilitarianism. And there was the son himself, John Stuart Mill (d. 1873). He began Greek and math at the age of three; at eight, he had read Aesop, Xenophon, and Herodotus in the original, together with masses of history; about twelve, he was grappling with Aquinas and Aristotle; at thirteen, political economy, Adam Smith. At twenty-one, he broke down, "victim of a dejection which robbed life not only of its pleasures but also of its purpose."[3] And the last word in that philosophical assault may have been succinctly written in 1871 by an English logician and political economist, William Stanley Jevons (d. 1882): "Value depends entirely upon utility." This, I am afraid, is a thesis that dominates much of American culture today: what is important is usefulness, the profit I can extract from an experience or a possession.

A second reason why contemplation has fallen on hard times goes back to the churning sixties. The world was challenging the Church: "Forget this fascination with another world. Come to us where we are. Help us make the passage into a technological age without the brutality of a new paganism. If you remain comfortably in your cloisters, God will become a stranger to contemporary culture."

The Catholic Church was framing an even more anguished plea. Take the opening sentence of Vatican II's *Constitution on the Church in the Modern World*: "The joys and the hopes, the griefs and the anxieties of the men and women of this age, especially those who are poor or in any way afflicted, these too are the joys and hopes, the griefs and anxieties of the followers of Christ."

In the agonizing call for action, contemplation suffered. Work *is* prayer. To serve God, to pray, you need not get down on your knees; the world is your kneeler.

The obstacles to contemplation are graphically summed up in a comic strip—mother inside the house, looking out a window, her little boy sitting in the yard with his back to a tree:

> Mother: "Ditto, what are you doing out there?"
> Ditto: "Nothing."
> Mother: "You must be doing something! Now tell me!"
> Ditto: "I'm not doing anything."
> Mother: "Ditto! You tell me what you're doing!"
> Ditto (to himself): "Good gosh!" (He tosses a stone.)
>   (out loud): "I'm throwing rocks!"
> Mother: "I thought it was something like that. Now stop it at once!"
> Ditto: "Okay."
>   (to himself): "Nobody will let you just do nothing any more."

Now turn to contemplation. What is it? Oh, not the popular sense of *contemplate*, which is instantly associated with *navel*. Contemplation in its profound sense is just as real as your navel but far more exciting. The contemplative Carmelite William McNamara once called it "a pure intuition of being, born of love. It is experiential awareness of reality and a way of entering into immediate communion with reality." And what is reality? "People, trees, lakes, mountains. You can study things, but unless you enter into this intuitive communion with them, you can only know *about* them, you don't *know* them. To take a long loving look at something—a child, a glass of wine, a beautiful meal—this is a natural act of contemplation, of loving admiration." The problem? "All the way through school we are taught to abstract; we are not taught loving awareness."

Never have I heard contemplation more excitingly described: a long loving look at the real. Each word is crucial: real . . . look . . . long . . . loving. The *real*, reality, is not reducible to some far-off, abstract, intangible God-in-the-sky. Reality is living, pulsing people; reality is fire and ice; reality is the sun setting over the Swiss Alps, a gentle doe streaking through the forest; reality is a ruddy glass of Burgundy, Beethoven's *Mass in D*, a child lapping a chocolate ice-cream cone; reality is a striding woman with wind-blown hair; reality is the risen Christ. Paradoxically, what alone is excluded from contemplation is abstraction, the "spaced out," where a leaf is no longer green, water no longer ripples, a man no longer breathes, and God no longer smiles. What I contemplate is always what is most real: what philosophers call the "concrete singular."

This real I *look* at. I do not analyze or argue it, describe or define it; I am one with it. I do not move around it; I enter into it. Lounging by a stream, I do not exclaim "Ah, H_2O!" I let the water trickle gently through my fingers. I do not theologize about the redemptive significance of Calvary; I link a pierced hand to mine. Remember Eric Gill's outraged protest? "Good Lord! The thing was a mystery and we measured it!" Kerr compared contemplation to falling in love: not simply knowing another's height, weight, coloring, ancestry, IQ, acquired habits; rather, "the single, simple vibration that gives us such joy in the meeting of eyes or the lucky conjunction of interchanged words. Something private and singular and uniquely itself is touched—and known in the touching."[4]

I am not naked spirit; I am spirit incarnate; in a genuine sense, I *am* flesh. And so I am most myself, most human, most contemplative, when my whole person responds to the real.

Many of us have grown up on a dehumanizing Anglo-Saxon legacy: passion is something to be ashamed of. Strong feeling is a sign of weakness; the manly reaction to reality is stoicism. Love, of course, but let not love enrapture you. Be afraid, if you must, but keep your teeth from chattering. Take joy from a sonata, but let it not thrill you. Death will always sadden, but you dare not weep. Detest sin, but never be disturbed by it. Protest injustice, but grow not black with anger.

No, to "look" wholly means that my whole person reacts. Not only my mind, but my eyes and ears, smelling and touching and tasting. Not senses utterly unshackled; for at times reason must temper the animal in me. But far more openness, far more letting-go, than we were permitted of old, in a more severe spirituality, where, for example, touch was "out," because touch is dangerous. No one ever thought of reminding us that free will is even more dangerous. Or cold reason.

This look at the real is a *long* look. Not in terms of measured time, but wonderfully unhurried, gloriously unhurried. For many Americans, time is a stopwatch, time is money, life is a race against time. To contemplate is to rest—to rest in the real. Not lifelessly or languidly, not sluggishly or inertly. My entire being is alive, incredibly responsive, vibrating to every throb of the real. For once, time is irrelevant. You do not time the Philadelphia Symphony; you do not clock the Last Supper. I shall never forget the Louvre in Paris and the haunting *Mona Lisa*. On the one hand, an endless line of tourists, ten seconds each without ever stopping; on the other hand, a lone young man at rest on a stone bench, eyes riveted, whole person enraptured, sensible only of beauty and mystery, aware only of the real.

But this long look must be a *loving* look. It is not a fixed stare, not the long look of a Judas. It demands that the real captivate me, at times delight me. Tchaikovsky's *Swan Lake* ballet or Lobster Cardinal, the grace of God's swans or the compassion in the eyes of Christ— whatever or whoever the real, contemplation calls forth love, oneness with the other. For contemplation is not study, not cold examination, not a computer. To contemplate is to be in love.

True, contemplation does not always summon up delight. The real includes sin and war, poverty and race, illness and death. The real is AIDS and abortion, apartheid and MS, bloated bellies and stunted minds, respirators and last gasps. But even here the real I contemplate must end in compassion, and compassion that mimics Christ is a synonym for love.

A long, loving look at the real. From such contemplation comes communion. I mean the discovery of the Holy in deep, thoughtful encounters—with God's creation, with God's people, with God's self—where love is proven by sacrifice, the wild exchange of all for another, for the Other. Thus is fashioned what the second-century bishop Irenaeus called "God's glory—man/woman alive!"

But how realize this capacity for contemplation? Especially in its profound religious sense, a long, loving look at the Real, oneness with Someone transcendent. Several suggestions.

First, some sort of desert experience. Not that contemplation is incompatible with the City; without a continuing contemplation, wherever you are, you may well perish. Rather that the process can best be initiated by an experience that brings you face to face with solitude, with vastness, even with powers of life and death beyond your control. That is why the physical desert runs through the Bible, through salvation history, through the Church's tradition—specifically the Hebrew people, Christ Jesus, the desert fathers. The desert is a place of trial and struggle, a proving ground (see Exodus 16:1–36, Matthew 4:1–11), where the values of life are presented in clear, stark terms, where you opt for living or nature destroys you.

I shall never forget how, decades ago, Father McNamara revealed in word and his own person how the desert evokes your capacity for initiative, exploration, evaluation; interrupts your ordinary pattern of life; intercepts routine piety; disengages you from the regular round of respectable human activities. You learn to be alert, perceptive, recollected, so that issues become clear, reality recognizable. You know yourself, not a statistically polled image of yourself. You know God, not abstractions about God, not even a theology of God, but the much more mysterious and mighty God of theology.

In the desert tradition one meaning persists above all others: the desert is where we encounter God, where God comes to meet us, where God visits God's people: "I will allure her, and bring her into the wilderness, and speak tenderly to her" (Hosea 2:14). The desert is not an escape, though it could be. Only the few abide bodily in the desert. In fact, for most the desert is not a place but an experience that takes hold of you, becomes part of you, turns you inside out, opens the City to contemplation, to a long, loving look at the real. Here you can face Kazantzakis' terrifying trinity: "love, death, and God—perhaps one and the same."

A second suggestion: develop a feeling for festivity. Here I recommend Josef Pieper's slender volume *In Tune with the World: A Theory of Festivity*.[5] With remarkable perceptiveness Pieper develops the thesis that festivity resides in activity that is meaningful in itself. I mean activity that is not tied to goals, to "so that" or "in order to." Festivity, therefore, calls for renunciation: you must take usable time and withdraw it from utility. And this you must do out of love, whose expression is joy. Festivity is a *yes* to the world, to the reality of things, to the existence of woman and man; it is a yes to the world's Creator.

It is only if you can say such a festive *yes* to the real that you will see, with Teilhard [de Chardin], how "God is as out-stretched and tangible as the atmosphere in which we are bathed." Matter and spirit, he insisted, are not two things glued into unity, but aspects of all created being. The divine milieu is not only the mystical but also the cosmic body of Christ; here it is that creative union takes place.

A third suggestion, closely allied to festivity, intrinsic to it: a sense of "play." I don't mean "fooling around." I mean what poet Francis Thompson meant when, in his essay on Shelley, he likened the poet's gifts to a child's faculty of make-believe, but raised to the nth power— whose box of toys is the universe, who "makes bright mischief with the moon," in whose hand "the meteors nuzzle their noses."

It demands a sense of wonder. With that sense we are born; but as we grow older, most of us lose it. We get blasé and worldly-wise and sophisticated. We no longer run our fingers through water, no longer shout at the stars, no longer make faces at the moon. Water is H_2O, the stars have been classified, and the moon is not made of green cheese. We've grown up. Rabbi Heschel saw it as our contemporary trap: "believing that everything can be explained, that reality is a simple affair which has only to be organized in order to be mastered. All enigmas can be solved, and all wonder is nothing but 'the effect of novelty upon ignorance.'"[6] The new can indeed amaze us: a space shuttle, the latest computer game, the softest diaper in history. Till tomorrow; till the new becomes old; till yesterday's wonder is discarded or taken for granted.

No, don't put everything under a microscope, don't program life in a computer. Let your imagination loose to play with ideas—what it means to be alive, to be in love, to believe and to hope. I shall always be grateful to a psychologist who, two decades ago, monitored a simulated Jesuit faculty meeting, watched us reach dead ends because we were enslaved to past solutions, and kept asking, "Where's the wild idea?"

A fourth suggestion, intimately linked to festivity and play: don't try to "possess" the object of your delight, whether divine or human, imprisoned marble or free-flowing rivulet; and don't expect to "profit" from contemplation, from pleasure. Here Kerr has written a paragraph that has influenced my living far beyond my ability to describe:

> To regain some delight in ourselves and in our world, we are forced to abandon, or rather to reverse, an adage. A bird in the hand is *not* worth two in the bush—unless one is an ornithologist, the curator of the Museum of Natural History, or one of those Italian vendors who supply restaurants with larks. A bird in the hand is no longer a bird at all: it is a specimen; it may be dinner. Birds are birds only when they are in the bush or on the wing; their worth as birds can be known only at a discreet and generous distance.[7]

A fifth suggestion: read, make friends with, remarkable men and women who have themselves looked long and lovingly at the real. The list is long and impressive; I list only a handful of personal favorites. But note what kind of folk these are: not solitaries, not neurotic escapists, but flesh and blood in a flesh-and-blood world—unique, however, because each smashed through boundaries and stretched human limits to the walls of infinity.

I mean biblical figures like Abraham and Mary of Nazareth, murmuring *yes* to Yahweh though they knew not where it would take them. I mean martyrs like second-century Ignatius of Antioch on his tortured way to the Colosseum: "God's wheat I am, and by the teeth of wild beasts I am to be ground, that I may prove Christ's pure bread." Martyrs like twentieth-century Martin Luther King, with a dream of black freedom he bathed in blood. I mean saints like John of the Cross, with the Carmelite interplay of dark night and radiant joy, of purgation and unifying likeness. Saints like Thomas More: "Man God made to serve Him wittily, in the tangle of his mind." I mean uncanonized women like Dorothy Day and Mother Teresa, arms embracing the homeless and the hopeless from New York to Calcutta. I mean Anne Morrow Lindbergh, with her counterculture conviction (expressed so sensitively in *Gift from the Sea*) that "this is my hour to be alone."

I mean Lao-tzu doing everything through being, and Rabbi Abraham Joshua Heschel doing everything through worship. I mean philosophers like Jacques Maritain, insisting that the culmination of knowledge is not conceptual but experiential: man/woman "feels" God. I mean Mr. Blue, Myles Connolly's New York mystic who flew kites and exulted in brass bands. I mean Nikos Kazantzakis, standing in old age before the abyss tranquilly, fearlessly: "There are three kinds of souls, three kinds of prayers. One: I am a bow in your hands, Lord. Draw me lest I rot. Two: Do not overdraw me. Lord, I shall break. Three: Overdraw me, and who cares if I break. Choose!" I mean short-story writer Flannery O'Connor, dead of lupus at thirty-nine, with her mature acceptance of limitation, with her God never far away, quietly loved, with so much Christlife in her frail frame—what I can best describe as grace on crutches. I mean Thomas Merton, always the contemplative but moving from renunciation to involvement, making contact with Hindu and Buddhist and Sufi, protesting Vietnam and violence, racial injustice and nuclear war.

Touch men and women like these, and you will touch the stars, will touch God.

A final word. To me, an ironic, scandalous facet of the contemporary search for the transcendent, for direct experience of the real, is that the searcher rarely seeks it in our Western culture, in Western Christianity. Ironic and scandalous because this is our ageless tradition. It goes back to Jesus, alone with his Father on the mountain, in the desert, in the garden. It goes back to the Fathers of the Church and the fathers of the desert: Gregory of Nyssa finding God in the image of God that is our inner self; Antony seeking God in community, Pachomius in solitude. It goes back to the medieval mystics, to Eckhart and Hildegarde, to Ruysbroeck and Julian of Norwich. It goes back to Teresa of Ávila ravished by a rose, to Ignatius of Loyola in ecstasy as he stares at the stars.

We have betrayed our tradition. Few of these contemplatives fled the world—even when they removed to a discreet distance. But for all their involvement with people and passions, they sensed one basic truth: our involvement, our activity, will be sterile, fruitless, unless we are men and women of prayer. There is a degree of truth in the adage, "To work is to pray." But it can be dangerously seductive. Unless there is a personal relationship between you and God, unless you can look upon things and persons and God with a long, loving look, your activity is likely to end in frustration and failure—and you a castaway.

The world is athirst for women and men who know God and love God; for only such women and men can give to today's paradoxical world the witness to a living God that this age demands. My personal failing—where I can be devastatingly lacking—is to me agonizingly apparent: at times I do not come through as a man who looks long and lovingly at the real. The consequence? Some men and women who touch me do not thrill to the touch, and so they abide in their loneliness, continue to experience the absence of God.

Contemplation, my friends, is not a luxury; it is the mark of a lover; it is the mark of a Christian.

NOTES

1. Walter Kerr, *The Decline of Pleasure* (New York: Simon & Schuster, 1962), 48. This paper is heavily indebted to Kerr's work, which is actually one of the most "useful" pieces I have ever read on contemplation.

2. Ibid., 49.

3. Ibid., 54.

4. Ibid., 210–11.

5. New York: Harcourt, 1965—ancient, if you wish, but not dated.

6. In *Between God and Man: An Interpretation of Judaism from the Writings of Abraham J. Heschel* (New York: Harper, 1959), 40.

7. Kerr, *The Decline of Pleasure*, 245.

Prayer as Conscious Relationship

William A. Barry, SJ

From *God and You: Prayer as a Personal Relationship*, 1987

A number of years ago I saw a photograph entitled "School Prayer." In it one sees first graders in prayer. Their faces are very serious, most have their eyes closed, and most have strained, tense, even squinty looks. Their hands are tightly folded. It is a rather funny picture until you begin to think about what we might be teaching children about prayer and about God. Most of us adults have had the same kind of teaching. When you think of prayer, what comes to mind? Going to church or chapel? Closing your eyes? Getting down on your knees? Thinking deep thoughts? Do you get a little nervous? Do you think about devotions and rosaries or the Book of Common Prayer? I suspect that most of us would figure that prayer is something holy people do a lot while we just occasionally do it. I wonder how many of us think of our Sunday church services as prayer.

While we may have some real qualms about prayer and wonder whether it is for the likes of us, at the same time we are curious. For instance, you have started to read this book. Books on prayer are becoming a hot item in publishing circles. Admittedly, they do not top best-seller lists, but they sell well enough that publishers are on the lookout for new ones. No need to go into the reasons for this renewed interest in prayer. Let us take it for granted and take your interest for granted. In this chapter I propose to discuss prayer as a conscious relationship with God and then in future chapters to spell out some of the implications of such an understanding of prayer. My hope is to help people to develop their personal relationship with God, in other words, to help people to pray.

In our creeds we affirm our faith in God as our Creator and Redeemer. We call God our Father, Jesus our Brother, and the Holy Spirit the Giver of life. We affirm that Jesus died for our sins and rose again for our justification. Let us just think for a few minutes about the implications of these creedal statements for prayer. Whether we know it or not, the creed says, God is in relationship with each and every created thing in the universe and in relationship to the whole of it. He continually creates and sustains in being everything and everyone in the universe. In the words of the theologian John Macquarrie, God lets-be every being. Hence, God is in relationship to every being whether that being is aware of the relationship or not. The same line of reasoning can be followed out for every other creedal statement about God. The Son of God, the Word made flesh, is brother to all human beings on the face of the earth whether they know it or not. The Holy Spirit is the Giver of life to those who are unconscious of the gift as well as to those who are conscious. So God, Mystery itself, is always and everywhere in relationship to us and to the whole universe, and, because he is God, consciously in relationship.

Does God want us to be consciously in relationship with him? Old and New Testaments and the experience of men and women down through the ages testify that he does. The Bible is a record of how God continually tried and tries to awaken human beings to the full reality of who they are, namely, his beloved children. Moreover, he wants us so awake and aware for our own good. Human beings who do not know their real father or mother, for example, suffer a lack that will probably show itself in a sense of rootlessness or of not knowing who they really are. So, too, unawareness of the God who is so intimately in relationship with us may show itself in occasional anxiety about the meaning of life, or in a frantic search for answers to life's mystery, or in overwork or overindulgence of some kind. Knowing who we are—in our depths—is salutary and freeing even if a bit daunting. So God does want us to be in conscious relationship with him. And conscious relationship is prayer, another way of saying that prayer is the raising of the mind and heart to God.

The remarkable thing about God is that he will not force himself on us. He continually tries to arouse our interest in him, to invite us to awareness and a deeper relationship, but he leaves us free to blind ourselves to his presence if we wish, or to refuse to respond even if we are aware of his presence.

First, however, let us say a few words about how God tries to arouse our awareness of him. You are riding in a car with someone else driving and you turn around and are stunned by the beauty of a sunset. You pick up a two-week old baby and feel a sense of awe and wonder as you touch her tiny hand. Your husband has just had a heart attack and is hovering between life and death in the intensive care unit; you start to pray for him but find yourself blurting out to God, "You don't give a rap for us!" and you sense a presence there in sympathy with you. You and your wife have just made love after a great evening together; as you lie beside her you are filled with a gratitude for all of life that brings tears to your eyes. You see a picture of an emaciated Ethiopian mother and child; your heart seems to stop beating for a second and you wonder what you can do. In these and many other ordinary events of life, God may signal his presence and his care.

As noted earlier, we are free to pay attention to these experiences, these possible overtures or communications of God, or not. We can let them drop out of awareness as quickly as we forget a stomach cramp when it goes away. Or we can wonder about the experience and its meaning. For example, I might note how I felt when I saw the sunset and realize that spontaneously I had whispered, "Wow!" and meant it as praise of God. I still feel rather exhilarated and have a desire to recover a relationship with God that has been on the back burner in recent years. In other words, such experiences may lead us to realize that we have been missing something in our lives and that we want something more.

What is the something more that we want? There may be a forest full of answers to that question. I may want to pass an exam, to find a new job, to meet a mate. I may want the cure of my sick mother. I may want a sense of purpose in life or the lifting of depression. I may want a family rift healed or the victory of the Democratic party. I may want to know that God cares for me personally. I may want to know Jesus and what he stood for better. I may want to become more like Jesus in my attitudes and values. Scratch any of these desires a little, even the seemingly most self-centered and materialistic, and we will find that we want to know something about God and his relationship to us.

If I seriously ask God to help me find a better job, for instance, what do I mean? At the surface, I suppose, I am asking God to make something good happen for me. If I think about the request a bit more, I may realize that what I most want is to know that he cares for me and has a loving providence in my regard. In other words, all our desires of God, even for material things, reduce to a desire for a sense of his relationship to us. We want to know how God is toward us.

Thus far we have established a working definition of prayer as conscious relationship. The relationship is based on God's actions to establish it and his desire that we become conscious of who he is and wants to be for us. Our consciousness depends on our willingness to pay attention to God's actions, or at least to experiences that might be the actions of God, and to let our desires for God be aroused.

Before ending this chapter, let me spell out a few implications of the working definition. First, when I become conscious of God's actions, no matter how dimly, then I am praying, even if I do not say a word. If you think of prayer as conscious relationship, any time of the day or night can be prayer time. I can be walking along with someone, both of us admiring the fall foliage, and it is a conscious relationship even if no words are spoken, as long as I am aware of the other's presence. So too with God. Second, we can make prayers of petition more understandable. Why ask God for something if he is all-knowing and loving? He does not need information, e.g., that my best friend is sick and I want him to get well. But if prayer is relationship, the issue is not information, but whether I believe he cares how I feel and whether I am willing to let him know what I feel and desire, that is, to reveal myself. Third, distractions in prayer are as normal and ordinary as they are in any relationship. You can be with someone you deeply love and be in a deep conversation and suddenly wonder if you put out the lights in the car. So too in prayer. Also distractions during a conversation with a friend sometimes come because you do not want to hear what the friend is saying or because you are bored with the friend. The same thing can happen during prayer. Finally, if prayer is just conscious relationship, it is not something esoteric, for saints and mystics. It is open to anyone, including the likes of us.

Rummaging for God: Praying Backwards through Your Day

Dennis Hamm, SJ

From *America*, 1994

About twenty years ago, at breakfast and during the few hours that followed, I had a small revelation. This happened while I was living in a small community of five Jesuits, all graduate students in New Haven, Connecticut. I was alone in the kitchen, with my cereal and the *New York Times*, when another Jesuit came in and said: "I had the weirdest dream just before I woke up. It was a liturgical dream. The lector had just read the first reading and proceeded to announce. 'The responsorial refrain today is, *If at first you don't succeed, try, try again.*' Whereupon the entire congregation soberly repeated, *'If at first you don't succeed, try, try again.'*" We both thought this enormously funny. At first, I wasn't sure just *why* this was so humorous. After all, almost everyone would assent to the courageous truth of the maxim, "If at first . . ." It has to be a cross-cultural truism ("Keep on truckin'!"). Why, then, would these words sound so incongruous in a liturgy?

A little later in the day, I stumbled onto a clue. Another, similar phrase popped into my mind: "If today you hear his voice, harden not your hearts" (Psalm 95). It struck me that that sentence has exactly the same rhythm and the same syntax as: "If at first you don't succeed, try, try again." Both begin with an *if* clause and end in an imperative.

Both have seven beats. Maybe that was one of the unconscious sources of the humor.

The try-try-again statement *sounds* like the harden-not-your-hearts refrain, yet what a contrast! The latter is clearly biblical, a paraphrase of a verse from a psalm, one frequently used as a responsorial refrain at the Eucharist. The former, you know instinctively, is probably not in the Bible, not even in Proverbs. It is true enough, as far as it goes, but it does not go far enough. There is nothing of faith in it, no sense of God. The sentiment of the line from Psalm 95, however, expresses a conviction central to Hebrew and Christian faith, that we live a life in dialogue with God. The contrast between those two seven-beat lines has, ever since, been for me a paradigm illustrating that truth.

Yet how do we hear the voice of God? Our Christian tradition has at least four answers to that question. First, along with the faithful of most religions, we perceive the divine in what God has made, creation itself (that insight sits at the heart of Christian moral thinking). Second, we hear God's voice in the Scriptures, which we even *call* "the word of God." Third, we hear God in the authoritative teaching of the church, the living tradition of our believing community. Finally, we hear God by attending to our experience, and interpreting it in the light of all those other ways of hearing the divine voice—the structures of creation, the Bible, the living tradition of the community.

The phrase, "If *today* you hear his voice," implies that the divine voice must somehow be accessible in our daily experience, for we are creatures who live one day at a time. If God wants to communicate with us, it has to happen in the course of a twenty-four-hour day, for we live in no other time. And how do we go about this kind of listening? Long tradition has provided a helpful tool, which we call the "examination of consciousness" today. "Rummaging for God" is an expression that suggests going through a drawer full of stuff, feeling around, looking for something that you are sure must be in there somewhere. I think that image catches some of the feel of what is classically known in church language as the prayer of "examen."

The *examen*, or examination, of conscience is an ancient practice in the church. In fact, even before Christianity, the Pythagoreans and the Stoics promoted a version of the practice. It is what most of us Catholics were taught to do to prepare for confession. In that form, the *examen* was a matter of examining one's life in terms of the Ten Commandments to see how daily behavior stacked up against those divine criteria. St. Ignatius includes it as one of the exercises in his manual *The Spiritual Exercises*.

It is still a salutary thing to do but wears thin as a lifelong, daily practice. It is hard to motivate yourself to keep searching your experience for how you sinned. In recent decades, spiritual writers have worked with the implication that *conscience* in Romance languages like French (*conscience*) and Spanish (*conciencia*) means more than our English word *conscience*, in the sense of moral awareness and judgment; it also means "consciousness."

Now prayer that deals with the full contents of your *consciousness* lets you cast your net much more broadly than prayer that limits itself to the contents of conscience, or moral awareness. A number of people—most famously, George Aschenbrenner, SJ, in an article in *Review for Religious* (1971)—have developed this idea in profoundly practical ways. Recently, the Institute of Jesuit Sources in St. Louis published a fascinating reflection by Joseph Tetlow, SJ, called *The Most Postmodern Prayer: American Jesuit Identity and the Examen of Conscience, 1920–1990*.

What I am proposing here is a way of doing the examen that works for me. It puts a special emphasis on feelings, for reasons that I hope will become apparent. First, I describe the format. Second, I invite you to spend a few minutes actually doing it. Third, I describe some of the consequences that I have discovered to flow from this kind of prayer.

A Method: Five Steps

1. *Pray for light.* Since we are not simply daydreaming or reminisc-
    ing but rather looking for some sense of how the Spirit of God
    is leading us, it only makes sense to pray for some illumination.
    The goal is not simply memory but graced understanding. That's
    a gift from God devoutly to be begged. "Lord, help me under-
    stand this blooming, buzzing confusion."

2. *Review the day in thanksgiving.* Note how different this is from
    looking immediately for your sins. Nobody likes to poke around
    in the memory bank to uncover smallness, weakness, lack of
    generosity. But everybody likes to fondle beautiful gifts, and
    that is precisely what the past twenty-four hours contain—gifts
    of existence, work, relationships, food, challenges. Gratitude is
    the foundation of our whole relationship with God. So use what-
    ever cues help you to walk through the day from the moment of
    awakening—even the dreams you recall upon awakening. Walk
    through the past twenty-four hours, from hour to hour, from
    place to place, task to task, person to person, thanking the Lord
    for every gift you encounter.

3. *Review the feelings that surface in the replay of the day.* Our feelings,
    positive and negative, the painful and the pleasing, are clear
    signals of where the action was during the day. Simply pay atten-
    tion to any and all of those feelings as they surface, the whole
    range: delight, boredom, fear, anticipation, resentment, anger,
    peace, contentment, impatience, desire, hope, regret, shame,
    uncertainty, compassion, disgust, gratitude, pride, rage, doubt,
    confidence, admiration, shyness—whatever was there. Some of
    us may be hesitant to focus on feelings in this over-psychologized
    age, but I believe that these feelings are the liveliest index to what
    is happening in our lives. This leads us to the fourth moment:

4. *Choose one of those feelings (positive or negative) and pray from it.*
    That is, choose the remembered feeling that most caught your

attention. The feeling is a sign that something important was going on. Now simply express spontaneously the prayer that surfaces as you attend to the source of the feeling—praise, petition, contrition, cry for help or healing, whatever.

5. *Look toward tomorrow.* Using your appointment calendar if that helps, face your immediate future. What feelings surface as you look at the tasks, meetings, and appointments that face you? Fear? Delighted anticipation? Self-doubt? Temptation to procrastinate? Zestful planning? Regret? Weakness? Whatever it is, turn it into prayer—for help, for healing, whatever comes spontaneously. To round off the examen, say the Lord's Prayer.

A mnemonic for recalling the five points: LT3F (light, thanks, feelings, focus, future).

Do It

Take a few minutes to pray through the past twenty-four hours, and toward the next twenty-four hours, with that five-point format.

Consequences

Here [are] some of the consequences flowing from this kind of prayer:

1. There is always something to pray about. For a person who does this kind of prayer at least once a day, there is never the question: What should I talk to God about? Until you die, you always have a past twenty-four hours, and you always have some feelings about what's next.

2. The gratitude moment is worthwhile in itself. "Dedicate your-selves to gratitude," Paul tells the Colossians. Even if we drift off into slumber after reviewing the gifts of the day, we have praised the Lord.

3. We learn to face the Lord where we are, as we are. There is no other way to be present to God, of course, but we often fool ourselves into thinking that we have to "put on our best face" before we address our God.

4. We learn to respect our feelings. Feelings count. They are mor-ally neutral until we make some choice about acting upon or dealing with them. But if we don't attend to them, we miss what they have to tell us about the quality of our lives.

5. Praying from feelings, we are liberated from them. An unat-tended emotion can dominate and manipulate us. Attending to and praying from and about the persons and situations that give rise to the emotions helps us to cease being unwitting slaves of our emotions.

6. We actually find something to bring to confession. That is, we stumble across our sins without making them the primary focus.

7. We can experience an inner healing. People have found that praying about (as opposed to fretting about or denying) feelings leads to a healing of mental life. We probably get a head start on our dreamwork when we do this.

8. This kind of prayer helps us get over our Deism. Deism is belief in a sort of "clock-maker" God, a God who does indeed exist but does not have much, if anything, to do with his people's ongoing life. The God we have come to know through our Jewish and Christian experience is more present than we usually think.

9. Praying this way is an antidote to the spiritual disease of Pelagianism. Pelagianism was the heresy that approached life with God as a do-it-yourself project ("If at first you don't succeed . . ."), whereas a true theology of grace and freedom sees life as response to God's love ("If today you hear God's voice . . .").

A final thought. How can anyone dare to say that paying attention to felt experience is a listening to the voice of God? On the face of it, it does sound like a dangerous presumption. But, notice, I am not equating memory with the voice of God. I am saying that, if we are to listen for the God who creates and sustains us, we need to take seriously and prayerfully the meeting between the creatures we are and all else that God holds lovingly in existence. That "interface" is the felt experience of my day. It deserves prayerful attention. It is a big part of how we know and respond to God.

Further Reading

To pursue Walter Burghardt's idea of contemplation further, consult what William Barry, SJ, and William Connolly, SJ, have to say about "the contemplative attitude" in *The Practice of Spiritual Direction* (New York: Seabury Press, 1982), 46–64. A recent book-length treatment of our modern problem and possible solutions is Ronald Rolheiser, OMI, *The Shattered Lantern: Rediscovering a Felt Presence of God*, rev. ed. (New York: Crossroad, 2001). Part 1 is entitled "Narcissism, Pragmatism, Unbridled Restlessness, and the Loss of the Ancient Instinct for Astonishment"; part 2, "Recovering the Ancient Instinct for Astonishment: Three Contemporary Traditions within Western Christian Thought."

The "Consciousness Examen" presented by Dennis Hamm in "Rummaging for God" is given book-length treatment by Timothy Gallagher, OMV, in *The Examen Prayer: Ignatian Wisdom for Our Lives Today* (New York: Crossroad, 2006).

For a fine compilation of Ignatius's own writings on prayer, consult Irish Jesuit Joseph Veale's "Saint Ignatius Speaks about 'Ignatian Prayer,'" *Studies in the Spirituality of Jesuits* (March 1996). David Lonsdale, professor of spirituality at the Jesuit-sponsored Heythrop College (of higher studies in philosophy and theology), University of London, devotes a chapter to "Ignatian Prayer" in *Eyes to See, Ears to Hear* (Maryknoll, NY: Orbis, 2000).

In *Close to the Heart: A Practical Approach to Personal Prayer* (Chicago: Loyola Press, 1999), Margaret Silf—British laywoman, spiritual guide, and retreat director—offers a superb introduction to prayer and its various ways, teaching the reader first of all to "listen" to her or his own experience. Her more recent *Gift of Prayer* (New York: BlueBridge, 2004) is written in poetic sense-lines to help the reader ponder what she is saying. Wilkie Au, also a wise teacher and practitioner of Ignatian spirituality, devotes a chapter of his *By Way of the Heart: Toward a Holistic Christian Spirituality* (Mahwah, NJ: Paulist Press, 1989) to prayer: "Open-Heart Prayer and the Divine."

A Hunger for God, edited by William A. Barry, SJ, and Kerry A. Maloney (Kansas City: Sheed & Ward, 1991) offers ten approaches to prayer. The first three chapters of Tim Muldoon's *The Ignatian Workout* (Chicago: Loyola Press, 2004) provide a very helpful introduction to praying for beginners. Especially noteworthy is the third chapter with its seven practices drawn from the Ignatian tradition and presented in language and example suited to young adults. The final chapters (24–26) of Dean Brackley's *The Call to Discernment in Troubled Times* are also worth attention. Two works by Philippines Jesuit Thomas H. Green are modern classics on prayer: *Opening to God: A Guide to Prayer* (Notre Dame, Indiana: Ave Maria Press, 1977) and *When the Well Runs Dry: Prayer Beyond the Beginnings* (Notre Dame, Indiana: Ave Maria Press, 1979).

Finally, something about a kind of prayer that is not traditionally Ignatian, because, if Ignatius were alive today, he might just recommend it as an antidote to the data- and activity-overload of our contemporary culture. Classic Christian teaching about prayer divides it into two fundamental types: *kataphatic* (with concepts, words, and images) and *apophatic* (without words). The former is Augustinian, Franciscan, Ignatian; the latter, Pseudo-Dionysian and Carmelite (in the persons of Teresa of Ávila and John of the Cross—near contemporaries of Ignatius). Apophatic prayer has been effectively taught in our time under the heading of "centering prayer" by two Trappist (a reform of Benedictinism in the direction of silence and contemplation) monks, Thomas Keating and Basil Pennington (*Centering Prayer: Renewing an Ancient Christian Prayer Form* [New York: Doubleday, 1980]). The Irish Jesuit William Johnston, who has spent most of his life in Japan and practices Zen regularly with Buddhist monks, has written extensively out of his experience beginning with *Christian Zen* (New York: Harper & Row, 1971).

In an appendix, Johnston has diagrams for a special kind of prayer bench that enables the pray-er who cannot sit in the traditional lotus posture (sitting on a tiny cushion with legs crossed underneath and knees touching the floor) to be grounded and centered nevertheless. I made one of these benches (called *seiza* benches) for my friend and classmate Justin Kelly, SJ. Some years later Justin told me that I had thereby done more for his prayer than many books and articles. All of which helps to remind us that Ignatius considered posture a very important aspect of prayer.

In the 1970s, the late Anthony de Mello, an Indian Jesuit, started offering guided awareness exercises (e.g., attentiveness to breathing) to Christians in India and, during summers, in the United States. These exercises were finally published in 1978 as *Sadhana: A Way to God—Christian Exercises in Eastern Form* (distributed in the U.S. by the Institute of Jesuit Sources [St. Louis, 1978]; this and most of de Mello's subsequent works are now published by Doubleday).

St. Louis University philosopher William Rehg, SJ, in "Christian Mindfulness: A Path to Finding God in All Things" (*Studies in the Spirituality of Jesuits* [May 2002]) rightly joins the apophatic (Buddhist "mindfulness") with the kataphatic (Ignatian "finding God in all things").

The Spiritual Exercises

Introduction

The Spiritual Exercises of St. Ignatius are the heart of Ignatian spirituality. An organized series of spiritual meditations and contemplations, Ignatius fashioned them out of his own personal experience and that of others to whom he listened. Eventually published in 1548, they were in use long before that as a powerful way of enabling people to encounter the living God and be nourished and transformed by that encounter. As a first glimpse into the distinctive character and power of these Exercises, we have the distilled wisdom of one of the great twentieth-century adapters of Ignatius, Ricardo Lombardi, SJ, creator of the "Better World Retreat," which sought to integrate contemporary theology (anticipating Vatican II's "The Church in the Modern World") with the Exercises:

> One who is familiar with the Exercises . . . knows they are an extremely compact collection of considerations, observations, and points that instead of being read must be experienced in a retreat, under the guidance of a person who knows their methodology and applies it to retreatants with power yet simultaneously with delicacy. In order to know these Exercises, it is necessary to practice them, to live them: one must add to the printed text the vital function of a guide and still more the intensive contribution of retreatants themselves. Especially noteworthy is the portion of the task left to them, since, properly speaking, they are the ones who *exercise themselves*. One who would be content with simply reading Ignatius' book from beginning to end would remain outside its marvelous world.[1]

The Exercises, at their most powerful, then, need a skilled and sensitive guide and retreatants who don't just read the book; they "exercise" themselves.

This section on the Spiritual Exercises consists of four short readings. We open with "What Are Spiritual Exercises?" by William Barry, SJ, who has guided scores of people through the Exercises and written extensively about the Exercises from that rich and privileged experience. Barry not only explains what the Exercises are but lays out a number of presuppositions that the Exercises have. Next we have "The Specificity of the Ignatian Exercises," by Javier Melloni, a Spanish Jesuit whose research into the antecedents of Ignatius in the Western spiritual tradition enables him to answer, quite convincingly, this question: Given all that Ignatius inherited, what was his original contribution? We follow this with "An Experience of the Contemporary Personally-Guided Spiritual Exercises" by James Fowler, then teaching at Harvard Divinity School and just beginning his research for what was to become a major work, *Stages of Faith*. Fowler's is a first-person account of his receiving Ignatian guidance or "coaching" during a time of great spiritual need. And we conclude with Irish Jesuit philosopher Patrick Heelan's foreword to *Powers of Imagining: Ignatius de Loyola* by Antonio de Nicolas, brother of the recently elected Jesuit superior general, Adolfo Nicolas.

As a way into these readings, let me review something of Ignatius's practice of the Exercises, later Jesuit developments away from that practice, and then the remarkable recovery of Ignatian practice in the second half of the last century.

Based on Ignatius's own spiritual experience and the discernment that he learned to practice with it, the Spiritual Exercises have as presupposition that God communicates with human beings through their (ordinary) experience, and people can "know" God and God's "will" in that experience. In simple and direct language, Barry draws an important corollary from this: "God . . . wants a personal relationship with each . . . individual."

Ignatius advises approaching God with "great desires," says Barry, "and also great expectations of what God wants to give me. . . . The path through the Exercises will not be smooth." But by gradually learning "to notice and talk about what happens interiorly, . . . [we will] learn to discern in our own experience what is of God from what is not of God."

Is this Ignatian way to God distinctive, new? Melloni concludes that "the Ignatian name for union with God is 'election,'"—the ongoing process of discerning/choosing/acting for God that "comes about . . . not through the flight from the world . . . of [the earlier] monastic tradition, but through the kenotic [self-emptying] movement of incarnation in the world and for the world."

The Exercises then are a kind of pedagogy (teaching method), inviting attentiveness to God's personal and unique communication with each human being. The power and effectiveness of that pedagogy in leading to behavioral change or conversion lay with Ignatius's ability to meet and coach each individual as such and to engage the whole person, not just the rational intellect.

It was unfortunate but not entirely surprising that, as the popularity of the Exercises grew over time, it became more "economical" to lead groups in the Exercises, instead of individuals, and to preach some parts of the content of the Exercises—letting go the fundamental Ignatian principle of adaptation to the individual person.[2]

Further, the kind of spiritual exercise which apparently assumed the smaller place in Ignatius's practice—namely *meditation*, or thinking and mulling over truths of the faith—gradually came to be taken as *the* Ignatian method. What tended to lose out in the age of rational Enlightenment (eighteenth century) and beyond was Ignatius's favored *contemplation*, or imaginative engagement in the story of Jesus as one's own story. Ultimately, of course, Ignatius was against imposing any particular way of praying, since that would encroach on a person's freedom and the guidance of the Holy Spirit.

In recent years, scholars and practitioners of the Exercises have been rediscovering what Ignatius intuitively knew. There are parts of the human person (e.g., the "right brain," the "unconscious")—crucial determinants of feeling, value, and action—that the rational, controlling mind does not touch. Rather are they reached when the rational mind is "in neutral," and contemplative, aesthetic, and imaginative modes of knowing are allowed to operate.

Fowler, in describing the spiritual condition that led him to seek out a guide such as his Jesuit students were suggesting, uses words like *Apollonian* (meaning "intellectual" or "heady" and therefore dominated by reason at the expense of feeling), *dry*, and *cast upon sand away from water*. Fowler's guide takes him on "an extended retreat" (i.e., a part-time "retreat in daily life" without withdrawing from home or work). Having listened well to what Fowler tells him, the guide suggests a way of praying that he has adapted from what Ignatius in the Exercises calls "Application of the Senses." It is designed to draw the retreatant into intimate contact with the gospel story (here Jesus' feeding of the five thousand). After some time, as Fowler tells it, "I discovered a porousness between my conscious and my unconscious mind. Images began to rise and meet images from the story. It was almost as if that part of me which is usually in control was in neutral. . . . I got in touch with my needs, with my hungers. I found a vulnerability. And I found a mediator. All this was in a way that I had not found from using my cognitive [purely rational] approach."

With his controlling rational mind "in neutral," Fowler is able to connect with parts of himself that had been closed off to him and therefore is also able to connect with Jesus and the Gospel story. How much courage it must have taken for Fowler, a divinity school profes-sor doing research on faith development and an ordained Protestant minister (therefore presumably better versed in the Scriptures than Catholics) to go to a Jesuit and ask for help!

What proved so efficacious for Fowler and what he understood of it in today's psychological terms is approached more historically and philosophically by Patrick Heelan in his foreword to Antonio de Nicolás's ninety-page essay on the powers of imagining.

NOTES

1. *Communitarian Dimensions of Ignatius: Communitarian Spiritual Exercises* (Silver Spring, MD: Movement for a Better World, n.d.), 259.

2. This is not to say that such preaching of the Exercises to a group has borne no fruit—far from it. Indeed, it can be considered a legitimate adaptation of the Exercises. I am simply pointing to a limitation in the use of this means. Ultimately, of course, God can communicate how and where God wills.

Understanding the Terminology:
Suggested Readings from *Do You Speak Ignatian?*

- spiritual exercises
- The Spiritual Exercises

What Are Spiritual Exercises?

William A. Barry, SJ

From *Finding God in All Things: A Companion to the Spiritual Exercises of St. Ignatius*, 1991

I suspect that most people in the world and even in the Christian world have never heard of *The Spiritual Exercises* of Ignatius of Loyola, Jesuit megalomania notwithstanding. That does not bother me. What does concern me is the fact that many, if not most, people who have heard about the Spiritual Exercises think of them as something esoteric, something reserved for novices or vowed members of religious communities, for holy people, or at least for people who can get away to a retreat house for an extended period of time. Such an image has, unfortunately, kept a treasure from broad use in the church. This book will, I hope, dispel that image and invite readers to consider how they might use the Spiritual Exercises to benefit their relationship with God. . . .

The book [of *The Spiritual Exercises*] essentially consists of notes or directions for the director of the Exercises. In it one finds directions for helping people to make a general and particular examination of conscience and to engage in various forms of prayer, ranging from vocal prayer and methods of saying vocal prayers to meditation and contemplation. It contains rules for the discernment of spirits, rules for eating, rules for thinking with the church.

The Exercises proper are divided into four "weeks," each division referring to a dynamic that may take more or less than a week's time to happen. The first "week" is taken up with the dynamic of letting God reveal to the retreatant his or her sins and sinful tendencies in order that the retreatant might repent of them and realize that, in spite of them, he or she is a loved sinner. The second "week" is devoted to the following of Christ, getting to know him better in order to love him more and to follow him more closely. In the third "week" the retreatant desires to share with Jesus the sufferings of his passion and death, and in the fourth "week" he or she desires to share Jesus' joy in his resurrection. Each "week" lasts as long as it takes for the retreatant to attain from God the grace desired.

Because his lack of theological training got him into trouble with the Inquisition of the time, Ignatius . . . decided to get a formal education in philosophy and theology and eventually went to the University of Paris. Here he met and became friends with other students, men like Francis Xavier, Pierre Favre, Nicholas Bobadilla, Alfonso Salmerón, and Diego Laínez. He directed each of them individually through the Exercises, and each of them decided to follow Christ unreservedly as did Ignatius. When these students made the Exercises they ranged in age from about eighteen to twenty-five. These young men were the founders of the Society of Jesus. I hope that it helps to dispel the mystique of the Spiritual Exercises to realize both how young these men were and that all but one were laymen at the time of making the Exercises.

What are the Spiritual Exercises? Here's what Ignatius himself says:

> By the term "Spiritual Exercises" is meant every method of examination of conscience, of meditation, of contemplation, of vocal and mental prayer, and of other spiritual activities that will be mentioned later. For just as taking a walk, journeying on foot, and running are bodily exercises, so we call Spiritual Exercises every way of preparing and disposing the soul to rid itself of all inordinate attachments, and, after their removal, of seeking and finding the will of God in the disposition of our life for the salvation of our soul (*Spiritual Exercises*, no. 1).

What Ignatius seems to mean, then, by spiritual exercises are any means by which we come into contact with God: means to overcome our resistances and to relate to God and, in the relating, to discover and to try to live out God's hopes for us. These Exercises are ways of meeting God and of discerning in our experience what is of God and what is not of God. Let's try to spell out some of Ignatius's presuppositions.

First, Ignatius learned from his own experience that God, the holy Mystery who is three in one, not only wants a personal relationship with each person, both as an individual and as a community, but also acts in this world to bring about such a personal relationship. Indeed, one can argue that the Ignatian Exercises rest on the theological assumption that God creates this universe precisely in order to invite other persons into the relational life of the Trinity. God's purpose or intention of inviting each person into the relational life of the Trinity is not episodic, occurring periodically in each person's life. God is always acting to bring about this intention.

Another way of making the same point is to say that God is always in conscious relationship with each one of us as our creator, our sustainer, dear father or dear mother, our brother, our savior, the Spirit who dwells in our hearts. Ignatius presupposes that at every moment of our existence God is communicating to us who God is, is trying to draw us into an awareness, a consciousness of the reality of who we are in God's sight. Whether we are aware of it or not, at every moment of our existence we are encountering God, Father, Son, and Holy Spirit, who is trying to catch our attention, trying to draw us into a reciprocal conscious relationship.

Second, the Spiritual Exercises are ways of helping us to become more aware of the reality of our existence as the objects of God's communication. Experience is an encounter between a being that exists and a person capable of being conscious of the encounter.[1] Faith tells us that God exists both as transcendent to and immanent in this world. So God is encountered. But we are not always conscious of, or alert to, the presence of God. The religious dimension of experience is supplied not only by the God who exists and is encountered, but also by a person of faith on the alert for God. The various exercises contained in the book of *The Spiritual Exercises* have as their purpose to heighten our awareness, to sharpen our ability to feel the "finger of God." These Exercises, then, are for anyone who wants to sharpen that awareness.

Perhaps some examples will make this more concrete. For the past several years, James Skehan, SJ, professor of geology and geophysics at Boston College, has been directing groups of people through the full Spiritual Exercises while they continue their ordinary lives. The retreat lasts about twenty-four weeks. Each retreatant takes time for prayer and reflection each day. In addition, they meet as a group for liturgy, dinner, and sharing of experience once a week. At the end of the latest retreat, I asked past and present participants to give me some reflections about what had happened. The retreatants have been faculty members, staff, graduate and undergraduate students, former students, and other people from the area, a cross section of the church, you might say.

One person wrote:

> The most powerful concept that occurred to me was that I am an actual member of the body of Christ and can participate with him in the transformation of the world. . . . Because I am a member of the body of Christ I am more aware of my own dignity and also of the presence of God in all people and all things.

Another said: "Perhaps the single greatest fruit of this retreat has been to discover what the Spirit wants me to do in following Jesus." A third wrote:

> Somehow, I cannot imagine that I will ever be the same person who started this retreat. My spiritual life up to then consisted of traditional prayer, often said without much thought. . . . These past several months of reflection and prayer I feel have become a very special part of me. The first reaction at this moment is to say that I am not afraid to die. Mind you now, I don't wish to die one second before my time. What I mean is that I never before was able to reflect on death and see

what might be the beginning of a better life and not just the end of a good one.

A fourth wrote:

> Silence and solitude now have meaning; they are no longer a space to be filled with activity or words but a time to listen and rest in peace and an ever-increasing sense of being loved. I now listen with a new awareness of every individual, and each interaction is not an isolated occurrence but a part of an ongoing conversation intending nothing less than that lovely Ignatian notion of seeing God in all things. Concretely I find myself smiling and laughing more often in the presence of others. . . . I feel my life is no longer an independent pursuit, for I must continually reach out in recognition of this human community.

These are wonderful testimonies to the power of the Spiritual Exercises in our own day.

Third among the presuppositions Ignatius makes is that the most important prerequisite for using at least some of these exercises is the desire to become more aware of the presence of God in one's life and to develop one's conscious relationship with this self-communicating God. One does not need any theological sophistication. Ignatius . . . was theologically illiterate when he first began the conscious development of his relationship with God. Nor does one need to be holy or even relatively far advanced in the spiritual life to make use of these exercises. Ignatius was, by his own admission, a spiritual child when he began the exercises at Manresa. In spite of these lacks, however, Ignatius had the one thing necessary to undertake the journey, namely, great desires. He distilled this concept in the fifth annotation at the beginning of *The Spiritual Exercises*:

> It will be very profitable for the one who is to go through the Exercises to enter upon them with magnanimity and generosity toward his Creator and Lord, and to offer him his entire will and liberty, that his Divine Majesty may dispose of him and all he possesses according to his most holy will (*Spiritual Exercises*, no. 5).

I take *magnanimity* and *generosity* to mean great desires and also great expectations of what God wants to give me during this period.

Fourth, Ignatius presupposes that the path through the Exercises will not be smooth. In fact, in the sixth annotation Ignatius tells the director to question carefully any retreatant who "is not affected by any spiritual experiences, such as consolations or desolations, and . . . is not troubled by different spirits" (*Spiritual Exercises*, no. 6). Ignatius began his own conversion when he noted the different emotional reactions caused by the two sets of daydreams, and he came to the conclusion that our hearts are something like a battleground. Not only is God trying to engage us in a dialogical relationship, but the evil one is also trying to draw us away from that relationship. If we give ourselves a chance to become aware of God's communications through making the Spiritual Exercises, we also open ourselves to the counter-attractions of the evil one. We will, therefore, experience internal ups and downs. So another prerequisite for making the Exercises is the ability to notice and talk about what happens interiorly while one is doing them. In the process of noticing and talking about these various movements of our hearts, we will have to learn to discern in our experiences what is of God from what is not of God.

One retreatant described the process of discernment in this way:

> I am extremely grateful that this retreat has brought an increase in my awareness of the abiding presence of God, and has done so by directing my attention to the only moment I have at any time, the present one. This has been reinforced by St. Ignatius's wise words to examine the day and what is moving through it in terms of spiritual light or spiritual darkness. All this is extremely important for me to practice because I would rather hope to find God in big and exciting events—yet then I would miss him in the simple and little events of each day.

The fact that the one who makes the full Spiritual Exercises has to be able to notice and talk about his or her inner life implies something about the relationship between the individual and the director of the Exercises. Sensible people will reveal their inner lives only to people they trust. Hence, the director of the Spiritual Exercises has to be a person who can be trusted. The trust obviously includes confidentiality and an ability to help with the relationship with God. But the director also has to be a "skilled helper," a person who knows how to help another to explore inner experience and to recognize emerging desires.[2] Moreover, the director needs to be someone who can adapt the Exercises to the needs and talents of the individual.

Many people think of the Spiritual Exercises as a planned and relatively fixed program of exercises to which a person submits. Indeed, many of us older people experienced the Ignatian Exercises in precisely this way. Those of us who made the full Exercises of thirty days prior to 1965 or so made them in groups. The director gave four or five talks each day in which he set out the matter for prayer for the four or five hours of prayer. There was little chance for individual direction because of the size of the groups. As a result there was a sort of lockstep movement through the thirty days. Until it was shown that originally the Spiritual Exercises were individually directed and only later adapted for groups, there were many who felt that the individually directed Exercises were a modern aberration.

Yet it was the genius of Ignatius to write a book that could be adapted to all sorts of people according to both their desires and capabilities and their availability. Ignatius put it this way:

> The Spiritual Exercises must be adapted to the condition of the one who is to engage in them, that is, to his age, education, and talent. Thus exercises that he could not easily bear, or from which he would derive no profit, should not be given to one with little natural ability or of little physical strength. Similarly, each one should be given those exercises that would be more helpful and profitable according to his willingness to dispose himself for them.
>
> Hence, one who wishes no further help than some instruction and the attainment of a certain degree of peace of soul may be given the Particular Examination of Conscience. . . .
>
> Similarly, if the one giving the Exercises sees that the exercitant has little aptitude or little physical strength, that he is one from whom little fruit is to be expected, it is more suitable to give him some of

the easier exercises as a preparation for confession (*Spiritual Exercises*, no. 18).

Adaptation is the name of the game, and the director of the Exercises has to be someone who has the art to make the appropriate adaptations to the persons involved.

Another misconception is that you have to go away to a retreat house in the country to make the Spiritual Exercises. Yet Ignatius gave the Spiritual Exercises to his first companions in the middle of the turbulent Left Bank of Paris. I have directed people in the full Exercises who lived in Boston and took the subway to see me each day. An acre of woods or seashore is not necessary to meet God.

Moreover, Ignatius conceived of a way for a person who could not take thirty days off from work to make the full Spiritual Exercises. In the nineteenth annotation, he writes: "One who is educated or talented, but engaged in public affairs or necessary business, should take an hour and a half daily for the Spiritual Exercises" (*Spiritual Exercises,* no. 19). Many people have made the full Exercises in this manner. They meet their director every week or every two weeks over a period of about thirty weeks. Thousands of people in Canada and the United States have made the full Exercises in this way in the past twenty years. A person can also make part of the full Exercises in this manner.

One of the hallmarks of Ignatian spirituality is the belief that God can be found in all things. Ignatius believed that we encounter God at every moment of our existence. The Spiritual Exercises are various methods to help us to become more and more aware of this everpresent God. If we want to, we can become contemplatives in action, people who are alert to God's presence in all our daily activities.

NOTES

1. Here I rely on John E. Smith, *Experience and God* (New York: Oxford, 1968).

2. See Gerard Egan, *The Skilled Helper: A Systematic Approach to Effective Helping,* 3rd ed. (Monterey, CA: Brooks/Cole, 1986).

The Specificity of the Ignatian Exercises

Javier Melloni, SJ

From *The Exercises of St. Ignatius Loyola in the Western Tradition*, 2000

As we have seen in the preceding pages, although at Montserrat and Manresa Ignatius received much traditional material which he would incorporate into his Exercises, it was in these places, too, that he lived through a personal experience of God which transformed the very content he had received. Many years would be needed for the elements of this experience to be structured in the salient themes of the Exercises: the principle that union with God comes about in the world through the continuous discernment of the will of God, that from this discernment emerges the shape of a personal vocation, specific to each individual and which it is for each to find; that the will of God can be found through discernment when someone puts themself wholly in a position to welcome it.

This attention to, and respect for, every individual's unique and non-interchangeable route gives to Ignatius's Exercises a distinctive and original feature with respect to the preceding Tradition: the book of the Exercises is conceived as "the book of the master," and is not intended for the direct use of the exercitant. That is to say, we have in the Exercises a guide for the person who is to give them and not a textbook for the person who makes them. What the giver proposes, the exercitants have to re-create out of their own experience and with their own words.

The Process of Mystagogy[1]

Yet it is a paradox of Ignatian mystagogy that there can be no access to the personal experience of the Exercises without accompaniment. Thus, on the one hand, the object of the Exercises is a personal and intimate meeting with God (*Spiritual Exercises,* no. 15), but on the other hand Ignatius insists that this meeting be tested in the Church through the companion who guides the exercitant's steps.

These steps trace a path which enters into the mystery of union with God through the relinquishment of self in the act of election, a putting-off which is a path to fullness. Here is the key to understanding the specific dynamic of the mystical union proper to *Ignatian mystagogy.*

Up to a point, we can indeed find a progression toward union in the actual sequence of the four weeks: from the purification brought about in the First Week through the interior knowledge of sin (*Spiritual Exercises,* nos. 57, 63) and the rejection of it, to the unitive conclusion of the *Contemplation for attaining Love* (*Spiritual Exercises,* nos. 230–237), passing in the Second Week through the illuminative elements of the "interior knowledge of the Lord who became human for me so that I may better love and follow him" (*Spiritual Exercises,* no. 104). However, as already indicated, Ignatius does not speak of the *via unitiva* explicitly.[2] At first sight, this might appear to suggest that the unitive way is not present in the Exercises and to support the argument that the Exercises, precisely as "exercises" (*askêsis*), belong within the frame of the active way and terminate at the point where the passive or unitive way begins.[3] This interpretation fails, however, to take account of the explicit "end" of the Exercises given by Ignatius: the search for the will of God in relation to one's own life in order to offer oneself to that will with all one's being. There is here a new step taken by Ignatius with respect to the entire previous tradition of which the significance might be epitomized by saying: *the Ignatian name for union with God is "election".* Such union comes about in the act and art of choosing in each moment in terms of God's will, which declares itself in history for the transformation of the world; an act and art of choosing which, the more profoundly they are exercised, the more they become in reality the act and art of "allowing" oneself to be chosen. This ultimately is what discernment is about: allowing oneself to be taken by God, allowing Him to act through oneself in every event of history. Thus, for Ignatius, union is always a quest and a tendency, never a definitive state.

To understand the contribution of the Exercises to the mystical tradition of the West, another point must be noticed: in Ignatius the movement of union is one of incarnation, not elevation, or more accurately, the form of elevation for Ignatius is that of a descent. The search for union with God—that aspiration which is within the heart of every human being—comes about for him not through the flight from the world (*fuga mundi*) of monastic tradition, but through the kenotic [self-emptying] movement of incarnation in the world and for the world. This "in the world" and "for the world" are contained in every act of choice: the will of God is nothing other than the recapitulation of all things in Christ, and Christ in the Father, so that God comes to be all in all (cf. 1 Corinthians 15:28). The will of God is the divinization of every creature; and it was to bring about this divinization that the One, who was in God and who was God, emptied himself (*ekénôsen*; cf. Philippians 2:7) in order to participate in our human condition and transform it from within.

Thus we can understand the Ignatian Exercises as the mystagogy which leads into this dynamic. The mystical search, the desire for union with God, for full participation in divine life, passes through the kenosis [self-emptying] of election. To perceive this kenosis as source of life, and way of union and of divinization, is the key to Ignatius's whole project and mystagogy. The Exercises are directed towards the configuration of the exercitant to the image of Christ Jesus. This comes about in two simultaneous ways: on the one hand, through the contemplation of Christ's life, passion, and resurrection, which imprints the image of Christ on the heart of the exercitant;

and on the other, by discerning the concrete form of this Christic configuration in one's own life (i.e., the "election," or the continuous decisions which have to be made) through the interior movements aroused by contemplation.

The Mystical Act of Election, Way of Union and of Unification

The foregoing presentation of what seem to be the most important sources of the general configuration of the Exercises enables us to perceive what is specific in the Ignatian approach, namely, "election" and the consequent discernment of the will of God in history, neither of which are to be met with before Ignatius. Certainly, the discernment of spirits is present in the tradition from the Desert Fathers on, but this discernment is not oriented towards a search of the will of God that converts human existence into a permanent "election."

The original and central character of the election has been established by many commentators, particularly by Gaston Fessard;[4] and study of the sources confirms that election is the most characteristic feature of the Exercises. However, what is being underlined in these pages is something more specific, that *election is precisely the unitive and mystical way proposed by Ignatius*. In this perspective, the act of election is understood to be an act of freedom because it is a mystical act. One must speak of the "act" because we are dealing with a movement which has to become concrete in time and space; but it is mystical because it is not one act among other acts, but the origin and source of all of them insofar as it proceeds not from the exercitant alone, but from the life of God which is in him or her. The Exercises of St. Ignatius are made precisely in order to prepare for and introduce this "act," which develops into a continuous attitude of receptivity and self-giving; an "act" which, located at a point in time, is also a continuous movement, a way of living. This way of life centered on the election is that of offering. Hence, the Exercises conclude with the "Take, Lord, and receive" of the *Contemplation to attain Love* (*Spiritual*

Exercises, no. 234). This offering is nothing less than the response to all that one has received, which is life itself and the very capacity to offer. It is a matter of exchange between the Lover and the Loved One (*Spiritual Exercises,* no. 234). Offering one's own life, one empties oneself (*kenôsis*), and receiving and welcoming the life of God, one comes to share in His nature, to be divinized (*theôsis*). The nature of God is Love, the capacity to give and to offer oneself and to welcome without limits. To be "divinized," then, means nothing other than to participate ever more profoundly in the act of giving. In the history of an individual life, the gift passes at each moment through an act of election.

Thus understood, the capacity of self-gift by means of the election is the participation in the divine life to which one is introduced by the mystagogy of the Exercises. So election and the unitive way of the preceding mystical tradition are not mutually opposed. On the contrary, election is the historico-kenotic dimension of that union. Election is kenotic, as the life of Christ with the Father was kenotic; in the space left by his self-emptying, the world is incorporated into Him to be transfigured. Through the whole course of the Exercises this kenotic aspect is present in the persistent contemplation of the "poor and humble Lord." "In poverty and humility"—such was the mode through which Christ was united with the Father through the Spirit, from His birth to His death:

> Watch and consider what they [Joseph and Mary] are doing, e.g., their travel and efforts, so that Christ comes to be born in extreme poverty and, after so many labors, after hunger, thirst, heat and cold, outrages and affronts, he dies on the cross. (*Spiritual Exercises,* no. 116)

The more Jesus relinquished Himself, the more He discovered the will of the Father. For the will of God is only love, and love is the gift of self without measure. Such is the "more" (*más* [in Spanish, *magis* in Latin]) contained in the Exercises; the "more" which belongs to a movement of steady descent: from the *Eternal King* to the *Two Standards,* and finally to the *Third mode of humility.* The unitive dimension begins, then, with incorporation into this descent of Christ, which turns to exaltation only in its lowest depths of abasement (cf. Philippians 2:8–11).

The mystical way of the Exercises consists in the grasp of such paradoxes as these, which implies the interior transformation prayed for—and to be prayed for ceaselessly—in the opening contemplation of the Second Week: "I ask for interior knowledge of the Lord who became human for me so that I may better love and follow him" (*Spiritual Exercises,* no. 104).

This interior knowledge is one of the keys of the Ignatian mystagogy; it implicates both the cognitive and the affective dimensions of the person. Both knowledge and affectivity are mobilized and worked on from the beginning of the Exercises. Both converge upon the act of election, where knowledge of the will of God is converted into a volitional impulse of the exercitant to commit him- or herself to it. Hence the way to union with the will of God implies simultaneously a progressive unifying of the whole person.

In the Ignatian plan, if it is understood in this sense, the mysticism of knowledge and the mysticism of love—also known as the mysticism of the will—are not opposed to each other. Rather one leads to the other, since knowledge is converted into love—the dynamism of self-giving; and love seeks knowledge of God's will, making life in its entirety a call to continuous discernment. All this is no more than another way of speaking of the Ignatian ideal of being a "contemplative in action."

Thus the Exercises, beyond the formal frame of eight, fifteen, or thirty days, constitute a way of living in God for the world and of living for God in the world. Such is Ignatius's contribution to the spiritual tradition of the West, and it is the way we have to offer to our contemporaries who, in their own manner, hunger and thirst for God.

NOTES

1. Mystagogy: As pedagogy, the art of teaching, is a way to knowledge, so mystagogy is a way to "mystical" knowledge, a way to knowledge of God and union with God.—Editor's note

2. Thus in the tenth Annotation (*Spiritual Exercises,* no. 10) Ignatius explicitly links the First Week with the purgative life and the Second Week with the illuminative life, but makes no mention of the unitive life.

3. It should be noted that union is the horizon onto which the final words of the Exercises open: "[filial fear] is wholly acceptable and pleasing to God our Lord since it is all one with divine love." *Eighteenth rule for thinking with the Church* (*Spiritual Exercises,* no. 370).

4. Gaston Fessard, *La dialectique des Exercices Spirituels de Saint Ignace* (Paris: Aubier, 1956), vol. 1, 23–41.

An Experience of the Contemporary Personally Guided Spiritual Exercises

James W. Fowler

Life Maps: Conversations on the Journey of Faith, 1978

Sam Keen: My essay "Education for Serendipity," which is published in *To a Dancing God*, was a start at saying what education would look like in a healthy society. I know a bit more now about education than I did when I wrote that, and I am more than ever convinced that the main thing that needs to be introduced is a more primitive approach. We need more techniques that touch the affective domain.

We need, for example, to teach people to stay in touch with their dreams. Dreams are the opening edge of our craziness. If you stay in touch with your dreams, you will probably not have to make a crazy journey.

Second, if we teach people to maintain touch with their own bodies, that will also help. Teaching direct experiential disciplines, like meditation and sensory awareness, or unconscious awareness and the reading of unconscious symbolism, will help. We know how to do this now, but it is being done largely under the guise of therapy rather than as education. This awareness is crucial to enable people to move through life without having to tear up everything around them to make their journey. They should have more gentle techniques at hand. The tragedy of our society is that so few of us (especially the elite who got there because their heads were hard as rocks) can learn to soften our heads without some other part of the body running away for a while.

JIM FOWLER: Sometimes these techniques lie in unexpected places or in places that are overlooked because of misunderstanding or excessive familiarity. I last discovered this (and one discovers it over and over) when I began working on the faith development project. I realized that I was getting awfully Apollonian and awfully dry. *Dry* is almost an understatement. I was virtually shipwrecked in terms of being cast upon the sand away from the water.

In my class that year there was a group of Jesuits. They kept saying in subtle ways that Ignatian spirituality was becoming very important to the Jesuits again. It might be important for me too. My image of Saint Ignatius was not an inviting one, but the Jesuits kept at it in a persistent, gentle, brotherly way. Finally, one of them gave me a copy of *The Spiritual Exercises*, written by Saint Ignatius. It is not a very edifying book to read, at least not prior to any experience in using it.

I went to a Jesuit spiritual director in Cambridge and said, "Look. I need some help. My own prayer life and my living with the Scriptures is all dried up. I'm in trouble."

He said, "I don't know if I can help you or not," but he took me on in an extended retreat. With great gentleness and in a unique relationship—not as a therapist or pastor in the sense of having answers, but more like a coach—he introduced me to the "new" method that he taught.

"I want you to take this story of the feeding of the five thousand, and I want you to mediate on it for three days. Just spend an hour a day. I want you to start off just mastering the thing. Use your cognitive abilities to get every detail of the story. Get everything down. Repeat it so that the narrative gets into you.

"The next day I want you to try to let loose of what you did the day before. Now I want you to read yourself into the story. I want you to sensually participate in it. I want you to smell the smells of that crowd. I want you to hear the sounds of their voices. I want you to feel them jostling up against you. I want you to see them and to see

Jesus. Above all, I want you to taste that food. Above all, I want you to taste it."

Some extraordinary things began to happen as I followed his directions. On the third day my task was to let my mind play. I was to let it be open to my own hungers. I was to ask myself what I was hungry for. Where did I need to be fed? Who feeds me? What food is there that I cannot get along without?

I discovered a porousness between my conscious and my unconscious mind. Images began to rise and meet images from the story. It was almost as if that part of me which is usually in control was in neutral. A new kind of transaction between myself and the text began to occur. I began to see how that tradition could be an instrument of the spirit in a way and degree that were different from anything I had known before.

I got in touch with my needs, with my hungers. I found a vulnerability. And I found a mediator. All this was in a way that I had not found from using my cognitive approach. I think that the sort of method found in the *Spiritual Exercises* is very promising for groups and for individuals. It is a native, Christian, and Western method of doing some of the things that we are learning about from other sources. Ignatius was very much like Carl Jung in his understanding of the way the unconscious produces symbols that can depict our situation, our needs, our directional tendency.

Foreword to *Powers of Imagining: Ignatius de Loyola*

Patrick A. Heelan, SJ

From Antonio de Nicolás, *Powers of Imagining: Ignatius de Loyola*, 1986

Many of the universities and libraries of Europe bear the IHS monogram of the Jesuit order, more properly called the "Society of Jesus." Such buildings were once owned by the Jesuits, among the greatest scholars, educators, patrons of the arts of their time. The first members of the order belonged to the generation of Nicolaus Copernicus, the generation that saw the beginnings of the scientific revolution, the generation that discovered infinite space and created the new sciences of the cosmos and of nature. This same generation paralleled the exploration of nature with the exploration of the earth, sending ships beyond Europe to extend the discoveries that had begun in the previous century. Such voyages were also missionary endeavors bringing both the new sciences and Christianity to the "new" lands. Even before the pilgrims landed in Massachusetts, the missionary and educational effort of the Jesuits had spread in this way to India, China, Japan, Mexico, and was soon to extend to Brazil, Paraguay, Canada, the Midwest of the United States, and California. The founder of this learned and powerful society was Saint Ignatius de Loyola.

Ignatius was born into a Basque family of minor nobility with no great wealth or important connections. His education was not extensive. He never rose to any high rank in the Church. He was not a charismatic preacher. Yet he became one of the great leaders and organizers of Counter-Reformation Europe. The instrument of his success was the *Spiritual Exercises*, a set of brief instructions for spiritual renewal that he composed during his convalescence after the siege of Pamplona and polished laboriously in the ensuing years.

The *Spiritual Exercises* do not teach doctrine nor morals. When used by an experienced master, they prepare a person to experience and to discern the affects that accompany the practice of living the "memory" of Christ's life, death, and resurrection. Such "memory" is not the memory of the scriptural scholar, nor of the scientist or historian, nor even that of the theologian or church fathers. The "memory" in question is of a special kind that is now largely forgotten, though it flourished for millennia when European culture was predominantly oral. This is the "memory" that Antonio de Nicolás calls the "powers of imagining."

The "powers of imagining" consist in calling on the sensuous imagination with great intensity—*exercising* the sensuous powers—in order to reenact, as it were, in one's own life the symbolic narratives of the past, so as to feel the affects of one's imagined present participation in the lives and events, in this case, of the founder of Christianity and of his disciples. Ignatian meditation, then, is not a form of rational (formal logical) analysis, nor does it seek historical and scientific accuracy. It is rather a manner of experiencing and then discerning, that is, evaluating, the spiritual affects of (what Ignatius called) "consolation" and "desolation," first in the course of such imaginative exercises, then in contemplating the world around that God made, and finally at the heart of daily human living. By the correct use of such discernment, one was enabled autonomously to come to those decisions that were (to use the motto of the Jesuit order) "for the greater glory of God."

Such a claim was rightly feared by some as tending toward a form of heterodox anti-ecclesiastical mystical "illuminism." However, unlike other forms of religious enthusiasm within and outside of the Roman Catholic Church at that time and later, Ignatian freedom to discern what was "for the greater glory of God" did not aim at replacing church authority in its own legitimate domain, but at supplementing the public administration of the church by training suitable people in the arts of spiritual discernment. Such people were taught to become aware of the inner life of the Holy Spirit shared by all Christians and to learn to respond autonomously to its demands. Such was the aim and the promise of the *Spiritual Exercises*. This little book molded the first companions of Ignatius and made possible the extraordinary expansion of the Jesuit order in the fifty years after Ignatius's death, and the effects of its pedagogy formed a worldwide bond such that, despite isolation from one another on five continents, the first generations of Jesuits seemed to be responding to a common, still, but commanding voice.

How is one to understand the claims to knowledge that are made by Ignatian meditation for the power of enactment (or reenactment) of our memories, particularly of our religious memories? Such practices, though they have long passed out of common use in scientific and academic circles, have nevertheless an important and respected place in the history of our culture and even in the development of modern science.

Modern science emerged in the seventeenth century as the creation of several quite different traditions. The view that nature was to be best understood as a machine or set of machines—the mechanical tradition—was the one that came to dominate nineteenth-century scientific thinking. In this view, a machine is something made up of interlocking (atomic or molecular) parts that perform cyclic motions, itself devoid of intrinsic purpose, in an otherwise empty space-time container. The mechanical view denies that there are in nature spiritual, rational, religious, or preternatural powers other than, perhaps, the human spirit.

Mechanical explanation, however, was scarcely used in antiquity. Both antiquity and the Middle Ages conceived the cosmos holistically as a living thing, full of finite powers and limited rational purpose. Such was the model defended, say, by Aristotle, whose authority was paramount in high culture during the period just before the scientific revolution. The holistic organic model persisted after the development of mechanical science right into the nineteenth century, particularly in the "lower sciences," such as biology and medicine, and is a second ingredient of development of modern science. Something of the holistic and purposive character of this model is presently being rediscovered in physical cosmology and in some other branches of modern science.

Both organismic and mechanical models of explanation are naturalistic models in that they do not rest on claims either to preternatural knowledge or to the existence of preternatural powers in the world. Although today we think of science as exclusively naturalistic, it would be a serious mistake to think that modern science sprang entirely from such roots, or continues in its most creative moments to spring from such roots.

The third important ingredient of the scientific revolution was the Hermetic tradition stemming in part from the Neoplatonic literary revival of the fifteenth-century Renaissance with its interest in numerology, and in part from even older Christian and non-Christian Gnostic sources in antiquity, particularly in Egypt and the Middle East.[1] Greatly dependent on this tradition were alchemy, astrology, and the science of mnemonics or memory. All of these sciences touched religion at one extreme and magic at the other. Their practitioners conceived themselves as operating in some way as agents of divine or preternatural powers in nature, either constraining such powers to serve private purposes (magic) or working in holy complicity with such powers for the greater glory of God (religion). Among the great figures of the scientific revolution, Copernicus, Kepler, Gilbert, and Newton saw themselves as such *magi*—that is, as engaged in solving the cosmic riddles which God uses both to display subtly and at the same time to guard the secret formulae to know which give control of nature's powers. Many others, from Francis Bacon to the Puritan divines who patronized science, were deeply under the influence of this tradition.

More important, then, than the division between the rival mechanistic and organismic explanations of nature, was the division between the purely naturalistic and the Hermetic traditions of scientific inquiry. To the extent, for example, that Protestantism favored the new sciences, it favored those with a strong Hermetic component, such as chemistry or alchemy, while it distrusted mechanical explanations as dangerously antireligious.[2]

Among the sciences closely related to the Hermetic tradition was mnemonics, or the science of memory, or—to use de Nicolás's words—the science of the "powers of imagining." The art or science of memory has roots both in ancient rhetoric and in religion.[3] The ancient treatises on memory from classical Roman antiquity, such as those by Quintilian and Cicero, described techniques for storing in memory and retrieving whatever could be useful in argument or for persuasion. One is advised to build in imagination, for instance, a "memory palace," where each room is the repository of information to be remembered. This was stored under the symbolic forms of pictures, statues, number diagrams, and other Hermetic displays, often exaggerated in tone or in caricature, placed at strategic locations in the rooms and corridors so as to facilitate recall.

Information, however, is power to act or to reenact, and in so being is feeling, sharing, learning from, and commanding in a mysterious way the powers that fill the cosmos. Here memory touches religion. For God makes plans for people and things—God's will, as it is called—and these seek fruition through the powers and gentle influences—the actual graces—that suffuse the universe. It was the practice of spiritual, mystical, or Hermetic disciplines associated with these beliefs that as, for example, in the case of Copernicus, Kepler, and Gilbert directed much of their scientific work. The abuse of such discipline was magic, or black magic to distinguish it from the proper use of such discipline which was called white magic. Magic—or black magic—was the use of memory to constrain the cosmic powers for selfish interests regardless of God's will.

The method of Ignatius belongs to the old tradition of mnemonics or the cultivation of memory.[4] Such a discipline was not exercised just for the sake of recall but—in its religious use—in order to learn God's will. God's will was communicated through reenacting, through making live in one's own experience, those mysterious memory symbols that spoke of salvation, of the cosmos, and of human history. Such a reenactment was directed in the first place toward feeling the affects that accompanied it, then toward learning to interpret these affects correctly, and then toward making life decisions in accordance with their guidance. Following Ignatius, after a suitable spiritual preparation, one started with the Christian memory of the life, death, and resurrection of Christ. From these one learned to recognize the true affects of "consolation" and "desolation." Then, one moved on to the natural and cosmological environment, learning to recognize the same spiritual affects in reenacting the mysteries of nature. And from there, one carried the principles of discernment into daily life.[5]

What is recovered by Professor de Nicolás in his work is the radical flavor of the original sense of the *Spiritual Exercises*. This radical flavor was lost gradually in the seventeenth century in the interests, perhaps, of adapting the Ignatian spirit to the environment of large institutional responsibilities. It was not until the 1950s, after a century and a half of persecution and repression that afflicted the Jesuit order in Europe, that the radicality of the Ignatian Exercises was rediscovered. . . .

De Nicolás's "powers of imagining" suggest that there is a deep fraternal bond among members of the human race, as well as an affective "sympathy" among people, nature, and historical circumstances made alive by "memory." At the birth of all original newness, such as a new religion, a new science, a new philosophy, a new art or poem, there the "powers of imagining" are at work exploring and "tasting" some new found "memory." Like Ignatius, like Plato, such creative persons choose to obey the demands of this inner "memory" rather than the established practices of their times. The lesson de Nicolás wants us to learn is that unless we discover how to use and develop our "powers of imagining," we surrender our own freedom; that is, we fail to know how to innovate while preserving the continuity of our "memories," which are ourselves.

NOTES

1. See, for example, Frank Manuel, *A Portrait of Newton* (Cambridge, MA: Harvard University Press, 1968); Frances A. Yates, *Giordano Bruno and the Hermetic Tradition* (Chicago: University of Chicago Press, 1964), Alexandre

Koyré, *Mystiques, spirituels, et alchemists* (Paris: 1955), and P. M. Rattansi, "The Social Interpretation of Science in the Seventeenth Century," in *Science and Society, 1600–1900*, ed. P. Mathias (Cambridge: Cambridge University Press, 1972), 1–31.

2. See Rattansi, "Social Interpretation. . . ."

3. See, for example, the excellent study of medieval and early Renaissance mnemonic art, *The Art of Memory*, by Frances A. Yates (London: Penguin, 1969).

4. See Jonathan D. Spence, *The Memory Palace of Matteo Ricci* (New York: Viking, 1984), chap. 1.

5. See Hugo Rahner, *Ignatius the Theologian* (London: Chapman, 1968).

Further Reading

Work on the Spiritual Exercises is so voluminous that all I can give here—in a longer than usual "Further Reading" essay—is just a taste.

Studies and interpretations: To follow up on Barry's "What Are Spiritual Exercises?" I suggest John O'Malley's fine treatment in the last part of chapter 1 of *The First Jesuits* (Cambridge, MA: Harvard University Press, 1993), 37–50. Because O'Malley writes in a fresh idiom, without much of the usual Jesuit jargon, one feels ushered into a new world. For a detailed commentary on Ignatius's text, consult *Understanding the Spiritual Exercises—Text and Commentary: A Handbook for Retreat Directors* (Leominster, UK: Gracewing, 1998), by the late British Jesuit Michael Ivens. In addition to his detailed commentary, Ivens gives each major topic in Ignatius's *Exercises* an introduction of several paragraphs or more.

Next I mention two modern classics of interpretation and two more that may well become classics:

Dutch Jesuit William Peters' *The Spiritual Exercises of St. Ignatius: Exposition and Interpretation* (Jersey City, NJ: Program to Adapt the Spiritual Exercises, 1968). Out of print; consult a Jesuit university library.

French Jesuit Edouard Pousset's *Life in Faith and Freedom: An Essay Presenting Gaston Fessard's Analysis of the Spiritual Exercises of St. Ignatius,* trans. and ed. Eugene L. Donohue, SJ (St. Louis: Institute of Jesuit Sources, 1980).

English laywoman Margaret Silf's *Inner Compass: An Invitation to Ignatian Spirituality,* 10th anniversary ed. (Chicago: Loyola Press, 2007). Silf is married and has a daughter. She was trained by Jesuits in the art of spiritual guidance. Her book "is surely one of the best translations of the dynamics of the *Spiritual Exercises* in contemporary lay language available today," says Dennis Hamm, SJ, of Creighton University.

Dean Brackley's *The Call to Discernment in Troubled Times: New Perspectives on the Transformative Wisdom of Ignatius of Loyola* (New York: Crossroad, 2004). Brackley is a New York Jesuit who volunteered to replace one of the six Jesuits slain at the University of Central America in San Salvador (1989). Don't miss the foreword by Ellen Calmus: "The Copyeditor's Conversion: A Foreword for Skeptics." Some parts of this work have been mentioned in the previous section and others will call for our attention in the next section of the reader.

A book-length interpretation that remains valuable today is the French-Canadian Jesuit Gilles Cusson's *Biblical Theology and the Spiritual Exercises: A Method Toward a Personal Experience of God as Accomplishing within Us His Plan of Salvation* (St. Louis: Institute of Jesuit Sources, 1988). Cusson came to be associated especially with the "Spiritual Exercises in Everyday Life," an adaptation which Ignatius foresaw and presented in the nineteenth Annotation (or introductory observation) at the beginning of the *Exercises*. This part-time way of making the Exercises, an alternative to the full-time, thirty-day retreat, spread rapidly across Canada and is more recently growing in the United States. Cusson deals with it in a second volume: *The Spiritual Exercises Made in Everyday Life* (St. Louis: Institute of Jesuit Sources, 1989). A shorter treatment showing how the "19th Annotation Retreat" has worked in practice is Jesuit L. Patrick Carroll's "The Spiritual Exercises in Everyday Life," *Studies in the Spirituality of Jesuits* (January 1990).

Guides for the Person Making the Exercises: Works described in this and the next paragraph, both in the genre of the Exercises in Everyday Life, are intended directly for the person making the Exercises, unlike Ignatius's original book, which was intended for the guide who coaches a person through the Exercises. In *Moment by Moment* (Notre Dame, IN: Ave Maria Press, 2000), Carol Ann Smith, SHCJ, and Eugene Merz, SJ, of Marquette University, present the Exercises in thirty-two "moments," with each moment given two pages (opposite each other) in the same format (questions for reflection, practical suggestions, and excerpts from scripture and the *Spiritual Exercises*). Thus, following Ignatius's directive, they refrain from the kind of fuller explanation that could inhibit the retreatant's doing the actual exercising. In *The Ignatian Workout: Daily Spiritual Exercises for a Healthy Faith* (Chicago: Loyola Press, 2004), Tim Muldoon of Boston College expands on the analogy that Ignatius draws at the beginning of the *Exercises* (nos. 3–4) between physical and spiritual exercises. Muldoon gives more explanation than Smith and Merz, in keeping with the likely principal audience—young adults—while still making it clear to readers that they are expected to make a commitment to doing these spiritual exercises.

Online Exercises: An amazing phenomenon of our electronic age are the "Online Exercises." Offered by Creighton University's Collaborative Ministry Office, this thirty-four-week process presents weekly suggestions and directions (fuller than those in Smith and Merz's *Moment by Moment*) for making the Exercises in everyday life. An individual or a group can start at any time and set the pace. Thousands and thousands of people from all over the world have done the Exercises with this great aid (www.creighton.edu/collaborativeministry/cmo-retreat.html).

Translations: For many years the 1951 English translation by Louis J. Puhl, SJ, (Chicago: Loyola Press) was the standard. There are still many things to recommend it, but, of course, Puhl knew nothing about inclusive language. That is remedied in the translation, accompanied by excellent notes and commentary, that George Ganss, SJ, made for his *Ignatius of Loyola: Spiritual Exercises and Selected Works* (New York: Paulist Press, 1991). The translation is also available in a separate volume from the Institute of Jesuit Sources (1992). And many have found the "Literal Translation and Contemporary Reading" (on opposite pages) of David Fleming, SJ's *Draw Me into Your Friendship* (St. Louis: Institute of Jesuit Sources, 1996) very helpful.

More of an adaptation than Fleming's "Reading" is a category I don't know how to name. With hardly an explicit mention of the Exercises and certainly no paraphrase of the text much less quotation, this kind of work, exhibiting remarkable creativity, captures the essence of the Exercises in the author's own words. The most famous of these is the Dutch Jesuit Peter van Breemen's *As Bread That Is Broken*, issued in a twenty-fifth anniversary edition in 1999 (Starrucca, PA: Dimension Books). It lends itself to prayerful reading and reflection, the fruit of which can be shared with a guide or in a small group. Another excellent work in this genre is British Jesuit Gerard Hughes's *God of Surprises* (1985), out of print but available from many Jesuit or other Catholic university libraries.

Guides for the Guide: The book of the *Exercises* itself, we remember, is a guide for the person accompanying the exercitant, the one making the Exercises. But very early in Jesuit history others began to compose directories or guides to Ignatius's guidebook (see Martin Palmer, SJ, ed., *On Giving the Spiritual Exercises: The Early Jesuit Manuscript Directories and the Official Directory of 1599* [St. Louis: Institute of Jesuit Sources, 1996]). And that practice continues in our own time, when more and more people who have made the full Exercises are empowered to guide others through them, first under professional supervision and later on their own. A classic in this genre is the Canadian Jesuit John English's *Spiritual Freedom: From an Experience of the Ignatian Exercises to the Art of Spiritual Guidance*, 2nd ed. (Chicago: Loyola Press, 1995). More recently, we have Joseph Tetlow, SJ's *Choosing Christ in the World* and *Light-works: Directing the Spiritual Exercises of St. Ignatius of Loyola* (Institute of Jesuit Sources, 1999). Finally, I recommend William A. Barry's *Letting God Come Close: An Approach to the Ignatian Spiritual Exercises* (Chicago: Loyola Press, 2001).

A Feminine Perspective: Starting in the 1960s with the rediscovery of the original Ignatian practice of personal, one-on-one guidance of the Exercises (first in France and Canada and later in the United States), a number of Jesuit centers were established to provide this kind of retreat and to train guides for it through an internship model (ones in Guelph, ON; Wernersville, PA; St. Louis, MO [later moved to Denver, CO]; Los Altos, CA; Cambridge, MA; Clarkston, MI; and Milford, OH come readily to mind). The most avid and numerous participants, both in making the personally directed retreat and in learning to guide others, were women religious (and somewhat later, laywomen). They have had a profound impact on the movement. After learning the art from men, these women came to the point of teaching their teachers, calling for some radical revision of the Exercises to make them more suitable for women. My first contact with this in print was Marie-Eloise Rosenblatt, RSM's "Women and the Exercises" in *The Way Supplement* (Spring 1991), a British Jesuit journal of spirituality. More recently, we have a superb book-length study by Katherine Dyckman, Mary Garvin, and Elizabeth Liebert, titled *The Spiritual Exercises Reclaimed: Uncovering Liberating Possibilities for Women* (New York: Paulist Press, 2001).

The Exercises and Ecological Awareness: Jesuit theologians Robert Sears of Loyola University Chicago and Joseph Bracken of Xavier University have written a thin, fine volume entitled *Self-Emptying Love in a Global Context* (Eugene, OR: Cascade Books, 2006), chapter 1, "The Environment in Theological History," and chapter 2, "Environment in the Spiritual Exercises." In the latter, they emphasize elements in Ignatius which are ecology-friendly and suggest alternative readings for those that are not. A larger work by New Zealand Marist Neil Vaney—*Christ in a Grain of Sand: An Ecological Journey with the Spiritual Exercises* (Notre Dame, IN: Ave Maria Press, 2004)—is rich in detail and example: Vaney's "own studies in environmental ethics and the theology of nature have given him a breathtakingly broad grasp of scientific theories and discoveries without taking him away from the heart of the spiritual quest. . . . [His] explanations of scientific discoveries [are] eye-opening and very helpful" (from the foreword by William A. Barry).

De Nicolás's *Powers of Imagining*: If Patrick Heelan's foreword to de Nicolás's work has whetted your appetite for more, the work is still in print more than twenty years after its first publication: Antonio T. de Nicolás, *Powers of Imagining: Ignatius de Loyola: A Philosophical Hermeneutic of Imagining through the Collected Works of Ignatius de Loyola, with a Translation of These Works* (Albany: State University of New York Press, 1986). De Nicolás's ninety-page introductory essay that precedes his translations is an important but also difficult piece of work.

Discernment

Introduction

Ignatius of Loyola came on the scene with his teaching about discernment just as the modern Western world, with its sense of the unique individual, was dawning. Today, once a person realizes that leading the Christian life *as an adult* demands a more sophisticated awareness of self and a more nuanced practice than just following rules and regulations, he or she has entered the world in which Ignatian discernment, the heart of Ignatius's spiritual teaching, can play a significant role. Whether or not we recognize it, most of us have practiced some kind of discernment in reading our own thoughts and feelings and in making the little or bigger choices of our lives. Here is an opportunity to reflect on that experience and to gain further knowledge about this crucial art.

The "Discernment of spirits," writes Timothy Gallagher, OMV—a reliable contemporary guide—has to do with "distinguishing among *the stirrings of our hearts* that which is of God and that which is not, and how to respond to these stirrings." This discernment—treated by Ignatius in his Rules for Discernment (*Spiritual Exercises*, nos. 313–36)—is not the same process as seeking to discern God's will (*Spiritual Exercises*, nos. 169–88), though facility in the discernment of spirits is an important, even necessary, aid in discerning God's will. It will help to keep the distinction between these two kinds of discernment in mind while reading the five selections here, for the authors—good as they are—do not always use the terms clearly and unambiguously.

In the first selection of this section, James Gaffney, longtime professor of theology at Loyola University, New Orleans, now teaching at the University of St. Thomas in St. Paul, Minnesota, shares his wisdom about Ignatius's distinctive way of praying, his focus in the Exercises on major life decisions, and his getting priorities right in the process. "For the point is not to see to it that one's ultimate values survive one's career," says Gaffney. "It is to see to it that they designate, stimulate, and animate one's career."

Next, William A. Barry, SJ, writes about discernment "as an act of faith"; that is, acting on a decision made involves—implicitly or explicitly—a conviction that God is leading the discerner in this direction. Barry illustrates this by a judicious choice of passages from the *Autobiography*, which he then correlates with key rules (better called "guidelines") for discernment in the *Exercises*. Thus he makes clear what we perhaps already know—that Ignatius learned the art of discernment largely from reflection on his own life experience.

The chapter on discernment in David Lonsdale's *Eyes to See, Ears to Hear* (London: Darton Longman & Todd, 1990; Chicago: Loyola University Press, 1991) is a fairly comprehensive introduction to current knowledge on the subject. Lonsdale, professor of spirituality at Heythrop College, University of London, starts by clearing away certain misconceptions (for example, about "God's plan" and "God's will") and then proceeds to deal with the way Ignatius himself learned discernment (by reflecting on his life experiences), with Ignatius's fundamental principles or guidelines, with contemporary cases for practice in discerning, and finally with the issue of confirmation of decisions made (no discernment is ever final and absolute, since new data may call for a revision of what has been decided in all good faith). The revised version of Lonsdale's book (DL&T and Orbis, 2000) makes no changes in the text of the discernment chapter.

The practice of discernment is a difficult and delicate art. Having read through a rather thorough presentation of the process with David Lonsdale, we proceed to another one of our longer readings: "Refining the Acoustics of the Heart," by Wilkie Au, professor of theological studies at Loyola Marymount University, and his wife, Noreen Cannon Au, faculty member of the C. G. Jung Institute of Los Angeles. In this chapter of their book *The Discerning Heart*, the authors pay special attention to the body-spirit unity of the person, developing the key Ignatian insight that discernment requires awareness of body and emotion and not just of mind. Their treatment nicely complements Lonsdale's. My only reservation in reprinting it here is that it is only one chapter from a book-length study of discernment and so does not do justice to the authors' full, extensive, and highly nuanced work.

With the perspective thus provided, we can begin to understand and appreciate the final, very brief selection that sums up "What Discernment Means," by Benedictine Suzanne Zuercher, a fine teacher and practitioner of Ignatian discernment. Let her speak in her own words, drawn more from contemporary body-psychology than from the language of Ignatius:

> Sometimes genuine discernment is wrongly seen as a mental decision about what is good followed by an act of will to carry out that good. I would say, rather, that discernment is the awareness of centered or not-centered energy in the organism. . . . This awareness comes from an accumulated awareness of who we fully and genuinely are. It is knowing where our center—and hence our life—resides, as well as where it does not. . . . As life builds up more and more sense of our total selves, more and more inclusion of body, mind, and emotion in our self-experience, it becomes less and less possible for us to choose against ourselves. . . . Discernment well made—that is, experience well known—makes choice natural, even easy. Choice is that decision either to retain boundaries of judgment manifested by blocked body energies or to risk letting in everything we are. . . . In doing so we abandon predictions of how life will turn out, judgments of what is good or bad, assessments of what does or doesn't fit. We simply live from our center.

Understanding the Terminology: Suggested Readings from *Do You Speak Ignatian?*

- Discernment

Ignatian Discernment

James Gaffney

From "Two Faces of Loyola," Loyola Day Address at
Loyola University, New Orleans, Fall 1987

This longing to spend time, and if possible a lifetime, in the Holy
Land reminds us that Ignatius's austerities were not merely feats of
strength, but feats of emulation, strivings to recapitulate legendary
glories of the saints and of their Lord. Ignatius read pious narratives
in a highly characteristic way, trying, as it were, to get inside them,
make himself part of them, let them become the vital matrix of his
imagination, so that his own story would be, in a sense, continuous
with theirs. Because for him the holy lives, and Christ's life above
all, were spiritually nutritive and normative, he cultivated a sense of
their actuality and immediacy. That was why being physically present on the ground where Jesus walked mattered so much. The same
disposition explains why Ignatius's Jesus is so much less a teacher and
preacher than he is a doer and sufferer. It explains also why to Ignatius
the traditional contrast between contemplative and active life did not
seem radically dichotomous. What he typically contemplated was
action. He contemplated it in such a way as to enter imaginatively into
the action. And he found that the result was to energize and orient his
own action. Thus his action tended to preserve and intensify rather
than supplant or obscure the contemplation from which it took rise.

This style of prayerful, practical imagination became a basic element in the guidebook Ignatius gradually put together to enable

others to profit from his experience, his *Spiritual Exercises*. The ideal result is a potent combination of strengthened self-control and heightened motivation. The motivation is not diffuse, since it always tends in the direction of doing as Christ and his saints typically did, and that evidently excludes a great deal. But it still encounters a wide range of unsorted possibilities, out of which specific practical objectives must be selected and actively pursued, if the outcome is to be more than a religious counterpart of the secret life of Walter Mitty. Accordingly, Ignatius was led to pay increasing attention to the matter of practical choice, of deciding what to do with one's reformed self.

The widest limits were, of course, set by morality and rationality. Certainly one must not do anything downright wicked or absurd. But that still left a multitude of alternatives, some of which could have enormously far-reaching implications. Some of them, moreover, once chosen, could not afterwards easily be relinquished, because of entailing contractual obligations and sacred duties. Thus Ignatius paid special attention to those broad, basic, decisive choices which, once made, impose their shape on all or much of life, in particular what we might call vocational or career choices. What chiefly concerned Ignatius about them was that such choices be determined by the highest value or ultimate goal of the one who made them, being embraced precisely as means to the realization of that value, the attainment of that goal. And for Ignatius, of course, the ultimate goal was the Christian one, of glorifying God by one's inward and outward living, and therein finding salvation.

What seemed to him the main obstacle is clarified by examples. They are examples of perfectly decent people making perfectly decent vocational choices—like marrying a certain spouse, or pursuing a certain office, or acquiring a certain property—accompanied in each case by the intention of living a good Christian life in the chosen circumstances. By Ignatius's standards, choices made in that way are corrupt and corrupting. And what makes them corrupt is their readiness to make ultimate purposes into pious afterthoughts. One should not, he insisted, plan or decide to be a good Christian husband, or wife, or proprietor, or official. That is to confuse means with ends. One's basic decision should be simply that of being a good Christian, which was for Ignatius indistinguishable from being a good human being. And that decision should thereafter determine what one ought to do about such options as marriage, property, and office. For the point is not to see to it that one's ultimate values survive one's career. It is to see to it that they designate, stimulate, and animate one's career.

Once that basic ordering of priorities is established, the main thing in making life's important choices is to be neither, on the one hand, misled by moods nor, on the other, unresponsive to inspirations. Ignatius's advice on this subject of interpreting and evaluating the affective components of consciousness—observing and diagnosing emotions, to translate his own phrase rather literally—has been much admired not only by religious thinkers but also by psychologists. Its relevance for moralists had until recently been largely ignored—even, surprisingly enough, by Jesuit moralists. Yet, as the theologian Karl Rahner was one of the first to point out, its importance should be evident in an age like our own, when we are constantly reminded how often the moral dilemmas of conscientious people do not fall squarely under plain rules of an accepted ethical code, but demand more personal and existential modes of resolution. Popular moral wisdom has always recognized the importance of being guided, not only by reasonable ethical directives, but also by one's "better feelings." Ignatius's thoughts about such matters are probably the ones that have most often persuaded modern thinkers that he has timely wisdom to impart even to an age so different from his own and to persons skeptical about many of his most confident assumptions.

It would seem consistent with that judgment that it was his treatment of these matters especially that made the (relatively) young Ignatius a suspicious character among conservative Catholics and brought him eventually under scrutiny and finally under arrest by the Spanish Inquisition. He seemed to them to be encouraging an individual reliance on private inspiration that fostered irresponsible subjectivism and ecclesiastical anarchy. Such threats from officialdom made Ignatius especially sensitive to his need, if he was to function effectively, for academic and ecclesiastical credentials. As with many of our own students, Ignatius's interest in schooling had nothing to do with scholarly tastes. And indeed the most lasting elements in his own teaching had been largely established before he ever occupied a bench in a lecture hall.

Discernment of Spirits as an Act of Faith

William A. Barry, SJ

From Spirit, Style, Story: Essays Honoring John W. Padberg, SJ, 2002

Recently, while directing a retreat, I realized that discerning the spirits requires an act of faith. One of the retreatants had stated early and quite openly that she hated retreats. I asked her why she continued to make them if this was the case. She said, "Because religious have to." She could pray in short periods, she said, but the idea of spending an hour at a time in prayer sent her into a tizzy. At the same time, she desired to experience the presence of God. The desire was strong enough to bring tears to her eyes as she spoke of it. Nevertheless, she did not have much hope that her desire would be fulfilled.

When I asked her what she liked to do, she told me that she enjoyed listening to music, doing puzzles, and going for walks in the woods. I suggested that she spend the day doing those things with the desire that God make his presence felt. She was afraid that she would feel guilty if she spent her retreat time in this way; it did not seem like prayer. Over the next day or so I prevailed on her to give enjoyment a try. She later recounted that on the evening of the third day she said to herself with a laugh, "I'm actually enjoying this retreat." She also had the sense that God might be enjoying it too. But the guilt feelings did not disappear; she still felt that this could not be the way a good retreat should go. During the session after this day we looked at the two different experiences: the enjoyment of the retreat and the feelings of guilt. I then asked her, "Which of these experiences are you going to believe in?" At that moment I had the insight that the discernment of the spirits is not complete until it ends up in an act of faith. I thanked her for helping me to arrive at this clarity. By exploring this insight I hope to help spiritual directors and others.

In *Jesus and the Victory of God*, the second of a projected three or four volumes on the New Testament and the question of God, N. T. Wright develops a historical hypothesis about the nature of Jesus' vocation and his self-consciousness. It is a Christology from below, as it were, but it arrives at a very high Christology. One of his statements concerns our topic. He notes that to speak of Jesus' vocation is not the same as to speak of Jesus' knowledge of his divinity. "Jesus did not . . . 'know that he was God' in the same way that one knows one is male or female, hungry or thirsty, or that one ate an orange an hour ago. His 'knowledge' was of a more risky, but perhaps more significant, sort: like knowing one is loved. One cannot 'prove' it except by living it."[1] In other words, Jesus had to take the risk of faith that any human being takes when he discerns a vocation from God. But Jesus' vocation, as he saw it, included within it actions that Israel's God had reserved to himself. Jesus, by entering Jerusalem on a donkey, symbolically enacted the return of Yahweh to Zion; Jesus took upon himself the role of Messianic shepherd, God's role. Jesus' discernment of his vocation, in other words, required an act of faith in a unique relationship with God. He "proved" it by living it. I am going to argue that every discernment of spirits is like this; it is not complete until we prove its truth by acting on it.

As many know, Ignatius of Loyola included rules for the discernment of spirits in the little book *The Spiritual Exercises*. We know from his memoirs, which he dictated to Luis Gonçalves da Câmara, that he developed these rules on the basis of his own experiences during his recovery at Loyola and his months of prayer at Manresa. At Loyola he engaged in two sets of daydreams. In one set he was a knight doing great deeds to win the favor of a great lady. In the other he was a follower of Christ after the manner of saints like Francis of Assisi or

Dominic. Both sets of daydreams gave him great pleasure while he was engaged in them, but after the first set he found himself "dry and dissatisfied," while after the second set he remained "satisfied and joyful." He continues:

> He did not notice this, however; nor did he stop to ponder the distinction until the time when his eyes were open[ed] a little, and he began to marvel at the difference and to reflect upon it, realizing from experience that some thoughts left him sad and others joyful. Little by little he came to recognize the difference between the spirits that were stirring, one from the devil, the other from God.[2]

Here, for the first time, Ignatius discerned the movements of his heart. Notice that his discernment meant an act of faith that God was acting to inspire him to follow Jesus. Insight must be followed by action for the discernment to be complete, and the action is an act of faith in God's direction of him. Like Jesus, Ignatius proves that he is being called by acting on his insights.

The next instance makes the act of faith even clearer. After some time of great consolation at Manresa, Ignatius of Loyola began to be deeply troubled by scruples. He wrote:

> But here he began to have much trouble from scruples, for even though the general confession he had made at Montserrat had been quite carefully done and all in writing . . . still at times it seemed to him that he had not confessed certain things. This caused him much distress, because although he had confessed that, he was not satisfied. . . . Finally, a doctor of the cathedral, a very spiritual man who preached there, told him one day in confession to write down everything he could remember. He did so, but after confession the scruples still returned, becoming increasingly minute so that he was in great distress.
>
> Although he was practically convinced that those scruples did him much harm and that it would be good to be rid of them, he could not break himself off.
>
> Once when he was very distressed by them, he began to pray, and roused to fervor he shouted out loud to God, saying, "Help me, Lord,

for I find no remedy in men nor in any creature; yet if I thought I could find it, no labor would be too hard for me. Yourself, Lord, show me where I may find it; even though I should have to chase after a puppy that it may give me the remedy, I will do it."[3]

Things got so bad that he was tempted to commit suicide. He decided to embark on a total fast to beg God for relief, and he did so for a week. When he went to confession the next Sunday, his confessor ordered him to break his fast. With some reluctance he did so and was without scruples for a couple of days. But on Tuesday the scruples returned with a vengeance. He then goes on:

> But after these thoughts [of all his sins], disgust for the life he led came over him with impulses to give it up.
>
> In this way the Lord deigned that he awake from his sleep. As he now had some experience of the diversity of the spirits from the lessons God had given him, he began to examine the means by which that spirit had come. He thus decided with great lucidity not to confess anything from the past any more; and so from that day forward he remained free of these scruples and held it certain that Our Lord had mercifully deigned to deliver him.[4]

Earlier, Ignatius says, he knew that these scruples were doing him great harm, but he did not, perhaps could not, act on this knowledge. He still believed in a God who was an exacting taskmaster, almost a celestial accountant who was waiting to catch him out. This was the faith he showed in practice. In effect, he could not believe in a God who wanted his peace. After the last bout of scruples, however, Ignatius came to the conclusion that he faced a choice. He may not have formulated the choice in terms of faith, but that is what it amounted to. Ultimately, Ignatius had to decide what God he believed in. When he chose not to confess his past sins again, he had no guarantee that he was right. He had to act in faith, hope, and love that God was not an ogre ready to pounce on mistakes and forgotten sins.

This incident in the life of Ignatius reminds us of the first two "Rules for the Discernment of Spirits" more suitable for the First Week of the Exercises:

The First Rule. In the case of the persons who are going from one mortal sin to another, the enemy ordinarily proposes to them apparent pleasures. He makes them imagine delights and pleasures of the senses, in order to hold them fast and plunge them deeper into their sins and vices.

But with persons of this type the good spirit uses a contrary procedure. Through their good judgement on problems of morality he stings their consciences with remorse.

The Second. In [the] case of persons who are earnestly purging away their sins, and who are progressing from good to better in the service of God our Lord, the procedure used is the opposite of that described in the First Rule. For in this case it is characteristic of the evil spirit to cause gnawing anxiety, to sadden, and to set up obstacles. In this way he unsettles these persons by false reasons aimed at preventing their progress.

But with persons of this type it is characteristic of the good spirit to stir up courage and strength, consolations, tears, inspirations, and tranquility. He makes things easier and eliminates all obstacles, so that the persons may move forward in doing good.[5]

From his experience (and perhaps from the experience he had in directing others who were very scrupulous, such as one of his first companions in Paris, Blessed Pierre Favre), Ignatius came to believe that God acts differently with people depending on their orientation in life. For those who are trying to lead a good life (those of the second rule), troubling, anxious thoughts about sin are not from God; rather, they emanate from the enemy of human nature, the evil one. Most people who want to make the Spiritual Exercises or who seek spiritual direction would surely be in this category, as Ignatius was after his conversion and during all his time at Manresa. Hence, they are asked to make an act of faith that God is not the author of their worried and anxious movements, that God wants their peace and deep contentment. (A sign that these anxieties are not from God, by the way, is that they put the focus on the self, not on God and God's activity.)

It was clear to us both that by the end of her retreat, the retreatant who occasioned these reflections was faced with this faith choice. Once again, we note that there is no guarantee that God will act in any given way with those who are trying to live a good life; one plants one's feet firmly in midair and marches on in faith, hope, and trust. The only verification we get is the continued peace and joy we experience on the journey. The "fruit of the Spirit is love, joy, peace, patience, kindness, goodness, faithfulness, gentleness, self-control."[6]

Of course, events can distort our discernment of how we are being led. Ignatius provides a good example of this. During his stay at Manresa, Ignatius determined that his vocation was to go to Jerusalem and live and "help souls" there. Some commentators believe that this decision was, for Ignatius, an election made according to the pattern for "The First Time" described in *The Spiritual Exercises*. In the section entitled "Three Times . . . suitable for making a sound and good election," Ignatius writes: "*The First Time* is an occasion when God our Lord moves and attracts the will in such a way that a devout person, without doubting or being able to doubt, carries out what was proposed. This is what St. Paul and St. Matthew did when they followed Christ our Lord."[7]

In his memoirs Ignatius makes it quite clear that he determined "to remain in Jerusalem, continually visiting those holy places; and in addition to this devotion, he also planned to help souls," although he kept this latter idea to himself. When he spoke to the provincial of the Franciscans who had charge of the holy places about his desire to stay, he was told that he could not remain because other pilgrims who had remained had been captured and enslaved and had to be redeemed at great cost. Ignatius replied to this that he was very firm in his purpose and was resolved that on no account would he fail to carry it out. He frankly insisted that even though the provincial thought otherwise, if there was nothing binding him under sin, he would not abandon his intention out of any fear. To this the provincial replied that they had authority from the Apostolic See to have anyone leave the place, or remain there, as they judged, and to excommunicate anyone who was unwilling to obey them, and that in this case they thought that he should not remain.[8]

We can see how strongly Ignatius believed that he was being led by God in his determination to remain in Jerusalem. But when he was threatened with excommunication, he concluded that "it was not Our Lord's will that he remain in those holy places."[9] Ignatius acted in faith that God was leading him to live and die in Jerusalem. Only by such an act of faith could he discover that he was in error with regard to his discernment. Note, however, that it took another act of faith to change his direction. Ignatius believed that God was speaking through the provincial who had the authority from the Holy See to excommunicate anyone who disobeyed him. In our own day, many a person has discerned a vocation and has been convinced that God inspired the decision, only to have events disconfirm it. For example, a young man discerns that he has a vocation to be a Jesuit priest but finds that the Society of Jesus will not accept him. He had to act in faith on his best lights and move forward with his application, trusting that he would discover in the process that he was correct in his discernment. How he now goes forward with his life will be a sign of how openly he is seeking what God desires.

Later Ignatius had other occasions to discern "spirits" and to note how the evil spirit cloaks himself as an angel of light for those who have advanced a bit in their journey into a deeper intimacy with God. For example, upon his return from Jerusalem he decided that he needed to study in order to be able to help souls:

So, returning to Barcelona, he began to study with great diligence. But one thing was very much in his way: when he began to memorize, as one must in the beginnings of grammar, there came to him new insights into spiritual matters and fresh relish, to such an extent that he could not memorize, nor could he drive them away no matter how much he resisted.

So, thinking often about this, he said to himself, "Not even when I engage in prayer and am at Mass do such vivid insights come to me," Thus, little by little, he came to realize that it was a temptation. After

praying he went to Our Lady of the Sea, near the master's house. So
when they were all seated, he told them exactly all that went on in his
soul and what little progress he had made until then for that reason; but
he promised this same master, saying, "I promise you never to fail to
listen to you these two years, so long as I can find bread and water in
Barcelona with which I might support myself." As he made this promise
with great determination, he never again had those temptations.[10]

In this instance Ignatius had to decide in faith that these "spiritual favors" were not from God. Such experiences lie behind his
fourth rule for discernment appropriate for the Second Week of the
Exercises.

It is characteristic of the evil angel, who takes on the appearance
of an angel of light, to enter by going along the same way as the devout
soul and then to exit by his own way with success for himself. That
is, he brings good and holy thoughts attractive to such an upright soul
and then strives little by little to get his own way, by enticing the soul
over to his own hidden deceits and evil intentions.[11]

Ignatius had to act in faith on his discovery that God is not the only
source of pious thoughts.

The discernment of the spirits rests on the belief that the human
heart is a battleground where God and the evil one struggle for mastery. Jesus of Nazareth himself believed this. In the desert he had been
tempted by the evil one masquerading as an angel of light. If these
were real temptations, then he, like us, had to discern the movements
inspired by God from those inspired by the evil one. He, too, had to
make an act of faith in who God really is, based on his experiences
and his knowledge of the Scriptures of his people. Jesus came to
recognize who the real enemy of God's rule is. He cast out demons,
and equated his power over the demons as a sign of God's coming to
rule: "But if it is by the finger of God that I cast out demons, then
the kingdom of God has come upon you."[12] The majority party of the
Pharisees and most Jews of the time saw the real enemy of Israel, and
therefore of God, as the pagans, and especially the Roman occupiers.
Over and over again Jesus warned his hearers that the real enemy was
Satan. Jesus faced this enemy and refused to use the strategies and

means of the evil one to carry out his vocation.[13] God's rule cannot come about through the means proposed by Satan. Jesus, like any faithful Jew, believed that God was acting in history to bring about his rule (this notion may be called "God's project" or "God's intention"). He also believed that whoever is not God's enemy "is for us."[14] John Meier puts the matter this way:

> It is important to realize that, in the view of Jesus, . . . human beings were not basically neutral territories that might be influenced by divine or demonic forces now and then. . . . Human existence was seen as a battlefield dominated by one or the other supernatural force, God or Satan (alias Belial or the devil). A human being might have a part in choosing which "field of force" would dominate his or her life, i.e., which force he or she would choose to side with. But no human being was free to choose simply to be free of these supernatural forces. One was dominated by either one or the other, and to pass *from* one was necessarily to pass *into* the control of the other. At least over the long term, one could not maintain a neutral stance vis-à-vis God and Satan.[15]

Jesus' own discernment of spirits rested on his Jewish belief that God was acting in history and that the evil one was acting to thwart God. Once again, we see that the discernment of spirits is a matter of faith put into practice.

Indeed, faith is not just an intellectual affirmation of truths; faith is a verb. Faith is a graced response to our self-revealing God. This goes for the faith of the church as well as for the faith of the individual who is trying to discern a path through life. Perhaps we can get a better grasp on how discernment requires an act of faith from the philosophy of the person of John Macmurray. In the first volume of his Gifford Lectures, Macmurray argues that the world is ruled by intention. He ends that volume with the following statement:

> If we act as if the world, in its unity, is intentional; that is, if we believe in practice that the world is one action . . . we shall act differently from anyone who does not believe this. We shall act as though our own actions were our contributions to the one inclusive action which is the

history of the world. If, on the other hand, we believe that the world is a mere process of events which happen as they happen, we shall act differently. Our conception of the unity of the world determines a way of life; and the satisfaction or dissatisfaction of that way of life is its verification.[16]

In other words, if we believe that the world is one action ruled by one intention, we are committed to a way of life in conformity with this belief. If we do not act on our belief, we act in bad faith. At the end of the second volume, Macmurray fleshes out this insight in more theistic terms:

> There is, then, only one way in which we can think our relation to the world, and that is to think it as a personal relation, through the form of the personal. We must think that the world is one action contained in it, subordinated within it, and necessary to its constitution. To conceive the world thus is to conceive it as the act of God, the Creator of the World, and ourselves as created agents, with a limited and dependent freedom to determine the future which can be realized only on the condition that our intentions are in harmony with His intention, and which must frustrate itself if they are not. . . .
>
> It would be a mistake to suppose that this vindication of the validity of religious belief in general constitutes an argument for the truth of any system of religious belief in particular. Religious doctrines are as problematic as scientific theories and require like them a constant revision and a continual verification in action. Their verification differs in this, that it cannot be experimental, since they are not merely pragmatic; they can be verified only by persons who are prepared to commit themselves intentionally to the way of life which they prescribe.[17]

In other words, all religious beliefs are only verified in action. Indeed, "religious beliefs" that do not issue in complementary action are not religious beliefs at all; they are thoughts about the world, not beliefs. Someone may object: "But I am a sinner and often do not act according to my beliefs." That is true, but the very fact that you know that you are a sinner who does not act according to your beliefs shows that you have beliefs that must be verified in action. If I say that I believe God acts with purpose in this world, that belief must lead to attempts, however feeble, to discern how my own actions might be attuned to God's one action. Moreover, these attempts to discern must lead to action; otherwise I will be acting with "bad faith" and will experience malaise, the pricking of conscience that Ignatius mentions in the first rule cited earlier.

Jesus did not leave us a list of truths to affirm but a task to carry out. We must try to discern in our time and place how God wants us to live our lives in this world in tune with God's Spirit, the one divine action at work in this universe. This is what the discernment of spirits is all about. Followers of Jesus have been given a task to carry out and the means to do it. Impelled by God's Spirit, they must try to live in this world with the conviction that with the life, death, and resurrection of Jesus all the needful has been done, that God has won the victory he intends. Our task, therefore, is to follow the prompting of the Spirit, who has been poured out in our hearts, to follow the way of Jesus, the way of peace, of love, of the cross. We discern the spirits in order to act as followers of Jesus, as believers. Every act of discernment is an act of faith in what God has done in Jesus of Nazareth and continues to do through the indwelling of God.

NOTES

1. N. T. Wright, *Jesus and the Victory of God* (Minneapolis: Fortress, 1966), 653.

2. Ignatius of Loyola, *A Pilgrim's Testament*, trans. Parmananda R. Divarkar (St. Louis: Institute of Jesuit Sources, 1995), 9–10.

3. Ibid., 34–36.

4. Ibid., 37–38.

5. Ignatius of Loyola, *The Spiritual Exercises*, trans. George E. Ganss (St. Louis: Institute of Jesuit Sources, 1992), 12, nos. 314–15.

6. Galalatians 5:22–23. All scriptural citations taken from the *New Oxford Annotated Bible with the Apocrypha: Revised Standard Version* (New York: Oxford University Press, 1977).

7. *Exercises*, 76, no. 175.

8. *Pilgrim's Testament*, 60–62.

9. Ibid., 63.

10. Ibid., 79–80.

11. *Exercises*, 126–27, no. 332.

12. Luke 11:20.

13. See Luke 4:1–13.

14. Mark 9:40.

15. John Meier, *Mentor, Message, and Miracles*, vol. 2 of *A Marginal Jew: Rethinking the Historical Jesus* (New York: Doubleday, 1994), 414–15.

16. John Macmurray, *The Self as Agent* (Atlantic Highlands, NJ: Humanities Press, 1978), 221.

17. John Macmurray, *Persons in Relation* (Atlantic Highlands, NJ: Humanities Press, 1979), 222–23.

Discernment of Spirits

David Lonsdale

From *Eyes to See, Ears to Hear: An Introduction to Ignatian Spirituality*, 2000

It is not always recognized that discernment lies at the heart of Christian spirituality. People are even suspicious about the word *discernment*. Some think that it is something so esoteric and technical as to be outside the scope of the ordinary Christian woman or man; others see it as another name for ordinary common sense enlightened by faith, and therefore not worth making a fuss about. In some religious circles, too, discernment jargon has become so overused that it is all but meaningless. We often readily recognize, however, that if we take being a Christian fairly seriously, it involves us in daily attempts to make truth and love concrete realities. And discernment in the true sense of the word is essential to that enterprise.

Today we are more ready than we have been in the past to acknowledge that being a Christian is more of a search for genuine truth and love than a secure position of certainty from which to survey the world and pass judgment. Trying to be a Christian means learning how to respond with love to God, to people, and to circumstances. It means searching for ways of living out the two great gospel commandments of loving God and our neighbor, while recognizing the imperfection of our attempts. It also means searching honestly for the most authentic truth; not just the knowledge that can be learned but makes little difference to how we live, but also the deeper gospel truth that makes little sense in fact until it becomes the truth which governs our lives.

The Christian's search for the way of truth and love, however, has another dimension which should not be forgotten, namely, that it takes place within the setting of a living relationship with God "who has loved us first," and who is seen as the source and revealer of the Christian way of truth and love. All genuine love implies a surrender. When I love another person I surrender all or part of myself to him or her; I allow part at least of my life to be, as it were, invaded and taken over by the other person. People say such things as: "My life is not the same since I met her," or "How Emma has changed since she met Frank." When I love I allow another person to exercise a control and influence on me and my life, which often astonishes both my friends and me by the radical changes it makes in the way I behave. And I make this surrender willingly and freely; it is not forced upon me. When the love is mutual, the surrender, the offering of oneself to another, is mutual and there is both giving and receiving.

If our relationship with God is a relationship of love, this too involves some form of surrender. If the relationship deepens, we relinquish control of our own lives and hand this over to God, usually little by little, to the extent that we are able. This is not to say that we immaturely hand over responsibility for ourselves and our actions to another, but that we choose to collaborate with God. We allow God increasingly to lead us, though normally not without a struggle. This is the setting which discernment presupposes: a willingness to look at and appreciate the signs of God's love for us and in response to listen to the voice of the Spirit of God and to follow where the Spirit leads.

Our search draws us then to look for ways of making truth and love real in the shapes that our lives take, in all the changing circumstances in which we find ourselves. Because circumstances constantly change and the gospel is a living gospel and not a dead letter, Christian love and truth have constantly to be embodied and expressed in different forms. There is continuity with the past, of course, but continuity does not mean simply repeating over and over again what has been done before. We have to find our own new ways of being Christians, of trying to live according to the gospel of Jesus, and discernment, rightly understood, is at the heart of this search for an authentic Christian discipleship.

Very briefly, discernment is the art of appreciating the gifts that God has given us and discovering how we might best respond to that love in daily life. It is a process of finding one's own way of discipleship in a particular set of circumstances; a means of responding to the call of Christian love and truth in a situation where there are often conflicting interests and values and choices have to be made. It is the gift by which we are able to observe and assess the different factors in a particular situation, and to choose that course of action which most authentically answers our desire to live by the gospel.

Discernment of spirits is often associated with "finding the will of God" and there are difficulties about how we understand this. Sometimes people talk about the will of God or the plan of God as if it were a large, immensely complex, ever-changing, living blueprint of what God "wants" to happen in the world. According to this model, finding the will of God means something like getting in touch with that small corner of the immense celestial blueprint that concerns us, and getting to know "what God wants us to do," so that we can comply and thus "do the will of God." Of course that short description is a caricature to some extent, but it contains enough truth about the model that many people seem to use in thinking and talking about "the will of God." And unfortunately it is a powerful cause of anxiety to many good Christians who spend much time and effort trying to "find out" God's will according to this model, and who become very distressed and anxious when, not surprisingly, they do not succeed. There are many reasons why this "management blueprint" model is unsatisfactory, but the principal one I would like to mention here is the fact that it constricts our freedom so much. The scope of our freedom is reduced to choosing to fit in, whether we like it or not, with what God has "planned" for us, once we think we know what that is. And that is very little freedom indeed.

A more satisfactory understanding of the will of God in connection with discernment of spirits gives greater value to our precious gift of freedom. God's will for us is that we should learn to respond in freedom to God's love for us, and to give shape to our individual and common lives in freedom by the choices that we make. In scripture, tradition, the Church, our own consciences and powers of judgment, and in many other gifts, God has given us aids to the responsible exercise of our freedom. God's will is that we should exercise our freedom responsibly and well by choosing what honestly seems the best course of action in a given set of circumstances, using all the relevant aids that we have been given for that purpose. There is a sense in which we create, in terms of concrete action in given circumstances, the will of God in this exercise of freedom. There is no blueprint in God's mind with which we have to comply. Discernment of spirits, within a living relationship with God, is one of the gifts that we have been given to help us to exercise our freedom in the choices that we make and so come to "find the will of God" for us.

Discernment in Ignatius's Life

It will help us to grasp the relevance of Ignatian discernment for ourselves if we look briefly at the part it played in the life of Ignatius himself. We have already seen that his conversion at Loyola awakened in him a deep attraction towards the person of Jesus, as he met him in Ludolph of Saxony's *Life of Christ*. And if we look at the life of Ignatius, it is clear that there were two different but related settings in which discernment was at the heart of his following of Jesus. The one is the setting of everyday life; the other is those occasions on which he had a very important decision to make.

During and after his convalescence at Loyola he was moved by love for God and for Jesus to the extent that he began to want to give himself over to the service of God. His recognition that this would mean surrendering control of his life to God seems to have dawned gradually. The desire "to find the will of God and to have the courage to carry it out" grew both more exciting and more insistent. He wanted to allow his life to be governed not by his own desires and ambitions but by God leading him in love, but it was some time before he learned exactly how he could put this into effect. He had to acquire a way of translating these powerful, even exhilarating, desires into practical decisions which would shape his life for the future. And that meant two things: learning—from "scratch," for he had no spiritual training to speak of—to grow in day-by-day responsiveness to God; and also to allow his major decisions about the direction of his life to be governed by the same openness to God's leading. In a word, he had to learn discernment.

It was not from books nor from consulting people wise in the ways of the spirit that Ignatius took the first steps in discernment, but by noting and reflecting on his own experience. During his convalescence he began to observe that different possible options open to him for the future evoked different responses in him. Thoughts of continuing to live as he had lived before, or daydreams in which he idealized himself as a romantic hero, though pleasant while they lasted, ultimately left him feeling sad and dissatisfied. On the other hand, when he pictured in his mind the wonderful things he might do for God—even difficult and painful things like walking barefoot to Jerusalem and eating nothing but herbs—he experienced deep feelings of joy which left him satisfied and cheerful. From noting and reflecting on these two sets of feelings, and on the direction in which they seemed to be leading him, he concluded that the way God wanted him to follow was becoming clear to him. God was speaking to him through his experience. He would go as a pilgrim to Jerusalem (*Autobiography*, 8).

There is not space here to give a stage-by-stage account of Ignatius's education in discernment.[1] Naturally some of his experiences—including the most painful ones—contributed more than others to his education. At Manresa he had to learn how to deal with (among other things) the onset of a real distaste for anything which had to do with God; persistent waves of discouragement about the way of life he was taking up; serious illnesses which brought him again to the point of death; scruples so bad that they nearly drove him to suicide; and "consolations" so powerful that they made his eyes hurt with weeping (Autobiography, 19–34). Then and later he also grew in the art of knowing how to distinguish between true and false forms of encouragement, enthusiasm, and other pleasant and satisfying feelings. In Jerusalem he discovered that, though he had been right to go there, it was impossible for him to stay as he had intended and he must find God's purpose for him over again. He was brought before the Inquisition for trial and put in prison more than once. Between Salamanca and Paris he was discouraged because his original group of companions broke up and dispersed. In Barcelona and Paris he enjoyed powerful spiritual insights which absorbed his attention and threatened to wreck his studies and deflect him from his purpose. Later on in Rome his concept of the Society of Jesus was threatened when the authorities objected to its lack of monastic or conventual structures and practices and actually imposed Office in choir for a time.[2]

That is by no means the whole story, but it is enough to see the kind of experiences Ignatius used to learn and practice discernment. Through these and other storms, as well as in smoother seas, he tried to find his own personal way and to be faithful to that. From the time of his stay at Manresa onwards, of course, he had opportunities to consult people skilled in discernment of spirits, and eventually he had access to books which could teach him the tradition and principles of discernment, particularly during his studies. But he began with his own experience, and his later reading added to, confirmed, and no doubt modified what he had learned there.

After his return from Jerusalem in 1523, his main intention was to devote himself to "helping souls." His writings on discernment, brief though they are, form one of his most valuable and original legacies for others who are engaged in pastoral work, and particularly in spiritual direction. Occasionally Ignatius himself wrote letters of direction in which he explained some of the principles of discernment.[3] But the *Spiritual Exercises* are the book in which he formally set out his guidelines for others to use. There the two sets of Rules for the Discernment of Spirits define some of the technical terms, explain the fundamental principles of discernment, and offer acute and sensitive guidance in dealing with typical situations that arise, especially when evil masquerades as good or the less good as the better. Here and there in the sections known as the Annotations and the Additional Directions, Ignatius also offers a few further helps towards discernment. And the sections of the *Exercises* that deal with an Election, taken in conjunction with these rules, provide the spiritual guide with a step-by-step approach to discernment, in the particular context of helping a person make an important decision. Taken together these are an original and extraordinarily thorough guide to discernment and Christian decision-making. They speak specifically to the context of giving and making the Exercises, but by no means exclusively, and they have been found to have much wider and very helpful application in daily life.[4]

Ignatian Discernment of Spirits: Principles and Practice

Discernment of spirits in everyday life involves us in a process of sifting our daily experience by noting and reflecting regularly on our affective responses to God and to life and its events. It means noting, for example, situations and events in which we experience joy or sorrow, peace or turmoil, attractions or revulsions, an opening out to others or a narrowing in on ourselves, a sense of God's presence or absence, creativity or destructiveness. The purpose of observing and reflecting on these patterns of responses is that they deepen our sense of ourselves and they can show us where, for each of us, our Christian path lies, where the Spirit of God is leading. Those are large claims and demand an explanation.

To help our explanation, I will make two more preliminary remarks. The first is that discernment of spirits is concerned with choices between two options or values, both of which appear to be morally good. The process aims at determining what is the right or better choice in particular given circumstances. Often it is a choice between two courses, both of which initially appear morally good and then later, when the discernment process has matured, one of them looks different. This different color may not be downright evil but might be such as to involve a spurning of love.

A second preliminary note has to do with the fact that the term *discernment of spirits* harks back to a previous age of psychology. The term itself comes from the time when the variety and changes of often contrary feelings within the human person were attributed to the presence and action of "good" spirits (the Spirit of God and the angels) and "evil" spirits (Satan and his minions). Naturally, Ignatius, being a man of his pre-Freudian time, accepted this framework unquestioningly and built it automatically into his writing on discernment. But of course we do not have to accept that particular theoretical framework in order to believe in and practice discernment. A difficulty is, however, that we have not yet found a very adequate terminology to replace the traditional one, and people still use the language of "spirits." So it is important to distinguish between this language and the outmoded theoretical framework from which it springs, and to know what we in fact mean if we use the language of "spirits."

With those observations in mind, we can now look more closely at the fundamentals of discernment in the Ignatian tradition. Though Ignatius and his companions also practiced "group discernment," our primary focus here is on the individual person rather than a group. Group discernment is largely an adaptation of the principles and process of individual discernment.

In the course of everyday life we experience a continuous, sometimes bewildering, succession and mixture of different affective movements: desires, revulsions, attractions, impulses, and feelings of varying intensity and power. We know, too, that we have different levels of feeling: some of our desires and responses are superficial; we recognize them and are affected by them, but they do not engage us deeply as persons. I can be moved even to tears, for example, by watching a romantic film, but the feelings which it evokes are usually fairly transient emotions which do not affect in a notable way my conduct or my more lasting attitudes and commitments. Other states of feeling, however, are far deeper and more significant: the experience of falling in love, for instance, can be a profound affective movement which alters my conduct more or less radically; touches me at the level of my most cherished beliefs, attitudes, desires, and commitments; and changes me permanently. In between these two levels of feeling, of course, there are many others. In discernment of spirits it is the deeper levels of affectivity that we are concerned with: those which actually influence our behavior; the areas where our affective life and the life of the spirit interpenetrate; the places from which spring our commitments, our most significant choices, and the fundamental directions that we give to our lives. Discernment is mainly about those more significant areas of our affective life.

These movements or states of feeling that we experience can be evoked by events and people in the external world or by our own thoughts, imagination, dreams, our own "inner world." Sometimes too their origin seems to be largely physiological, as in some kinds of depression. Often enough we do not know where the feelings come from or why we feel as we do. In discernment of spirits it is not the origin of a particular affective state or movement that is the main issue, though to know that can be helpful. Discernment has to do more with the spiritual interpretation and evaluation of feelings, and particularly with the direction in which we are moved by them.

Ignatius identified two contrary kinds of feelings or affective movements among those which we experience. They are contrary in that, when they affect us, they move us in opposite directions. In the tradition of discernment which Ignatius grew familiar with, they are called "consolation" and "desolation." (Ignatius's own descriptions of consolation and desolation are in sections 316–17 of the *Spiritual Exercises*.) Very briefly, consolation is any affective movement or state that draws us to God or that helps us to be less centered upon ourselves and to open out to others in generosity, service, and love. We might feel, for example, a sense of gratitude to God that leads us to a deeper faith, trust, and love; or a joyful awareness and appreciation of the presence and action and gifts of God in people, in events in our own lives or in some other part of the world; we might experience a state of peace and quiet in the knowledge of God and God's gifts, and so reach out to others in reconciliation and trust. All these, and others, are examples of the kind of movements of feeling that the umbrella term *consolation* includes. The main feature of them is that their direction is towards growth, creativity, and a genuine fullness of life and love in that they draw us to a fuller, effective, generous love of God and other people, and to a right love of ourselves.

The feelings and affective movements that come under the heading of "desolation" are the contrary of these. Their characteristic tendency is to draw us away from God and things which have to do with God, and to lead us to be self-centered, closed in, and unconcerned about God or other people. These feelings move us in the opposite direction from the previous ones. So, for example, we might feel a depressing inner darkness and restlessness; life ceases to have meaning; God and other people seem to count for nothing; paralyzing feelings of failure, guilt, and self-hatred can threaten to set us on a downward spiral of neglect of ourselves, other people and God; or we might experience other states and movements of feeling which seem to undermine our capacities for faith, hope, and love and to lead us into destructive forms of behavior towards others and ourselves.[5]

The crucial issue therefore in interpreting and evaluating our feelings in discernment is not so much where the movement of feeling is coming from (though knowledge of this can of course be helpful), nor even what exactly the feeling is: joy, anger, guilt, confusion, and so on. It is rather the direction in which the feelings are leading. But it is also very important to realize that in discernment our interpretation and estimate of the spiritual value of any affective movement depends upon the context in which it occurs. Let us take an example. Peter is a man who takes his Christian life fairly seriously, wants to deepen as far as he can his relationship with God and to live out the consequences of his discipleship in his attitudes towards other people and the world and in his dealings with them. That is the general direction of his life, and normally he will find joy and peace in events and people and choices which are consistent with these desires. If he experiences movements of feeling that we usually associate with desolation, it could be an indication in him of a resistance to this direction; some inner movement that is contrary to this general direction and thus causing him to experience conflict within himself; something that is threatening to deflect him from his commitment.

Mark, on the other hand, is a man who has little time for God and little consideration for other people. On his own admission, he is mainly interested in "looking after 'number one'" as much as he can, and is not averse to exploitation and manipulation of other people, with an eye to the main chance. If he finds himself experiencing feelings we usually associate with desolation—restlessness, confusion, sadness, and depression, for instance—it can be a sign that there is a movement within him that is contrary to this general direction of his life and wants him to change it. The human spirit seeks goodness and truth rather than the opposite and tries to reassert those values in people who neglect them.

The main point about the two examples is that the same feelings—in this case, restlessness, confusion, disturbance, lack of peace—have opposite significance for discernment. In the case of Peter they indicate a destructive movement to draw him away from living out faithfully his Christian commitment, whereas for Mark the same kind of feelings show the presence of a movement towards growth through taking more notice of the kinds of values we associate with Christianity.

The decisive difference lies in the general direction in which the two men's lives are moving. In the old terminology, Peter interprets these feelings as evidence of the "evil spirit" trying to lead him towards what is less good; in Mark's case they are signs of a "good spirit" trying to move him to a better way. Most commonly in discernment we are dealing with a person like Peter, one who wants to grow in Christian discipleship. In this case, "consolation" will mean pleasant feelings of joy, peace, delight in God, and in the following of Jesus, and "desolation" will mean unpleasant feelings: confusion, sadness, moods of depression, distaste for the things involved in the following of Jesus.

There is another important point to make about desolation. It is natural to judge any kind of desolation as bad, because the experience is usually painful, and for a committed Christian the direction in which it is leading is destructive. Ignatius is at pains to insist, however, that desolation, far from being necessarily harmful and bad, can in fact be an experience of growth if it is handled well (Exs 318–22). The feelings of desolation, whatever form they may take, are not in themselves destructive. But if we begin to act and to make choices under the influence of feelings of desolation, that is when it becomes destructive for ourselves and for others. Ignatius's advice therefore is that we should not make any changes or any decisions in time of and under the influence of feelings of desolation, precisely because they could be destructive and lead us away from God.

The process of discernment of spirits therefore is one of looking at and sifting our present and past experience, taking note especially of the events, people, and situations that are associated with or evoke the moods and feelings of consolation and desolation. When we look at the present and immediate future in this way, the aim of discernment is to help us to make choices which encourage and build on the events and situations that are associated with consolation. The reason behind this is that it is characteristic of the Spirit of God to produce consolation, to work for that which is life giving, creative, joyful, peaceful, and so on—the fruits of the Spirit. So our past experiences of consolation show us times when the Spirit has been at work in our lives. And in the present and future our path of truth and growth in discipleship is to choose those ways of being, those courses of action that bring consolation, for that is to respond to the Spirit's leading.

Let us look at another example. Pauline was a teacher for ten years and then took a job in administration in industry. The salary was higher, she had less distance to travel to work each day, and the administrative post matched her qualifications. Five years later, in the course of a retreat, she begins to reflect on her present and past experience because she feels dissatisfied, unhappy, restless, and out of place in her work. Her reflection on her experiences of "consolation" and "desolation" brings home to her that her feelings of consolation are in fact associated with teaching, and her opposite feelings are associated with her present work, although there seemed to be excellent reasons for changing jobs when she did. For her teaching was creative, life giving, a source of joy and peace, while her present job now appears to be destructive. Her way forward might be to look at possible job options which could allow her to find work which was once again a source of consolation. On the other hand, once she has realized what has been happening, she might also be able to approach her present job in such a way that she begins to find consolation where previously she found the opposite.

There are other depths and vagaries of the human heart that Ignatius lays bare, especially in his second set of guidelines for discernment (Exs 329–36). In particular, he highlights the fact that feelings of consolation can be deceptive: "the devil hath power to assume a pleasing shape."[6] Feelings of consolation—joy, peace, encouragement, enthusiasm, delight—can in fact lead to a result which is less good and even destructive.

This fact, that there is false as well as true consolation, is obviously very important to remember in discernment. And Ignatius records an experience of it in his own life which helps to clarify it for us. During the time of his studies, both in Barcelona and again in Paris, the insights that he had into spiritual matters were one of his sources of great delight (*Autobiography,* 55, 82). He found he could spend a long time thinking about these things with great joy, peace, and satisfaction: they were a source of consolation to him and good things in themselves. The disadvantage, however, was that they distracted him from his studies to the extent that he could not concentrate on the lectures. (Perhaps what he felt was the effect of an unconscious resistance within himself to the prospect of going back to secondary school at his age and in real poverty. In the circumstances, his desire to escape into his "spiritual thoughts" is understandable!) Eventually he came to the conclusion that they were what he called a deceptive form of consolation. Though good in themselves they were in fact drawing him away from his better purpose, which was to study in order to be able to help other people. The wise and successful step that he took to be free of the deception was to tell one of his teachers what was happening to him, and to promise "never to fail to attend your class these two years, as long as I can find bread and water for my support" (*Autobiography,* 55).

The advice that Ignatius offers for such instances in his guidelines is no doubt based on this and similar experiences. Deceptive consolation is subtle. We often only recognize that it is deceptive and harmful after some time when its true, destructive effect becomes clear, by its "serpent's tail," as Ignatius says (Exs 334). By then, of course, harm may have been done. The response that Ignatius advises is two-fold. First we should trace back from the harmful effect the whole chain of thoughts and feelings to the point where things started to go wrong (Exs 333–34). This will also help us to notice the deception more easily in the future. And the second piece of advice is to tell somebody about what is happening. This enables someone who is outside the situation to look at it more objectively and not to be taken in so easily by the deception. Or, as Ignatius puts it with much more color and drama:

> Our enemy may also be compared in his manner of acting to a false lover. He seeks to remain hidden and does not want to be discovered. If such a lover speaks with evil intention to the daughter of a good father, or to the wife of a good husband, and seeks to seduce them, he wants his words and solicitations kept secret. . . . In the same way when the enemy of our human nature tempts a just soul with his wiles and seductions, he earnestly desires that they be received secretly and kept secret. But if one manifests them to a confessor, or to some other spiritual person who understands his deceits and malicious designs, the evil one is very much vexed. For he knows that he cannot succeed in his evil undertaking, once his evident deceits have been revealed. (Exs 326)

Discernment and Choices: The Election

Ignatius recognizes the fact that a person who is making the Spiritual Exercises might come to the point of making a fundamental decision about her or his own life in the course of the Exercises. So in the material for the Second Week he offers a series of aids for making what has come to be called the Election (i.e., the choice or decision). These aids, taken together, make up a process of Christian decision-making based on discernment of spirits. And although these aids are set in the particular context of the Exercises, the principles and methods they embody are also very helpful when adapted for decision-making in everyday life. I am going to discuss Ignatius's guidelines in some detail here because I believe that the help that he offers towards making good decisions is one of his more distinctive and valuable contributions to Christian living, with undoubted application to our circumstances today.

The context of the Exercises is a particularly helpful one for making an important decision. The person who is making the Exercises is living in an atmosphere of prayer and reflection in which he or she is able to be more open than is usual in everyday life to God and to the various inner movements which we have been discussing in this chapter. These movements and their significance have been the subject of daily conversations between the one who is making the Exercises and her or his "director." During the First Week, those who are making the Exercises have become more aware of the interior and exterior bonds which impede them in their responses to God's love and faithfulness, and in their attempts to follow Christ in freedom. We can hope too that in the process they have also become at least a little more free from the destructive effects of those bonds, though this kind of liberation also continues long after they have finished making the Exercises.

At the beginning of the Second Week, they have looked in some detail at the fundamental demands and framework of discipleship of Jesus when contemplating at length and repeatedly (Exs 118–31) the Call of the King (Exs 91–98), the story of the Incarnation (Exs 101–9), the nativity of Jesus (Exs 110–17), and aspects of his early life (Exs 132–34). They are therefore coming to the point of looking again at the life and teaching of Jesus in the Gospels, the world in which they live and their own lives, and noticing resonances and discords, harmonies and disharmonies between them. In the contemplation on the Call of the King and in subsequent periods of prayer over several days, they have been invited to offer themselves generously to follow and serve Jesus (Exs 98), and they have prayed repeatedly for "an intimate knowledge of Our Lord . . . that I may love Him more and follow him more closely" (Exs 104). In the Meditation on Two Standards and at other times, they have contemplated personal and social dimensions of the setting in which their lives are placed in the light of the Gospels and the mission of Jesus. They may therefore be in a position to examine and choose (or renew a choice already made of) the way in which they hope to put into effect their commitment to Jesus in the particular circumstances of their own lives. And that, in some form, is usually the basic material of the Election.

As the decision is about how a person is going to follow Jesus in his or her own life, the process of discernment in the time of decision-making, as indeed throughout the Exercises, goes on within the framework of that person's understanding of himself or herself in relation to the larger world together with daily contemplation of Gospel events from the life of Jesus. The inner, affective movements of consolation and desolation, therefore, are responses to the Gospel accounts of Jesus' life, death, and resurrection, to the exercitant's own life and to the world generally. Jesus' way is kept firmly in view all the time, however, and the decision is made in very close relation to that. To help discernment still further, Ignatius sets out the Contemplation on Two Standards (Exs 136–48). There he asks the one who makes the Exercises to look at again and try to understand more fully discipleship of Jesus, and especially the contrary objectives and ways of operating of Jesus and "the enemy of our human nature": the one life-giving, the other destructive.

Throughout his guidelines for the Election, Ignatius is concerned that circumstances should be right for making a decision (Exs 170), and that the person faced with the choice should be motivated as far as possible by a single intention: "the service and praise of God our Lord and the salvation of my soul" (Exs 169). So he offers for repeated consideration a series of examples, some of them short parables, which illustrate bad, good, and better choices (Exs 149–56, 165–68), culminating in this statement of the worthiest grounds for choosing:

> Whenever the praise and glory of the Divine Majesty would be equally served, in order to imitate and be in reality more like Christ our Lord, I desire and choose poverty with Christ poor, rather than riches; insults with Christ loaded with them rather than honours; I desire to be accounted as worthless and a fool for Christ, rather than to be esteemed as wise and prudent in this world. So Christ was treated before me. (Exs 167)

The Election

Ignatius's step-by step guidance for the Election is discernment in slow motion. We should remember, of course, that throughout the Election the one who is making the Exercises is discussing his or her inner affective movements daily with the person who gives the Exercises. Ignatius envisaged three different situations in which a person might come to a decision:

1. He takes into account first the possibility that the Spirit of God simply moves a person to make the right choice "so that a devout soul without hesitation or the possibility of hesitation, follows what has been manifested to it" (Exs 175). His own examples of this are Matthew the tax-gatherer in the Gospels and Saul on the Damascus road.

2. The second situation, which is obviously more usual, happens when a person experiences different affective and spiritual movements of consolation and desolation such as we have been discussing. Discernment here means observing and reflecting on the pattern of those experiences and making the choice which is associated with feelings of consolation (cf. Exs 176).

3. It can happen of course that the person who is making the decision experiences not the seesaw of two contrary kinds of feeling but "a time of tranquillity, that is, a time when the soul is not agitated by different spirits, and has free and peaceful use of its natural powers" (Exs 177). This third situation is the time when it is appropriate and even necessary to use some different methods of approaching the decision.

    3.1. The first of these is a systematic consideration, not this time of the *feelings* that are evoked by the decision, but of all the *reasons* for and against the various options, the advantages and disadvantages of each possible choice (cf. Exs 178–83).

3.2. In the second of these methods for "a time of tranquility" Ignatius suggests some exercises by which those who are making the Election, by use of the imagination, can place themselves in circumstances where they would want to make the right choice (Exs 184–88). Having done that, they should consider what decision would be right, and allow themselves to be guided by that.

The wise purpose behind Ignatius's guidelines for a decision in "a time of tranquility" is that he is trying to ensure that three necessary elements are present. The first of these is that the person who is making the decision not only reflects on how he or she *feels* about it but also weighs carefully all the circumstances and factors that are relevant to the decision, and especially all possible reasons both for and against each of the options. This helps to avert the danger of making a wrong choice under the influence of powerful feeling such as enthusiasm or depression, without attempting a realistic appraisal of the situation. His second purpose is to try to ensure as much objectivity as possible on the part of the person making the choice (Exs 185–87 especially). And thirdly he tries to make sure that this person knows as well as possible his or her motives and objectives in the decision. To help to achieve this, he repeatedly points out what he sees as the most worthy grounds on which good choices can be made (Exs 177, 179, 180, 181, 183, 184, 185, 189).

Offering and Confirmation

In the Exercises, the Election takes place in an atmosphere of prayer, as is fitting for any important decision which a Christian person makes. Prayer is part of the process of decision-making in a distinctive way. We have seen how the decision is made during a time of repeated contemplation of the life and teaching of Jesus as presented in the Gospels, so that Jesus is a constant reference-point. Moreover the person who makes the decision looks at all the advantages and disadvantages of his or her options in a time of prayerful tranquillity and is constantly begging God for help and guidance. And the exercises which Ignatius proposes as part of the Election itself are prayer exercises.

Prayer also becomes an essential part of the Election in one other very important way. Ignatius advises that when the choice has been made, we should repeatedly offer our choice to God "that the Divine Majesty may deign to accept and confirm it, if it is for his greater service and praise" (Exs 183; cf. Exs 188). The offering is a sign of the desire to choose what we believe will most give praise and service to God.

Once the decision has been made, Ignatius expects that we will experience confirmation of the rightness of our choice, and that this confirmation will come through experiences of consolation. This will assure us that the decision we have reached is coherent with and a concrete expression of our commitment to being disciples of Jesus.

In the context of the Exercises, the Third and Fourth Weeks are very important as the setting in which the decision is confirmed. Contemplation of the passion and death of Jesus in particular can be a time when our commitment to Jesus and our faithfulness to the decision we have made are severely challenged by the cross, as we contemplate more fully the implications of our choice. Consolation at that time can be a very encouraging confirmation. Outside the Exercises, confirmation of our right choices comes with time: sometimes in prayer, equally also in the continuing experience of consolation in daily life, as we try to live out our choices and commitments in circumstances which are never ideal. A wrong choice will be expected to lead in these same circumstances to experiences of desolation. For these reasons it is very important that discernment continues after an important decision has been made.

Reflections

It should now be easier to see why discernment is at the heart of Ignatian spirituality, and to understand the claim that it also lies at the heart of any genuine Christian spirituality. We have been used to thinking that spirituality has mainly to do with the "inner life," prayer, mysticism, and so on. But these things form only a part of it, though a not unimportant part. They are incomplete except within a broader setting in which disciples of Jesus try to live their disciple-ship in committed, honest, and coherent ways. And discernment is at the heart of discipleship, because when we walk a disciple's path we are constantly faced with changing situations in which we have to discover how to be faithful to the gospel and the leading of the Spirit, and true to ourselves.

This involves us constantly in making choices, in our attempts to integrate prayer and life. Some of them are the great decisions involved in our fundamental commitments or when we make signifi-cant changes of direction. But there are also the lesser, daily choices by which, within the larger context of our basic commitments, we give shape to our everyday lives. We have seen in this chapter what Ignatius has to offer to us in both the larger and the smaller choices.

Finally, because of common misapprehensions, it is important to remind ourselves that Christian discernment and decision-making are not automatic or mechanical processes. The guidelines offered by Ignatius are not like the instruction manual for using the word pro-cessor on which I have written this chapter. With the manual, so long as the instructions are correct and I follow them accurately and the machine is functioning properly, the word processor will store and eventually print the chapter. Ignatius's guidelines are not a manual for operating a machine, nor are they a magic spell for infallibly producing a right answer. It is not true to say that if I follow to the letter the instructions about decision-making set out in the Exercises I will automatically come out with the guaranteed "right" decision. Decision-making on a particular occasion by discernment of spirits presupposes a living relationship with God and a background of daily life in which I am trying to be responsive and faithful to the Spirit's leading. That is the only context in which Ignatius's guidelines have meaning and use. And a "right" decision about a course of action I should take is not a matter of finding out some so far undiscovered item of "God's plan" and putting it into effect. Rather the "right" decision is what appears to be the best in the circumstances and is the expression of the deepest truths of ourselves within the setting of this day-to-day relationship with God.

NOTES

1. Nicholas King, "Ignatius Loyola and Decision-making," *The Way Supplement* 24 (Spring 1975), 46–57, traces the growth of Ignatius's experience of discernment with regard to choices.

2. See, e.g., Candido de Dalmases, SJ, *Ignatius of Loyola, Founder of the Jesuits: His Life and Work*, trans. Jerome Aixala, SJ (St. Louis: Institute of Jesuit Sources, 1985), 169–72, 285–87.

3. His most famous letter on discernment is that to Sister Teresa Rejadell, in *Letters [of St. Ignatius Loyola*, trans. William J. Young, SJ (Chicago: Loyola University Press, 1959)], 18–25; other letters which deal with some aspects of discernment can be seen in ibid., 126–30, 179–82, 196–211, 257–58, 420–21.

4. A good book which in a helpful way translates Ignatius's guidance in discernment from the setting of the Exercises to that of daily life is John English, *Spiritual Freedom:[From an Experience of the Ignatian Exercises to the Art of Spiritual Guidance*, 2nd ed. (Chicago: Loyola University Press, 1995)].

5. Gerard W. Hughes has a useful chapter on interpreting and evaluating these feelings in *God of Surprises* (London: Darton, Longman & Todd, 1985 [out of print]). He writes of consolation and desolation in terms of "creative moods" and "destructive moods."

6. William Shakespeare, *Hamlet*, 2.ii.

Refining the Acoustics of the Heart

Wilkie Au and Noreen Cannon Au

From *The Discerning Heart: Exploring the Christian Path,* 2006

Listen carefully . . . with the ear of your heart.
—Prologue, *Rule of Saint Benedict*

It is only with the heart that one sees rightly;
what is essential is invisible to the eyes.
—Antoine de Saint Exupéry, *The Little Prince*

To know something important "by heart" is an experience of wholeness. The term *heart* is a traditional image for a way of perceiving, feeling, and loving that engages the total person. To Saint Augustine, the word signifies "our whole interior and spiritual life, and it includes mind and will, knowledge and love."[1] Heart, when used to symbolize spiritual discernment, indicates that following God is not something primarily heady, action oriented, or moralistic. Rather, it is a matter of being caught up in a dynamic, loving relationship with God and others. A heart-centered approach to discernment is holistic.

In the New Testament, the word *holistic* (from the Greek *holus*) means "total" or "whole," as in the story of the widow's mite, in which Jesus commends the woman for putting her *holon ton biou* ("all she had to live on") into the treasury (Mark 12:44). Like the dance called the hokey pokey, which invites us to "put your whole self in," holistic discernment invites us to put our whole self into the process. A holistic approach is inclusive and takes seriously the knowledge-bearing capacity not only of the mind but also of the body, emotions, senses, imagination, feelings, intuition, and dreams. "Two fundamentally different ways of knowing interact to construct our mental life," states psychologist Daniel Goleman. "One, the rational mind, is the mode of comprehension we are typically conscious of: more prominent in awareness, thoughtful, able to ponder and reflect. But alongside that there is another system of knowing: impulsive and powerful, if sometimes illogical—the emotional mind."[2] The research findings in the field of neurology, Goleman argues, show that how well we do in life is determined by both rational and emotional intelligence. "The old paradigm," he states, "held an ideal of reason freed of the pull of emotion. The new paradigm urges us to harmonize head and heart."[3]

Holistic discernment revolves around a form of knowing that goes beyond cold rationality. This mode of knowing is reflected in the Hebrew verb *yadah*, signifying the kind of intimate knowledge resulting from the unification of intellect, feeling, and actions. Ignatian spirituality speaks of it as *sentir*, a felt knowledge that pervades the whole of one's being. As Paul Tillich puts it, it is not so much "grasping the truths of faith" but "being grasped by the Truth of faith." In his autobiography, C. S. Lewis provides a vivid description of a time when philosophical and intellectual constructs of Christianity came to life for him in this holistic way of knowing:

> As the dry bones shook and came together in that dreaded valley of Ezekiel's, so now a philosophical theorem cerebrally entertained, began to stir and heave and throw off its gravecloths, and stood upright and became a living presence. I was to be allowed to play at philosophy no longer. . . . Total surrender, the absolute leap in the dark, were demanded.[4]

Holistic knowing enables us to "listen to the messages from all the self's aspects: the mind, the heart, the genitals, the viscera, the spiritual sensitivities."[5] "Various forms of existential therapy value this holistic mode of knowing; these therapies try to restore the place of feelings where rationality has been the exclusive mode of operating. Gestalt therapy, for example, "undercuts language, the tool of thought, and clears the way for an approach that is explicitly *organismic.*"[6]

An organismic approach is holistic because it places the body, with its movement and sensations, on the same level as the mind and its abstract thoughts and verbal symbols. This approach recognizes the body-spirit or psychosomatic unity of the person and affirms that bodily expressions often reveal interior states pertinent to making a choice. Hardly an esoteric concept, the psychosomatic unity of the person can be observed whenever bodily reactions reveal affective states. Blushing, sweaty palms, and accelerated heart rate are common examples of these physical manifestations of emotions. Gestalt therapists, for example, rely heavily on body language for an indication of psychological states. They generally believe that the body conveys how a person feels more truthfully than words. Because our bodily posture and gestures often unconsciously express our interior states, awareness of them can reveal what is going on in us.

Gestalt therapist James Simkin recounts a case that illustrates this organismic approach. Once, when working with a man struggling to decide whether to remain in a business venture recently begun with a friend, Simkin asked the client to imagine sticking with his business commitment. As the client imagined concretely what this option would entail, Simkin directed him to attend to his bodily sensations. When he imagined remaining with the business, the client's stomach tied up in knots. Then Simkin directed him to fantasize dropping the commitment. As the client did so, his stomach began to unravel and relax. The therapist then asked him to continue to shuttle between the two different fantasies, while simultaneously paying attention to his bodily reactions. As the client did so, he discovered a recurrent pattern: whenever he imagined staying with the business venture, his body was filled with stress; whenever he imagined abandoning the business deal, his body began to relax. Simkin concludes:

Being able to self-validate what is the correct solution through one's own body language is a tremendous help in the economy of psychotherapy. Many of the transference and countertransference difficulties can be avoided, as well as the pitfalls of interpretation, through teaching oneself and one's patients how to use their symptoms—how to listen to their own body language.[7]

Simkin's case demonstrates how useful the data produced by the imagination, senses, bodily sensations, and feelings can be in decision-making. "My total organismic sensing of a situation is more trustworthy than my intellect," states psychologist Carl Rogers in support of a holistic approach. Testifying to this "wisdom of the organism," Rogers states: "As I gradually come to trust my total reactions more deeply, I find that I can use them to guide my thinking. . . . I think of it as trusting the totality of my experience, which I have learned to suspect is wiser than my intellect. It is fallible I am sure, but I believe it to be less fallible than my conscious mind alone."[8]

Attention to Interior Movements

What psychologists such as Rogers and Simkin say of decision-making is equally true of discernment. A holistic approach to discernment maintains that we must be alert to how we are being touched by God in all areas of our lives, because no aspect escapes the influence of the divine Spirit. When thought is the coin of the realm, other important sources of information, like feelings, bodily reactions, and intuitions, can be overlooked. A purely rational approach to discernment is impoverished because it fails to recognize God's influence in religious and affective experiences. Like holistic decision-making, good discernment must take into account one's total, organismic sensing of a situation. A society dominated by science and technology often mistrusts feelings and touts a coldly dispassionate approach as the only intelligent way to make decisions. Nevertheless, recent neurological findings have verified what common sense has told us long ago: feelings have a crucial role in navigating the endless stream of decisions we must make for satisfying living.

> While strong feelings can create havoc in reasoning, the *lack* of aware-
> ness of feeling can also be ruinous, especially in weighing the decisions
> on which our destiny largely depends: what career to pursue, whether
> to stay with a secure job or switch to one that is riskier but more inter-
> esting, whom to date or marry, where to live, which apartment to rent
> or house to buy—and on and on through life. Such decisions cannot be
> made well through sheer rationality; they require gut feeling, and the
> emotional wisdom garnered through past experiences. Formal logic
> alone can never work as the basis for deciding whom to marry or trust
> or even what job to take; *these are realms where reason without feeling is
> blind*[9] (emphasis added).

Ignatian spirituality goes further in asserting the importance of feelings by connecting our emotional awareness with our ability to decipher how we are being moved by God. Ignatius "came to rec-ognize that human experiences of joy and desolation, of enthusiasm and depression, of light and darkness, are not just human emotions which vary like the wind in a storm, but are the means by which we recognize the movements within our spirit stirred by the Spirit of Jesus."[10] Thus, in the *Spiritual Exercises* Ignatius instructs the director of a retreat to focus on the interior movements and experiences of the retreatant. If the retreatant reports not being affected by any move-ments, either of consolation or desolation, it is important that the director inquire into this (no. 6). For Ignatius, the director's central question to the retreatant throughout the experience of the *Spiritual Exercises* is: "How were you *moved* in prayer?"

Integrating Reason, Affect, and Religious Experience

Ignatius's approach to discerning life choices reflects the organismic approach of Gestalt therapy and can be considered as an early form of holistic decision-making. Like the organismic approach of Gestalt therapy, Ignatian guidelines for deciding or "making an election" emphasize the integration of thought, affectivity, imagination, and sensation. Ignatius's *sentir* or felt knowledge is equivalent to Gestalt therapy's idea of "emotional insights."[11] These emotional insights help decision-making because they are based on an expanded awareness of one's relationship with the environment, accompanied by positive feelings and a sense of discovery.[12] For example, when an obese person is able to persevere in a weight-loss program for an extended period, he may happily discover that his power to control his eating is greater than he had thought. Or a student struggling with self-doubts may realize, with the help of a counselor, that her consistent success in science and mathematics classes makes it realistic for her to dream about being a physician like her mother. These examples of emotional insights differ greatly from purely intellectual insights that have no impact on life decisions because they are not rooted in one's actual experiences. The case cited by Simkin above is a clear illustration of how Gestalt therapists lead clients to emotional insight by teaching them how to attend to their actual bodily reactions and emotions when deciding. In a similar way, Ignatius attempts to help retreatants making a decision detect God's influence as it impinges on their minds, hearts, and bodies.

Ignatius's Three Times of Making an Election

In the *Spiritual Exercises*, Ignatius describes three times or ways in which God can guide people faced with choice. The first time occurs when God "so moves and attracts the will that a devout soul without hesitation, or the possibility of hesitation, follows what has been manifested to it" (no. 175). Ignatius cites the responses of Saint Paul and Saint Matthew to Christ's call in order to illustrate this first time of election. Phenomenologically, this first time can be viewed as a moment of peak religious experience when individuals feel overwhelmed by an inner sense of certainty about their decisions. At such moments they may experience something deep within "click into place," providing an intuitive sense of how they must proceed. Everything points in one direction, and they feel no contrary movement. Or they may perceive such a total congruence between their sense of internal requiredness (what they feel they must do) and God's will (what they think God wants of them) that the course to be followed is unambiguously clear. Sometimes, quite apart from any deliberation, a personal "moment of truth" can spring suddenly upon the person without any antecedent cause, like a forceful flash of insight, removing any further need for deliberating.[13]

The second time of decision-making suggested by Ignatius emphasizes the knowledge-bearing capacity of feelings. It occurs when individuals must rely on their affective states of consolation or desolation to detect the influence of God regarding the decision to be made (no. 176). In the case of people progressing earnestly along the spiritual path,[14] Ignatius understands consolation as a complex of positive feelings that encourages, supports, and confirms a prospective decision as being "right." He sees desolation as a complex of negative feelings that discourages, questions, and calls into doubt a prospective decision, suggesting that it is "not right." The assumption underlying this second time of election is that emotions can be indicators of God's guidance.

The third time of decision-making highlights the process of reasoning (nos. 177–87).[15] Picturing oneself on one's deathbed and recalling God's purpose for creating us (that we might live in loving relationship with God by praising, reverencing, and serving God [no. 23]), the person is asked to list the pros and cons of various options (no. 186). This third time presupposes that God's guiding influence can be felt in the process of reasoning.[16] Like the values-clarification exercise that asks people what they would do if they had only a week to live, this Ignatian method relies on the truth that can come at death's door to provide a perspective for present choices. In other words, it asks people to anticipate which decision they would ratify or regret when facing death. In this third time of election, Ignatius also provides an example of heeding one's inner wisdom when he suggests imagining a person coming to us for help in making a choice similar to one we are facing. We should listen carefully to what we counsel this person to do and then follow our own advice (no. 185). This Ignatian exercise contains a twofold value: it increases clarity through objectification (telling our own story in the third person) and it encourages us to honor our inner authority.[17]

The genius of Ignatius, theologian Michael J. Buckley points out, was not that he counted transpersonal influences, or the attractions of affectivity, or the process of thinking as critical factors in securing the guidance of God. Others also shared this inclusive view. Ignatius's explanation of the dynamics of these three often interrelating factors within a person's religious experience is unique. "What Ignatius provided," maintains Buckley, "was a structure within which each of these finds a significant place; none is dismissed out of hand. A coordination among them is established so that they reach an integrity of effect and one is taught how to recognize and reply to each."[18]

Choice and Confirmation:
The Twofold Ignatian Dynamic

The phrase *integrity of effect* aptly describes the desired outcome of Ignatian discernment. Presuming the person is genuinely committed to doing the will of God and is free from inordinate attachments that destroy freedom, the decision is integral if it emanates from an integration of feelings and thoughts. Ignatius sought this integration by building into the second and third times of decision-making a complementary dynamic. He directs the person who makes a decision based on the rational approach of the third time to seek affective confirmation by prayerfully attending to his or her feelings as suggested by the second time of election (no. 183). In other words, following a decision the person should stay in close touch with the feelings that arise as a result of the decision and determine whether they confirm the rightness of the choice or cast doubt on it. After a period of testing, if positive feelings (for example, peace, joy, hope, confidence) dominate, it is clear that affectivity has joined with intelligence to produce a harmonious effect. However, if negative and disturbing feelings (such as doubt, fear, anxiety, discouragement) persist, then a closure would seem premature and the person should continue the process until an inner harmony is produced through the alliance of head and heart.

Conversely, a person who makes a decision based on the affective approach of the second time should also seek rational confirmation through a method of the third time. William Peters, in his commentary on the *Spiritual Exercises*, cites the *Directory of 1599* to substantiate this point. He notes that Juan de Polanco, a close friend of Ignatius, called the second time of election "more excellent" than the third, but adds that it might be wise to check the result of an election made in this time by one of the methods of the third.[19] Concretely speaking, when we make a decision based on a pattern of consolation surrounding a specific choice, we are still encouraged to strengthen that choice by thinking of all the pros that support that choice. At this point in the discernment process, we should play down the cons and put them on the back burner and not permit them to sabotage the decision that has just been made peacefully through consoling experiences in prayer. This approach allows us to invest wholeheartedly in the direction we have chosen in consolation without being hampered by any nagging voice of negativity. Of course, we need to monitor our ongoing experiences of consolation or desolation as we actually live out our choice in order to confirm its rightness or wrongness in concrete experience.[20] Choice and confirmation make up the two-part dynamic of the Ignatian method of discernment.

Clearly, the second time of decision-making, based on affectivity, and the third time, based on reasoning, were designed by Ignatius to function in a complementary dynamic. The Ignatian process seeks to ground life choices on felt knowledge, not on theoretical abstractions. This process, according to Ignatian scholar John Futrell, involves paying attention simultaneously to "the continuity of thoughts during reflection, the concomitant feelings constantly reacting to these thoughts—feelings which confirm or call into question the orientation of the reflection—and the growing understanding which involves both the thoughts and feelings—felt-knowledge."[21]

Grounding Ignatius's Three Times of Election in Contemporary Thought

Ignatius's first time or way of making an election, when a person is so touched by God that he or she knows deeply the path to be followed without any need for deliberation, finds contemporary support in the distinction made between religious truth and scientific truth. Whereas truth-claims in science need to be backed up by reproducibility, a religious truth may be based on a single, unique, irrepeatable religious experience. According to the scientific method, a truth-claim can be empirically verified only if an experiment produces the same results over and over again under the same conditions or variables. A religious truth, however, requires no such reproducibility to establish its claim to validity.

According to psychologist Joseph R. Royce, "The scientific enterprise is objective and it moves in the direction of making generalizations. Religion, on the other hand, demands personal involvement or subjectivity. . . . It recognizes that such individual involvement may be unique rather than a general phenomenon."[22] Existential validation, not empirical verification, grounds a religious truth. Existential validation occurs when we experience deeply the meaning, significance, and well-being produced by what we know through a religious experience. Theologian Paul Tillich illustrates how such a religious truth can come in a powerful experience of being "struck by grace":

Do you know what it means to be struck by grace? . . . We cannot transform our lives, unless we allow them to be transformed by the stroke of grace. It happens or it does not happen. And certainly it does

not happen if we try to force it upon ourselves, just as it shall not happen so long as we think, in our self-complacency, that we have no need
of it. Grace strikes us when we are in great pain and restlessness. It
strikes us when, year after year, the longed-for perfection of life does
not appear, when despair destroys all joy and courage. Sometimes at
that moment a shaft of light breaks into our darkness, and it is as though
a voice were saying: "You are accepted. You are accepted," accepted
by that which is greater than you, and the name of which you do not
know. Do not ask for the name now, perhaps you will find it later. Do
not try to do anything; do not perform anything; do not intend anything. Simply accept the fact that you are accepted. If that happens to
us, we experience grace. . . . Sometimes it happens that we receive the
power to say "yes" to ourselves, that peace enters into us and makes us
whole, that self-hatred and self-contempt disappear, and that our self is
reunited with itself. Then we can say that grace has come upon us.[23]

Tillich's description of the experience of being struck by grace
resembles Ignatius's description of consolation without a previous
cause. "I said without previous cause," states Ignatius, "that is, without
any preceding perception or knowledge of any subject by which a soul
might be led to such a consolation through its own acts of intellect and
will" (no. 330). Like Tillich's description of grace, this consolation
described by Ignatius is characterized by its total gift nature. Unlike
scientific knowledge that is engendered by a controlled experiment,
religious knowledge is simply received as a gift from God. "It belongs
solely to the Creator to come into a soul, to leave it, to act upon it,
to draw it wholly to the love of His Divine Majesty," states Ignatius in
his "Rules for Discernment of Spirits" (no. 330). Those who make an
election in Ignatius's first time have clearly been struck by an amazing
grace that eliminates the need for any discernment process, since they
sense deep within, without any doubt or contrary inner movement,
the course they must pursue.

However, when such an experience of consolation is not accompanied by a deep clarity about choices to be made, it is critical to
note Ignatius's caveat that people who have experienced consolation
without a previous cause "must consider it very attentively, and must

cautiously distinguish the actual time of the consolation from the period which follows it. At such a time the soul is still fervent and favored with the grace and aftereffects of the consolation which has passed. In this second period the soul frequently forms various resolutions and plans which are not granted directly by God" (no. 336). In this time of "afterglow," the plans and choices we make cannot be attributed directly to God, as was the actual moment of consolation, but have their source in our own fallible human reasoning and judgments. As such, they are susceptible to error.

Ignatius's three times of making an election can also be further understood in light of the theological distinction between God's transcendent and immanent nature. This distinction underpins his three ways of being influenced by God in our discernment. The first time of election highlights the transcendent nature of God, while the second and third times of election emphasize the immanent nature of God. When we refer to God's transcendence, we are acknowledging the fact that God is illimitable Mystery, totally beyond and dissimilar to any created reality and far beyond our human comprehension. Sovereign over all of creation, God can intervene in our lives to influence our choices without the mediation of thoughts, feelings, and images. When we speak of God's immanence, we acknowledge that God communicates to us not through mystical or ecstatic experiences alone, but also through the normal human faculties of knowing and experiencing. When we acknowledge that God is both transcendent and immanent, we affirm God's indwelling presence within the world while maintaining that God is wholly other and irreducible to any aspect of creation.

A Discernment Process Based on the Ignatian Tradition

IDENTIFY the decision that faces us or the issue we need to resolve

EXAMINE the underlying values (human, Christian, spiritual) and personal concerns involved

Through reflection, we clarify the values that are at stake in the decision (values clarification) and ask whether they are worth pursuing (value critique).

STRIVE for Ignatian indifference

Ignatian indifference is a state of inner freedom, openness, and balance that allows us beforehand not to incline more toward one option than to another but to allow our preference [to] be shaped by the single criterion of what will enhance our ability to love God and to embody that love for others in the concrete context of our lives.

Not easy to attain, indifference is a poised freedom that preserves our ability to go one way or another depending on the indication of God's lead. By calling for indifference, Ignatius is calling for a willingness right from the start to be influenced in the process by God's guidance.

Unfortunately, *indifference* is a bad choice of a word to convey Ignatius's meaning, since it often connotes apathy and complacency. For Ignatius, it has nothing to do with the absence of feelings; nor does it mean disinterest in people and situations. The sculpture of the discus thrower is a helpful image in understanding Ignatian indifference. Manifesting taut muscles ready to be sprung and pent-up energy ready to be released, the statue captures at once the paradoxical combination of action and rest. It is as if the discus thrower has been caught at a moment when he is ready to hurl the discus but is in waiting. Similarly, Ignatian indifference calls for a spiritual posture that imitates that of the discus thrower. We are called to be ever ready to embody the love of God in any way we can, but we must have the inner discipline to wait and to withhold action until we get an indication of directionality from God.

If unable to achieve indifference, discussing the matter in spiritual direction can help us understand what we are struggling with and what the next peaceful step might be in our discernment.

TAKE time to pray over the matter, paying attention to how we are being drawn or led

This moves our reflection into the context of prayer; we ask for God's guidance and try to be sensitive to how we are being drawn when the matter is brought to prayer.

Here it is important to remember what was said above regarding the interplay of reason, affect, and religious experience in the decision-making process. God can influence us through our thoughts as well as through our feelings of consolation and desolation in prayer.

MAKE a choice based on both the results of our "head work" and our "heart work"

"Head work" includes weighing the matter with our reasoning process by which we research the relevant information, consult with resource persons when necessary, listen to all the different aspects of our being (needs, wants, desires, and so on), and consider the pros and cons of the different options.

"Heart work" entails sitting with the choice that our reasoning has determined to be the best and checking for affective confirmation, that is, whether our feelings go along with what our mind has decided. If, over a period of time, the feelings that surround the choice we have made are predominantly enlivening and positive (Ignatian "consolation"), we can consider this a sensible way to proceed. If, however, the feelings are predominantly stifling and negative (Ignatian "desolation"), then we must keep the process open until we can arrive at a decision that head and heart can jointly embrace.

The feelings we are monitoring here are not the fleeting feelings that are our immediate responses to stimuli that impinge upon us throughout the day. That level of feelings is like the fluctuating waves on the surface of the ocean. The feelings that are relevant to this process of affective confirmation are similar to the more stable currents between the surface and bottom of the ocean. This mid level of feelings is more constant and stable and thus more relevant in determining whether our feelings confirm or call into question the decision we have made through our thinking process.

Addressing the importance of this affective confirmation, Pierre Wolff articulates a theological affirmation that is central to the Ignatian approach: "Within ourselves, by the process of discernment we offer the results of our intellectual search to the Spirit. If our Divine Guest indicates agreement with us through enlivening echoes produced at the core of our being, we may say that, at that level, we and the Spirit are in tune with one another and that we are deciding *together* our will. What we want at this depth is what God wants for us: God's will for us is what we decide."[24]

DISCUSS the matter with a spiritual companion

Because discerning the movements of God can often be a complex task requiring assistance, this step calls for sharing our deliberation with a trusted friend, counselor, or minister—someone who is committed to helping us be truthful, patient, and persevering in our search for God's call. Because we are all liable to self-deception, we need help to be objective and honest.

DIALOGUE with those who will be intimately affected by the decision being made

Too often decisions that affect spouses, children, and other loved ones are made unilaterally, without engaging the participation of those who have a right to be involved. These decisions, for example, may pertain to changing jobs, selling the house and moving, or caring for aging parents. It is important to make an effort whenever appropriate to ensure that important decisions are not made alone but shared with the significant people in our lives.

LIVE out our decision with courage, hope, and trust

This step requires us to trust in God and to decide, even in the absence of certitude. Sometimes fears and doubts can paralyze us and cause us to procrastinate in making important decisions. As Christians we are called to live boldly and decisively. We must act, even though our carefully discerned decisions may be tinged with some uncertainty due to variables beyond our control. We are called to trust in God's power at work bringing good out of everything. As Saint Paul says in Romans, "We know that all things work together for good for those who love God, who are called according to his purpose" (8:28).

It is also important to keep in mind that Ignatian consolation and desolation refer primarily to our relationship with God and should not be understood in terms of the pleasure-pain axis. Hence, a well-discerned choice can entail enduring periods of struggle and pain while at the same time be supported by a deep sense of God's presence and love.

Here we should also remember Ignatius's caveat about not making any significant decision when experiencing desolation (no. 318). For Ignatius, desolation is a time when we feel distant from God, confused and anxious. This time of darkness is not a good time to alter decisions that were freely made when in a state of consolation, a time when we experience an increase of faith, hope, love, and trust in God.

Friedrich von Hügel's Theory of Integrated Religious Development

An understanding of religious development that supports a holistic approach to discernment can also be found in Friedrich von Hügel's two-volume work *The Mystical Element of Religion*, first published in 1908.[25] According to von Hügel, who was Evelyn Underhill's spiritual director, healthy spiritual growth includes three aspects of religion: the institutional, the critical, and the mystical. The institutional dimension of religion is of central importance in the early stages of personal development, when children depend on sense impressions, memory, and instruction from others for their apprehension of religious belief. In the institutional stage of faith development, people believe because they have been taught by those whom they trust. They are the beneficiaries of a tradition, the recipients of the wisdom of a faith community. At this stage, "the External, Authoritative, Historical, Traditional, Institutional side and function of Religion are everywhere evident."[26]

The second stage, that of the critical, is a period of "trustful questioning, but still of questioning, first others, then oneself."[27] In this critical stage, which often characterizes adolescence, the human spirit's "reasoning, argumentative, abstractive side" demands recognition and "religion answers this demand by clear and systematic arguments and concatenations: this and this is now connected with that and that; this is true or this need not be false, because of that and that."[28] Finally, the third stage of religious development calls for the cultivation of an inner life and sensitivity to the world of interior experiences. "Here religion is rather felt than seen or reasoned about, is loved and lived rather than analyzed, is action and power, rather than either external fact or intellectual verification."[29]

According to von Hügel, there are clear historical examples of these three aspects of religion. In Judaism, "we find a severe and ardent external, traditional, authoritative school in the Pharisees; an accommodating and rationalizing school in the Sadducees; and . . . the experimental, ascetical, and mystical body of the Essenes."[30] Furthermore, he groups the New Testament writings according to the predominance of one of the three moods: the Petrine school illustrates the traditional, historic, external; the Pauline exemplifies the reasoning, speculative-internal; and the Johannine reflects the experimental, mystical-internal. Von Hügel concludes that ideal faith development in adults requires all three dimensions of religion:

> I believe because I am told, because it is true, because it answers to my deepest interior experiences and needs. And, everything else being equal, my faith will be at its richest and deepest and strongest, in so far as all three motives are most fully and characteristically operative within me, at one and the same time, and towards one and the same ultimate result and end.[31]

Von Hügel's understanding of integrative religious development lays the foundation for a holistic approach to discernment. Honoring the traditional guidance of one's faith community, his institutional stage validates the importance of a careful consideration of the wisdom of the group as handed on by tradition and taught by recognized authority. His stress on the importance of the critical dimension of religion affirms the necessity of adult reflection and questioning in the making of good decisions. Finally, von Hügel's mystical stage encourages Christians to value the data of their inner life and personal religious experience. The attractiveness of von Hügel's theory lies in its inclusiveness and balance. His stages are like sections of a tripartite bridge that help people journey through life. Each section must remain in place throughout the journey if the bridge is not to fall apart. Thus, he insists on the "joint presence" of the institutional, critical, and mystical aspects of religion, for "each of these three forces and elements is indeed necessary, but ruinously destructive where it more or less ousts the other two."[32]

When the institutional element predominates to the exclusion of the other two aspects, the result will be an infantilization of Christians and a loss of freedom; religion will then

> inevitably degenerate into more or less of a Superstition,—an oppressive materialization and dangerous would-be absolute fixation of even quite secondary and temporary expressions and analyses of religion; a ruinous belief in the direct transferableness of religious conviction; and a predominance of political, legal, physically coercive concepts and practices with regard to those most interior, strong yet delicate, readily thwarted or weakened, springs of all moral and religious character,— spiritual sincerity and spontaneity and the liberty of the children of God.[33]

Von Hügel's words, enunciated almost a century ago, sound remarkably contemporary and aptly express the feelings of the many people who fear the tyranny of the institutional in today's church. He points to the Spanish Inquisition as a clear example of the institutional element gone awry in religion.

When the critical aspect is apotheosized, the results are equally harmful. The worship of the god of reason leads to a destructive one-sidedness, "a Rationalistic Fanaticism, only too often followed by a lengthy Agnosticism and Indifference."[34] The critical element left alone is liable to produce rationalists rather than religious persons, people whose devotion to an intellectual system replaces their devotion to God. Those who foster the critical and neglect the other two elements are often suspicious of anything emotional and will tend to be out of touch with the mystery of their own inner thoughts and feelings, which are too complex to be captured in abstract concepts. Frequently rigid and dogmatic, such people are prone to be obsessed with the question of orthodoxy and with exposing those whom they consider to be theologically unfaithful.

Finally, when the mystical dimension is cultivated at the expense of the institutional and the critical, distortions arise. In its worst form, the mystical element, unchecked and cut off from the institutional and critical, can produce dangerous fanaticism and extremism, as the example of Jim Jones and the mass suicide of his [Jonestown] cult followers clearly illustrate. Adrift from the critique of the community, the mystical element can isolate Christians and lead to the mindless rejection of formal prayer and worship, the abandonment of doctrinal and moral teachings, and the growth of an emotionalism that cannot be understood because it refuses to submit itself to the critical element. When personal experience is canonized as the only legitimate source of discernment, the doors to anti-intellectualism and self-deception are left wide open.

Using von Hügel's Theory as a Discernment Tool

Von Hügel's three stages of integrated religious growth lend themselves easily to a simple, yet inclusive approach to sorting through issues. When faced with a decision, for example, we can use his stages as a process guide.

- *In the institutional phase, we inquire whether our faith community or social group has any relevant data to offer regarding the issue.*

This first step invites us to tap into the wisdom of a tradition-bearing community and thus benefit from the experiences and reflections of our predecessors. We might call this the hermeneutics [that is, the interpretation method] of retrieval stage, in which we try to access our group's best thinking on the issue. To skip this step would be to deprive ourselves of possibly valuable input for our discernment.

For mainline Christians today, this institutional aspect has been complicated by the existence of two very different ways of viewing the tradition. This difference has divided the contemporary church on such issues as the ordination of women, the union of gays and lesbians, and the path to salvation. Marcus Borg discusses these two competing views of being Christian. Labeling them as the "earlier" and the "emerging" paradigms, he concludes that "neither can claim to be *the* Christian tradition. Both are ways of seeing the tradition." These two ways of Christianity are so different, according to Borg, "that they almost produce two different religions, both using the same Bible and language."[35] Central to their radical difference is their understanding of biblical interpretation and the Bible's function in Christian life.

- *In the critical phase, we assess the data of tradition and the wisdom handed on by our community.* The teachings of tradition are important aspects of discernment because God's guidance can often be embodied in them. Of course, even tradition must be examined critically, with what theologians call a hermeneutic of suspicion, because the community too has made errors in the past from which much can be learned.

- *In the mystical phase, we pay close attention to the data of our own inner world of feelings, intuitions, gut-instincts, fantasies, desires, and aspirations.* As we sit with the various options before us, as well as the teachings of our community, we try to get a sense of which option best commands the agreement and consent of the whole self, resulting in the harmony of head, heart, and gut. The desired result is a decision that is based on a holistic knowing grounded in external authority, critical reasoning, and felt experience.

This method based on von Hügel's theory is holistic because it allows us to blend outer authority with inner authority. A holistic discernment process encourages us to benefit from the wisdom of the community, which has accumulated a storehouse of insights about life's issues and problems based on shared experience. Dialoguing with others of common faith and values provides a healthy check on our internal process, opens us to feedback, and helps ensure that we do not slide down the slippery slope of self-deception. However, discernment falters if it does not include paying serious attention to our inner life and honoring our inner authority. This prayerful attention to how God might be leading us through our thoughts and feelings, fantasies and desires, dreams and drives, bodily sensations and intuitions is what Christian spirituality refers to as solitude of heart. Solitude of heart entails cultivating a quiet inner center, a receptive space, where we can tune in to our inner voices and the voice of God within. Holistic discernment encourages us to befriend our inner life because it is a source of self-knowledge and a storehouse of personal wisdom.

Personal Reflections and Spiritual Exercises

Working with Our Inner Wisdom Circle

As a practical way of deepening an awareness of God's voice speaking within, it is helpful to imagine an inner wisdom circle in which a meeting of the various parts of the self is taking place. Of course, each person's inner circle has a personal configuration. Holistic discernment requires us to pay careful attention to the dynamics of our inner deliberation.

- Are all the legitimate representatives of the self given a respected place and a fair say in the meeting? Which parts are typically left out and need to be invited to participate?
- Which part(s) typically exercises power and control?
- Which part(s) typically experiences difficulty in being heard and respected?
- Is any part given to monopolizing and dominating the conversation?
- How is the guidance of divine Wisdom typically made known in our inner wisdom circle?

In this inner dialogue or conversation among the various aspects of the self, it is important that each part of the plural self feels that it has had its say and has been understood. It is also important that no one part monopolizes the discussion and tries to force its way on the self.

In a culture that worships reason and the scientific, objective mind, for example, it is critical to remember that, in the words of psychologist Carl Rogers, people are wiser than their intellects. When we face a decision, we might ask ourselves whether our feelings are being taken into account. Or do we say to ourselves: "Let's be objective; stick to the facts and keep feelings out of this"? Women's liberation has also happily liberated men. When feelings and hunches were once denigrated as merely women's intuition—not a solid basis for making decisions—everyone lost a potentially important resource. Ignoring feelings simply makes them go underground and operate outside of reasonable control, undermining the decisions in which they were given no say. On the other hand, we need to ask ourselves whether or not we allow our feelings to drown out the other voices in that inner wisdom circle. Either case—refusing to give feelings their say or letting feelings dominate—makes for poor discernment. The proper function of reflection is not the suppression of spontaneity, wants, and feelings, but rather the liberation of wants and feelings from impulsive reactions to immediate stimuli.

NOTES

1. Thomas A. Hand, *St. Augustine on Prayer* (Westminster, MD: Newman Press, 1963), 71.

2. Daniel Goleman, *Emotional Intelligence* (New York: Bantam Books, 1995), 8.

3. Ibid., 29. The research of cognitive psychologists "has resulted in models [of decision-making] which outline procedures facilitating 'well made' decisions and those which promote 'faulty' ones. In all these developments cognitive (mental) processes take center stage, while affect or emotions seem to receive attention only when they confound good decision making" (Michael J. O' Sullivan, "Trust Your Feelings, But Use Your Head: Discernment and the Psychology of Decision Making," *Studies in the Spirituality of Jesuits* [September 1990], 16).

4. C. S. Lewis, *Surprised by Joy* (Fort Washington, PA: Harvest Books, 1966), 227–28.

5. James B. Nelson, *Between Two Gardens: Reflections on Sexuality and Religious Experience* (New York: Pilgrim Press, 1983), 10.

6. Joel Kovel, *A Complete Guide to Therapy: From Psychoanalysis to Behavior Modification* (New York: Random House, 1977), 118.

7. James Simkin, "The Introduction of Gestalt," in *The Live Classroom: Innovations Through Confluent Education and Gestalt Therapy*, ed. George Brown with Thomas Yeomans and Liles Grizzard (New York: Viking Press, 1975), 39.

8. Carl Rogers, *On Becoming a Person: A Therapist's View of Psychotherapy* (Boston: Houghton Mifflin, 1961), 22–23.

9. Goleman, *Emotional Intelligence*, 55.

10. Paul Robb, "Conversion as a Human Experience," *Studies in the Spirituality of Jesuits* (May 1982), 11–12.

11. John B. Enright, "An Introduction to Gestalt Techniques" in *Gestalt Therapy Now*, ed. Joen Fagan and Irma Lee Shepherd (New York: Harper & Row, 1970), 119.

12. Ibid.

13. Making a case for a more nuanced understanding of the Ignatian rules of discernment in light of the findings and theories of social and cognitive psychologists, Michael O'Sullivan states, "Given the interaction between cognition and emotion, it becomes evident that a substantial amount of cognitive processing of information occurs in both Ignatius's First and Second Times of Choice (*Spiritual Exercises*, no. 175f.). Because of the psychological factors

involved in God-attributions, in the first time of choice it seems prudent to slow down and carefully examine the data upon which one has based the conclusion that it is 'God who has so moved and attracted one's will'" ("Trust Your Feelings," 30–31).

14. According to Ignatius, "In souls that are progressing to greater perfection, the action of the good angel is delicate, gentle, delightful. It may be compared to a drop of water penetrating a sponge. The action of the evil spirit upon such souls is violent, noisy, and disturbing. It may be compared to a drop of water falling upon a stone. In souls that are going from bad to worse, the action of the spirits mentioned above is just the reverse." The underlying rationale for Ignatius's interpretation is the principle of the opposition or similarity of these souls to the different kinds of spirits. The influence of spirits that are similar and compatible to ourselves registers in a quiet and peaceful way because we are "kindred spirits," while the influence of spirits that are dissimilar or contrary to ourselves causes disturbing and noisy commotion in us (no. 335).

15. O'Sullivan notes that "when we identify the second time of election as the 'affective' way and the third time as the 'rational' way, the discussion easily can isolate emotions from thought and thereby fail to recognize how interdependent and interactive they are." Thus, he suggests "that directors need to attend to how counselees' cognitive processes affect their feelings of consolation and desolation" ("Trust Your Feelings," 19). In other words, spiritual directors should not, according to O'Sullivan, concentrate "primarily on just the affectivity" but "would do well to pay ample attention to how people are thinking, processing information, and establishing mental procedures for their decisions" (ibid., 20).

16. See O'Sullivan for rational models of decision making based on contemporary psychological theory and their relevance to Ignatius's third time of making a choice (ibid., 27–30).

17. Ignatius provides a third scenario that can help a person trying to make a decision with the use of reasoning (no. 187). He suggests that the person imagine himself or herself standing before God on the day of judgment. From this perspective Ignatius invites the person to deliberate about what present choice he or she would most be able to validate at the time of judgment before God. In pastoral practice this Ignatian suggestion is generally avoided because of the concern that it would activate negative images of God as a harsh judge or

demanding deity, a distorted image that plagues many. Such an image of God commonly engenders a fear that contaminates the discernment process.

18. Michael J. Buckley, "Rules for the Discernment of Spirits," *The Way Supplement* 20 (Autumn 1973), 25–26.

19. William Peters, *The Spiritual Exercises of St. Ignatius: Exposition and Interpretation* (Jersey City, NJ: The Program to Adapt the Spiritual Exercises, 1967), 127.

20. Here it is important to note what O'Sullivan calls "the confirmation bias, also known as the positive-test strategy," [which] "involves searching only for positive evidence. Research has clearly demonstrated that people show a persistent bias that favors gathering information which confirms their beliefs, decisions, and conclusions, rather than challenging or refuting them" ("Trust Your Feelings," 34).

21. John Futrell, "Ignatian Discernment," *Studies in the Spirituality of Jesuits* (April 1970), 57.

22. Joseph R. Royce, *The Encapsulated Man: An Interdisciplinary Essay on the Search for Meaning* (Princeton, NJ: D. Van Nostrand, 1964), 27.

23. Paul Tillich, "You Are Accepted," in *The Shaking of the Foundations* (New York: Charles Scribner's Sons, 1948), 161–62.

24. Pierre Wolff, *Discernment: The Art of Choosing Well* (Ligouri, MO: Ligouri/Triumph, 2003). Wolff's book is a very clear and helpful guide to integrating reason and affect in a discernment process based on the Ignatian tradition.

25. Baron Friedrich von Hügel, *The Mystical Element of Religion as Studied in Saint Catherine of Genoa and Her Friends*, 2 vols. (London: J. M. Dent & Sons, 1902).

26. Ibid., 1, 51.

27. Ibid., 52.

28. Ibid.

29. Ibid., 53.

30. Ibid., 61.

31. Ibid., 54.

32. Ibid., 2, 387.

33. Ibid., 287–88.

34. Ibid., 389.

35. Marcus Borg, *The Heart of Christianity: Rediscovering a Life of Faith* (New York: HarperCollins, 2004), 2, 15.

What Discernment Means

Suzanne Zuercher, OSB

From *Enneagram Spirituality: From Compulsion to Contemplation*, 1991

Sometimes genuine discernment is wrongly seen as a mental decision about what is good followed by an act of will to carry out that good. I would say, rather, that discernment is the awareness of centered or not-centered energy in the organism.[1]

This awareness comes from an accumulated awareness of who we fully and genuinely are. It is knowing where our center—and hence our life—resides, as well as where it does not. It assumes experience has revealed how and where we flee in efforts to control life, to be our own god. It unmasks those dynamics by which we exaggerated perception or feeling or activity because they were instinctive to us. Discernment also lays open the parts we had to bury to maintain this false picture of ourselves.

As life builds up more and more sense of our total selves, more and more inclusion of body, mind, and emotion in our self-experience, it becomes less and less possible for us to choose against ourselves. We become less influenced by the fear that caused us to resist growing and developing into the persons we were meant to be. We come to accept ourselves and to know the Divine experientially, and this experience invites us again and again into life/Life. Discernment necessitates a decision to flow with life or to resist it. We can either pull away from our true center and up to that exaggerated center we have used as a basis for defining who we think we ought to be, or else we can relax trustingly and let life lead. The choice is ours.

But life becomes increasingly irresistible. It becomes harder and harder in the second part of our lives to violate our own selves, our very word, because we have learned how self-violation feels and how self-regard and self-dignity are preferable to it. When we learn to discern our genuine experience of being off-center and on-center, we grow increasingly aware of what it means to live. Once one has "seen God," the scriptures say, one finds God nearly impossible to resist. Life, "godliness," is so desirable that it takes immense energy to hold it off.

Discernment well-made—that is, experience well-known—makes choice natural, even easy. Choice is that decision either to retain boundaries of judgment manifested by blocked body energies or to risk letting in everything we are. When we can accept what we previously denied, we move beyond the fear of dying and into the dark and mysterious experience of living. In doing so we abandon predictions of how life will turn out, judgments of what is good or bad, assessments of what does or doesn't fit. We simply live from our center.

Now becomes the acceptable time, the day of salvation. We learn to live there more and more, not because it is law or rule or duty to grow in awareness, to have a more contemplative attitude, but because it gives us a sense of wholeness and centeredness, of living from the self. At this place of self, our true center of balance, we find our life/Life.

God is no longer in our past experience, helpful as it may have been along the way to remember life there. Nor is God in our plans and visions for the future, because there is nothing of future life we can predict, let alone experience. We are only creatures in time who meet reality moment by moment. We only have the poverty and emptiness—and fullness as well—of the present.

Our entire organism feels content with what is, like a weaned child is content, as the psalmist says, on its mother's lap (Psalm 131). We live as relaxed as that child, and we are nourished by the Divine

Mother at the center of who we are, body and spirit, incarnate being, human organism.

NOTES

1. Roberto Assagioli speaks about "the energized I" and discusses the qualities of the person who is in touch with this flow of energy (*The Act of Will*). I am especially indebted to Roger Evans of the London Psychosynthesis Institute for clarifying Assagioli's theories during a workshop sponsored by the Canadian Psychosynthesis Institute in 1978. Both Assagioli's and Evans's presentations appear consonant with the theory of discernment described by St. Ignatius Loyola in his *Spiritual Exercises*.

Further Reading

The German Jesuit Karl Rahner, the great Catholic theologian of the twentieth century, wrote a modern classic in his treatment of discernment: "The Logic of Concrete Individual Knowledge in Ignatius Loyola" (*The Dynamic Element in the Church* [New York: Herder & Herder, 1964], 84–170). As his title suggests, Rahner is concerned most of all with defining and carving out a place among types of human knowing for the special kind of knowing involved in discernment. First of all, such knowing is not merely the application of general moral norms to specific instances—as it were, a kind of deduction. Rather, Rahner positively teaches that people can come to know a right—or even better—course of action for themselves in all their particulars of personal history, personality, and present circumstances. In greater matters, such a discernment process amounts to the hearing of a personal and unique call or invitation from God. Avery Dulles, SJ, provides a clear summary of this difficult Rahner essay in "Finding God's Will" (*Woodstock Letters* [Spring 1965],139–52; the journal can be found in many a Jesuit university library). The late Christian ethicist William Spohn finds some limitations in Rahner's presentation and supplements it with insights from H. Richard Niebuhr and Jonathan Edwards, among others ("The Reasoning Heart: An American Approach to Christian Discernment," *Theological Studies* 44 [1983], 30–52).

Another classic on discernment is the article "Discernement des esprits" in volume 3 of the *Dictionnaire de Spiritualité d'Ascetique et de Mystique* (Paris: Beauchesne et Ses Fils, 1957). It has been published as a separate monograph in English entitled *Discernment of Spirits* by Jacques Guillet and others (Collegeville, MN: Liturgical Press, 1970). Though long out of print, it also can be found in many a (Jesuit) university library.

More recent, Dean Brackley's fine, concrete treatment of discernment is spread out over a number of chapters in *The Call to Discernment in Troubled Times*, namely, chapter 6 (the last chapter dealing with First Week material) and chapters 14–17 (together entitled "Discerning and Deciding").

Several years after publishing the chapter on discernment included in this reader, David Lonsdale wrote an entire little book on discernment: *Listening to the Music of the Spirit: The Art of Discernment* (Notre Dame, IN: Ave Maria Press, 1993). German Jesuit Stefan Kiechle, currently director of novices (young Jesuits in the first two years of spiritual formation), makes frequent use of concrete details— "cases"—in expounding *The Art of Discernment: Making Good Decisions in Your World of Choices* (Notre Dame, IN: Ave Maria Press, 2005). An older contribution, a classic still in print, is *Weeds among the Wheat: Discernment, Where Prayer and Action Meet* (Notre Dame, IN: Ave Maria Press, 1984) by Thomas H. Green, a New York Jesuit who has spent most of his life in the Philippines.

For commentary on Ignatius's "Rules for Discernment, I & II," in the book of the *Exercises*, see Michael Ivens' *Understanding the Spiritual Exercises*, mentioned previously in the section on the Exercises; *A Commentary on Saint Ignatius's Rules for the Discernment of Spirits: A Guide to the Principles and Practice*, by Jules Toner, SJ (St. Louis: Institute of Jesuit Sources, 1982); and Toner's *Spirit of Light or Darkness: A Casebook for Studying Discernment of Spirits* (St. Louis: Institute of Jesuit Sources, 1995).

Even more accessible and thorough commentary on the Rules can be found in two volumes by Timothy Gallagher, OMV: *The Discernment of Spirits: An Ignatian Guide for Everyday Living* (New York: Crossroad, 2005) and *Spiritual Consolation: An Ignatian Guide for the Greater Discernment of Spirits* (New York: Crossroad, 2007). The first volume deals with Rules for the First Week of the Exercises, the second with Rules for the Second Week (for people who have a more developed spiritual life). In both volumes, Gallagher uses an effective combination of lucid commentary on the Ignatian text and concrete examples ("cases"); the commentary and the examples illuminate each other. Gallagher's goal, he says, is to facilitate "the spiritual liberation to which [Ignatius's instruction on discernment] leads." The second volume concludes with a four-page bibliography of most of the important work done on Ignatian discernment—not only in English but also in Spanish, French, and German (some of the best studies on the subject are not in English). Gallagher is both a judicious scholar and a fine teacher.

Among all these suggestions, my highest recommendation goes to the entire book by Wilkie and Noreen Au, *The Discerning Heart: Exploring the Christian Path* (New York: Paulist Press, 2006), from which the fourth reading in this discernment section was taken. The book was awarded first place in the Pastoral Ministry category for 2007 by the Catholic Press Association of the United States and Canada.

The treatment here of Ignatius and Ignatian spirituality is now complete, but before moving on to the final section ("Theology to Support the Spirituality"), I want to mention three studies that come at our subject from the perspective of other disciplines: German Jesuit Willi Lambert's *Directions for Communication: Discoveries with Ignatius Loyola* (New York: Crossroad, 2000); former Jesuit and former J. P. Morgan executive Chris Lowney's *Heroic Leadership: Best Practices from a 450-Year-Old Company That Changed the World* (Chicago: Loyola Press, 2003); and Jesuit psychiatrist W. W. Meissner's *To the Greater Glory: A Psychological Study of Ignatian Spirituality* (Milwaukee: Marquette University Press, 1998). As his title suggests, Lambert looks at Ignatius and Ignatian spirituality from the point of view of communication theory and practice, Lowney from that of management and personal leadership, and Meissner from psychology. These other perspectives lead to new insights and fascinating interpretations of the Ignatian material.

Theology to
Support the
Spirituality

Introduction

The single reading in this section—"Living Conversation: Higher Education in a Catholic Context"—was originally delivered by Boston College theologian Michael Himes, a diocesan priest, to all six gatherings in round one of the "Western Conversations," meetings of faculty from the six Western Jesuit universities, with each school hosting one meeting. In readily accessible language for which Himes is justly famous, he lays out a theology of God (e.g., the least inadequate way to talk about God is as "the activity of loving," as "pure and perfect self-giving"), a broad sacramental theology ("sacramentality"), an explanation of the Incarnation (God's becoming human in Jesus), and its astounding implication ("whatever makes you more human makes you more like God"). And he explores belonging to a living tradition, to a continuing conversation, that is inclusive, that cuts across time and place ("you are freed from being merely a child of your [own] time and place"), and that engages in action toward social justice and reflection on that action (loving others as the only way to know God). Here, in a few short pages, is a compendium of theology and spirituality.

Understanding the Terminology:
Suggested Readings from *Do You Speak Ignatian?*

- God
- Jesus
- Gospel

Living Conversation:
Higher Education in a
Catholic Context

Michael Himes

From *Conversations on Jesuit Higher Education*, 1995

I intend first to lay a theological foundation for what I'm going to say and then to build upon it four points that I consider to be very important for people engaged in higher education within a Catholic context to consider.

The Foundation

I'm convinced that any theology that pretends to be Christian must show its rootedness in two central doctrines: the Trinity and the Incarnation. If what a theologian says cannot be shown to be rooted in these two doctrines, it may be very interesting, valuable, and true, but it is not Christian theology. Anything claiming to be Christian theology must necessarily relate to those two doctrines.

To begin, what do we mean within the Christian tradition by the word *God*? *God* is not anyone's name. There is not some person out there someplace, much older, much wiser, much more powerful than you or I whose name is *God*. God is not the name of a class of which there happens to be only one member.

The word *God* is a bit of shorthand, a stand-in which functions in Christian theology almost as *x* functions in algebra. When working an algebraic problem, one's central concern is *x*. But *x* is the stand-in for the thing one doesn't know. That is how God functions in Christian theology. It is the name of the Mystery that lies at the root of all that exists. We must never forget that we are talking about mystery. That is a salutary reminder, by the way, for anybody doing theology, since our temptation is to natter on as though we know what we're talking about.

Now, we must be clear about what I mean by Mystery. I do not mean the mystery in Agatha Christie, the *Murder, She Wrote* sense of the word. I am not talking about mystery as a puzzle for which we do not have all the pieces but which, if we could find all the clues and juggle them into the right order, would click into place. Then we would know that the butler did it, and the mystery would be solved. No, the Mystery that I mean is much more like asking you who you are.

Who are you? That's a very puzzling question, because as we all know (on excellent authority) "a rose by any other name would still smell as sweet." So when I ask who you are, I'm not asking you for your name. I'm not asking when or where you were born, who your parents are, whom you are married to, where you went to school, what you do, or where you live. That is all description, and I'm not asking for a description but for a definition. And the definition I want is not that of a *human being* but of *you*.

Who are *you*? And of course, the more one thinks about it, the more one discovers that one does not have an adequate answer. Indeed, most of the questions for which we do have adequate answers are relatively trivial. When we come to the great questions, the central concerns of our lives, we find that we are at a loss to answer them fully and finally. I mean questions such as *why* you married the person you married. You might well reply that it was because he or she is good, kind, loving, patient, and a host of other wonderful things. But here, I retort, are 356,812 good, kind, loving, patient, *et cetera*, people. Why did you choose this one rather than one of these others? It is very difficult to say *this* is the reason, isn't it?

I am frequently asked why I became a priest. And my standard answer is that to dig I am not able and to beg I am ashamed. In fact, I can't give an answer to that question. Certainly there is nothing more important in my own life than my decision to be ordained, but I cannot tell you with any definiteness why I made that decision. Was it twelve percent my mother's influence, ten percent my father's, seventeen percent the time and place that I was born, eight percent the example of this pastor, six percent the work of that teacher? I don't know. In fact, I'm still uncovering the reasons why I am a priest.

What I am aiming at is a Mystery that is mysterious not because it is so distant that it is hard to draw an angle on it, so remote that we cannot get the data needed. If you are as nearsighted as I am, you will understand at once that something can be impossible for me to read if it is too far away from me. Without my eyeglasses, everything from the elbow out vanishes into the mist. But something may also be unreadable if it is held too close. If I bring a book up to my nose, the print is as unreadable as if it were at arm's length. And the Mystery I mean is rather like that. It is mysterious because it is too close, too intimate, too central to us. It is in this sense that God is Mystery. God is Mystery as you and I are mysteries.

Having heard that, you may well say to yourself, "Well, if that's so, that God is Mystery and therefore you cannot finally speak about God, then sit down and shut up, Himes!" But, like any great religious tradition, the Christian tradition does think that, while it cannot say everything about Mystery, it can say something, even if falteringly. And what is it that the Christian tradition claims about the absolute Mystery that we call "God"? What is the fundamental metaphor that Christianity offers as the least wrong way to talk about God? I say "the least wrong way" because there is no absolutely right way. The least wrong way to imagine God, the Christian tradition says, is to think of God as love. The New Testament documents repeat this over and over again in parable and preaching, but it is said most forthrightly in one of its very late documents, the one we call the First Letter of John. In chapter 4, verse 8 and again in verse 16, we read that "God is love," but a very particular kind of love, for the word chosen in the Greek text is *agape*. It is not *eros*, which is a love that seeks fulfillment in that which is loved, nor *philia*, which is companionable love or friendship. *Agape* is a purely other-directed love, a love that seeks no response and demands no return, a love centered totally on the beloved. Because the English word *love* carries so many meanings, I prefer to translate *agape* as "self-gift," the gift of oneself to the other without any regard to whether the gift is accepted or returned. And the First Letter of John maintains that God is self-gift. Now I could demonstrate at length that this metaphor is fundamental to the New Testament; I could cite text after text, example after example, to show that it appears again and again in the core documents of the Christian tradition, even if not as succinctly as in 1 John 4:8 and 16. But for brevity's sake, I ask you to accept that *agape* is the fundamental Christian metaphor for the Mystery that is God.

Let me point out something very odd about that fundamental metaphor. Notice the First Letter of John does not say that God is a lover. It does not claim that the least wrong way to think about God is as one who loves. Rather, it says that God is love. Love, however, is not the name of a person or an agent, but of a relationship. It is more like an action than an agent. In other words, within the Christian tradition, the word *God* is really more of a verb than a noun, the name of something one does rather than of someone who does. It is the name of a relationship.

"Ah," you say, "we've been willing to listen to you this far, Himes, but what are we to make of this silliness about God being a relationship?" Well, as it happens, Christianity has made this claim again and again. The problem is that most of the time we don't take it seriously. That, alas, is too often the case with religious claims that we repeat again and again, especially religious statements about absolute Mystery and most especially religious statements that we address to absolute Mystery in prayer. Indeed, if we stopped to listen to some of the things that we say when we pray, we might cease to pray at all because we would find ourselves unsure of what our words mean. One of the things that we say in prayer most often is that what we are about to do is done "in the name of the Father and of the Son and of the Holy Spirit." There you have it: we are talking about a relational God, not the One but the relatedness of the Three. That is what we mean by the doctrine of the Trinity. I think I can say, without too great an exaggeration, that the entire doctrine of the Trinity is an enormous gloss on that phrase in the First Letter of John that God is self-gift. From that metaphor spins out the whole of Trinitarian theology.

Unfortunately, most of us don't take the Trinity terribly seriously. For most Christians, including most Catholics, the doctrine of the Trinity functions as a sort of divine test of faith, as though God were saying, "I'll tell them I'm one God in three Persons, and if they can believe that, they can believe anything." The Trinity doesn't make much *difference* to people. I have often remarked to students that if I and my fellow preachers mounted our pulpits some Sunday and announced that we had a letter from the Vatican saying that there are not three Persons but four, most people in the pews would simply groan, "Oh, when will these changes stop?" But to most of them it would cause no problem other than having to think about how to fit the fourth one in when making the sign of the cross. And that is a tragedy, for we are dealing with the deepest claim that Christianity offers about the Mystery that undergirds our existence, that is least wrongly named as the relationship of self-gift. That claim shifts everything. It is a unique way of thinking about reality. What we say about the Trinity affects the way we live marriage, raise children, choose professions, spend money, vote, and, I hope, teach. You have noticed, I am sure, that the Trinity is not an item in the creed but rather the basic form of the creed. We do not say that we believe in the Trinity along with a number of other doctrines. Instead, we say that we believe in the doctrines of Christianity in terms of the Trinity: "We believe in one God the Father who . . . ," and then we profess faith in the doctrines of creation and providence, "and in the Son who . . . ," and then we proclaim the Incarnation and redemption, "and in the Holy Spirit who . . . ," and then we affirm the Church, the sacraments, and the eschatological doctrines. We never actually say that we believe in the Trinity. The Trinity is not a doctrine next to other doctrines of the faith; it is the *only* doctrine, and all the others are expansions and explanations of it. The Trinity, which is the unfolding of the fundamental Christian metaphor that God is self-gift, is the clue to everything.

If that is true, then it is also the answer to that whopping good question that students seem so often to ask and that Martin Heidegger maintained was the origin of metaphysics: why is there being rather than nothing? The Christian response to that question is based on its fundamental claim about the Mystery that lies at the heart of all that exists. Christianity answers that the reason that there is something rather than nothing is that it is loved. All that exists is loved into being. All that exists, *everything* as well as *everyone*—you and I, the chair you're sitting on, the pen you're holding, the podium that I'm standing at, your pet cat, the farthest supernova, and the rhododendron outside the window—all that exists is loved *absolutely*.

Why absolutely? Because that, you see, is how God does things. God being God does not do things partially. What God does, God does *as God*, which means absolutely. Everything that is loved by God—and that is everything there is—is loved totally, completely, perfectly, absolutely. And that is why it exists. Not to be loved by God is not to be damned; it is simply not to be. The opposite of being loved by God is not damnation; it is nonexistence. Saint Thomas Aquinas (always a good source for a Catholic theologian to trot out) raised the question: if God is everywhere, is God in hell? His answer is, yes, God is in hell. Then, with his usual rigor, Thomas asks the next question: what is God doing in hell? And he replies that God is in hell loving the damned. The damned may refuse to be loved and they may refuse to love in response, but the damned cannot cause God not to love them; they cannot make God be not God. They exist because they are loved and loved absolutely.

One way I like to put this is that from God's "point of view" there is no difference between Mary and Satan. God loves both perfectly. The difference is that Mary is thrilled and Satan hates it. From God's perspective, everything is loved. As chapter one of Genesis insistently tells us, "God looked at it and saw that it was good."

Now, there is a traditional theological name for this "agapic" love that undergirds all that exists, a name for the self-gift of God outside the Trinity: *grace*. Grace is the love of God beyond the Trinity. To quote the most important Catholic theologian of the twentieth century, Karl Rahner, there is "grace at the roots of the world." The universe is rooted in grace. It exists because it is loved absolutely.

Sacramentality

The first point that I wish to draw from the claim that everything exists because it is engraced is that to appreciate anything in its depth is to see it as revelatory of grace. Illustrating this, there is a wonderful story told of Teresa of Ávila, the great sixteenth-century Spanish mystic and reformer. The story is, I must admit, probably apocryphal [doubtfully authentic], but a good story is a good story nonetheless. The tale is that, later in her life, Teresa was seated in the courtyard of one of the monasteries she had reformed with a group of younger women gathered around her. They were asking her questions about prayer. One of these younger nuns said, "Mother, you have written so much and so powerfully about contemplation and I simply do not understand it." What, she asked, was she supposed to be contemplating—a verse from the scripture, an incident in the life of Jesus, a mental image, a statue, or picture? Teresa picked up a brown and withered leaf that had fallen from a tree in the courtyard and replied, "If you really knew what it meant to say this leaf exists, you could contemplate it for eternity." Truly to know what it means to say something exists—because there is no intrinsic reason for its being, because it is held in being at this instant by the perfect love of God for it—is to encounter a miracle that can be contemplated eternally.

This is a very powerful claim, and Catholic theology has a name for it: sacramentality. I am not now speaking of the seven great sacraments acknowledged and publicly celebrated by the Christian community. Those are powerful communal sacramental moments. But I am speaking now about sacramentality on a wider and deeper level, one that encompasses but is not exhausted by those seven communal sacraments. For anything—any person, place, thing, event, any sight, sound, taste, touch, smell—anything that exists *can* be sacramental *if* one views it in its rootedness in the grace of God. So, how many sacraments are there? How many things are there in the universe?

Here I must quote a great Jesuit poet, in his sensibility Catholic to his fingertips, Gerard Manley Hopkins. One of his most frequently anthologized poems is "Hurrahing in Harvest." Thinking about the changing of the seasons, Hopkins realizes that he had not truly observed the natural glory around him. In the next to the last line of the poem he writes, "These things / These things were here and but the beholder wanting." I don't know a better and certainly not a more beautiful statement of the Catholic ideal of sacramentality than that. Grace is here. What is needed is someone to see it. What is wanted is the beholder.

The entirety of Catholic liturgical life—indeed, of Catholic spiritual, intellectual, and ethical life—is geared toward producing sacramental beholders, people who see what is there in its full depth. That should sound familiar to educators. Is it not true in every field, whether we teach philosophy or chemistry, literature or finance, that we strive to lead people to see what is there to be seen? I am suggesting that the Catholic sacramental principle supports this with the conviction that what is there to be seen in its depth is grace. Consequently, to teach any discipline or field is a holy activity. All teaching can produce sacramental beholders, even when the teachers do not know that this is what they are doing. And I suggest to you that sacramental beholders are what Catholic universities and colleges are supposed to be producing.

Before I move on to my second point, I must clarify this statement about Catholic education with the help of one of the most remarkable Catholic intellects of this century, Frederick von Hügel. Von Hügel, who despite his Austrian name was an Englishman, was invited to address a group of religiously interested students at Oxford in 1902. In the course of his talk, he referred to the person whom he regarded as the most extraordinary example of asceticism in the century that had just ended. It must have startled his hearers to learn that von Hügel's example of asceticism, which most of them undoubtedly associated with fasting, penitential discipline, and mortification, was

Charles Darwin. And why Darwin, o[f] all people? Because, Baron von Hügel said, Darwin had been willing to submit his wonderful intellectual powers and his great energy over a long period of time to the patient and painstaking observation of the development of barnacles, to the shapes of pigeons' beaks, and the varieties of organisms. For asceticism is not about self-punishment; it is the gradual stripping away of the self so that one can see what is there. Not to see what one would like to be there, or what one hopes is there or fears is there, or what one has been told by others is there, but to see what is, in fact, there. My favorite way of putting this is that asceticism is learning not to look in the mirror long enough that one might begin to look out the window. That is, we stop seeing what we would like the world to be or fear the world to be and see instead what the world is. That is why Baron von Hügel thought that religious people ought to take Darwin as their example of ascetical practice: to learn the discipline of submitting themselves to reality.

If this is so, then it is impossible to educate people in the sciences without training them in asceticism. Most scientists, I suspect, do not see themselves as ascetics. But if they are any good as scientists, they are. And scientific asceticism is a necessary training for sacramental beholding, for seeing what is there in its fullness and depth.

Whatever Humanizes, Divinizes

The Christian tradition claims that absolute *agape* (which is the least wrong way to think about the Mystery that we name God) is fully, perfectly expressed in human terms in the life, death, and destiny of one particular person, Jesus of Nazareth. We call this claim the Incarnation. In the Incarnation, absolute *agape* has taken flesh and walked among us. In the life, death, and destiny of Jesus, we see what perfect *agape* looks like in human terms. I cannot overemphasize how important this is to the whole Catholic intellectual tradition because in it we maintain that, if one takes the Incarnation seriously, God, the absolute Mystery, does not act human or pretend to be human or take on some aspects of humanity; rather, we maintain that the absolute Mystery is human.

Indeed, I doubt that this has ever been given more radical expression than in what is quite possibly (as far as we know) the earliest expression of the Christian faith. In St. Paul's letter to the Church at Philippi, chapter 2, he quotes a hymn. Now, recall that Paul's letters predate the gospels and that in this instance Paul seems to be citing a hymn that predates his letter. Thus it may very well be the first expression of the Christian faith which we still have. The hymn at the point at which Paul begins to quote it (Phil. 2:6–7), says, "Although he [the eternal Logos] was in the form of God he did not think being equivalent to God was anything to be held onto, so he emptied himself taking on the form of a servant and becoming like all other human beings." That is unquestionably the most radical statement of the dignity of the human person that has ever been made.

Notice: the Christian tradition does not say human beings are of such immense dignity that God really loves them. It does not say that human beings are of such dignity that God has a magnificent destiny in store for them. Nor does it say alone that human beings are of such dignity that they have been fashioned in the image and likeness of God. No, the Christian tradition says something far more radical; human beings are of such dignity that God has chosen to be one. God does not think being God is anything to be grasped; God empties himself and becomes human like all other human beings.

That statement opens up the truth of the observation made by G. K. Chesterton, that if one truly understands Christianity, only one good reason exists for not being a Christian: it is too good to be true. And sometimes to be sure it does seem difficult to believe that human beings are as important as Christianity insists that they are. If one makes this claim of the Incarnation—and it is one whopping great claim to make—then this principle inevitably follows: whatever humanizes divinizes. That is to say, whatever makes you more genuinely human, more authentically, richly, powerfully human, whatever calls into play all the reaches of your intellect, your freedom, energy, your talents and creativity, makes you more like God. This is how we encounter God in our incarnational tradition: not "out there" somewhere, but here being human along with us. Whatever makes you more human makes you more like God.

If one accepts this, it becomes perfectly obvious why Christianity had to give rise to universities in the Middle Ages. How could it not? It is perfectly obvious why Christians had to be concerned about health care, about feeding and clothing and housing people, and, of course, about educating people. Because in reverencing humanity we reverence what unites us with God. Whatever makes us more richly human makes us more like God.

Let me give a remarkable example of this from the second century, an example made more remarkable because it is so early in Christianity's history. In his *Dialogue with Trypho*, Justin Martyr describes Christianity as living in accord with the Logos—the Word, which he identified with the Word of which the Fourth Gospel spoke in its prologue: "In the beginning was the Word." We Christians, Justin says, live in accord with the Logos, we are "logical." Therefore, Justin maintains, anyone who is "logical" is, in some sense, Christian, whether or not he or she ever claims that title. Thus, he can write, not only were Abraham and Moses and Elijah Christians because they lived "logically," so too were Socrates and Plato and Pythagoras. Isn't that astonishing? By the middle of the second century, a mere hundred years after Paul wrote, Justin already lays claim to the whole of classical antiquity as being Christian at its best and wisest. How? Because anything that makes you more genuinely human makes you more like God. So, if philosophy makes you more human, then it is logical and, therefore, Christian. Extraordinary! Saint Thomas Aquinas described theology as *sacra doctrina*, a "sacred" science. And so of course it is. But so too, in the deepest sense, are biology and economics, history and literature and chemistry. For whatever expands the mind opens the imagination, frees the will, enlarges our capacities as human beings, makes us more like God. And if *that* is not what makes a *doctrina* to be *sacra*, I don't know what does. Whatever humanizes divinizes.

In passing, let me advance here a strong claim. I do not hesitate to tell undergraduate students in my theology courses that I am perfectly aware that many of them are at Boston College because they want to study chemistry or business and that they find themselves studying theology and wondering, "why in God's name am I studying this junk?" But, I remind them, Catholic universities need not justify the teaching of theology nor the requirement that all students study it. We're not the new kids on the block. We've been around since Salamanca and Paris and Oxford. The schools that don't require theology—they're the newcomers. They're the ones who have to justify themselves. They've only been around for two hundred years. Those of us who have been around for a millennium wonder how one can pretend to talk about the ultimate issues engaged in human experience and *not* deal with theology. We wonder how anyone can imagine that students can be introduced to the history of the Western world and not talk about the great religious issues, images, ideas, and symbols that have motivated the Jewish, Christian, and, in large part, Islamic communities for the last thousand years. It does seem to be rather like saying, "We run a fine university here, but we don't teach physics." Well, then, there is one whopping great hole in your curriculum. And the same is true if you don't teach theology. Catholic universities have nothing to be embarrassed about in proclaiming our religious affiliation. But other universities have a lot of explaining to do.

The Continuing Conversation

What enables someone to become more fully, richly human? Hanging out with human beings. You recall Aristotle's discussion in the *Nicomachean Ethics* of virtue as lying between two vices? Thus, generosity is midway between prodigality and miserliness, courage midway between rashness and cowardice. But if that is where virtue is to be found, then Aristotle obviously is confronted with a problem, namely, if all these good qualities are found in this "golden mean," what is the virtue that enables a person to find that midpoint and how is that virtue acquired? Aristotle suggests that this virtue is prudence. But, of course, one cannot say that prudence is found by locating the point midway between two vices, because that begs the question. Aristotle's solution is wonderful. It is, "Find a prudent person and hang out with that person." The way to find the virtue that enables you to determine other virtues is by living with virtuous people. To become virtuous, live among the virtuous and imitate what they do. And I suggest that the way to become authentically human is to live among the authentically human.

But how is that done? Let me refer once more to G. K. Chesterton. On one of the many occasions when he was asked why he had become a Catholic, Chesterton replied that he became a Catholic because Catholicism is a community with a deep and rich sense of tradition. And, he said, belonging to a community with such a sense of tradition is extremely important because only then can one be freed from the most degrading of all forms of servitude—that of being merely a child of one's time. That is, I think, immensely wise. Being part of a tradition means that you do not have to speak with North Americans alone; you can speak with South Americans and Africans and Europeans and Asians and Australians. It also means that you are not confined to speaking only with late-twentieth-century people; you can speak with Plato and Emily Dickinson and Mozart and Teresa of Ávila. You can speak with Dante and Madame Curie, with Newton and Euclid and Jane Austen. You can talk with all sorts of people who are not of your own age and clime. You are freed from being merely a child of your time and place. In the Catholic tradition, we call this the communion of saints. That communion or conversation has been going on for a very long time—and you and I are invited to participate in it.

Let me share with you my favorite image of teaching. (I teach theology, but the image applies as well for any field, I think, in the sciences or humanities.) One of the sorriest inventions of the twentieth century is the cocktail party. There are three elements to a good party: eating, drinking, and talking. At a cocktail party, one can't do any of them effectively. Trying to converse while balancing a glass and a little plate of canapés—it is the antithesis of a good party. But for purposes of my image, put aside the quite understandable complaints about the form, and imagine yourself arriving at a large cocktail party. There you are at the door of a room in which hundreds of people are milling about. You are wondering how you can possibly enter into this sea of humanity. And then over to you comes the host or hostess whom you will never forget and says, "Wonderful to see you! So glad you could come! Now let me introduce you to so-and-so, a very interesting person who is involved in such-and-such. And here's someone else, the well-known whatever. And this is yet a third who has recently been engaged in . . ." And after you have begun to talk with enough people who lead you to still others, the host or hostess can leave you to make your own progress deeper and deeper into the crowd and can return to the door to begin introducing someone else. Well, it seems to me that teachers are the hosts and hostesses at what is at this point a four-thousand-year-old cocktail party. Students are the newcomers standing at the door wondering how to begin the conversation, and we are the ones who take them by the arm and say, "Wonderful to see you! Let me introduce you! Here's Socrates—fascinating fellow, you're going to love Socrates. And this Shakespeare—what a character! And Einstein—great with numbers! And Emily Brontë! And Bach! And Kant! And Augustine! And . . ." We introduce people into an enormously immense conversation with people of different places and extraordinarily different times. One of the richest elements in the Catholic intellectual tradition is its notion of the communion of saints, and within the Jesuit educational tradition one of the richest elements is the insistence on engaging in a trans-temporal as well as a trans-spatial conversation. Our students desperately need such traditions so that they are not limited to their own contemporaries for companionship. This is a very important issue for those of us who teach in those traditions to consider: how do we introduce people into a living tradition, whether within the sciences or the humanities (and, I hope, both)?

Social Activism and Reflection

I am inclined to think that one of the wisest principles of education that I have ever come across is what William James used to tell his students at Harvard at the beginning of this century. He called it "the pragmatic principle." As James summed it up, the pragmatic principle is, "if it's true, it makes a difference; if it makes no difference, it's not true." Every term I urge my students to make that the measuring-rod of everything I say, they say, or we read together in the courses I teach. If, for example, you can't possibly imagine what difference it makes that God is triune, that is, if it makes no difference to anyone, anywhere, anywhen (as James liked to put it), then effectively it is not true. One has to be able to see or, at least, to imagine, what difference any statement makes in order to declare that statement true. This pragmatic principle, I suggest, is bred into Americans; we get it with our mother's milk. And therefore it must be taken with great serious-ness in the Catholic intellectual tradition as that tradition is lived out in this country. Thus, we cannot allow the formation of future intellec-tuals (and whom else are we teaching?) within the Catholic tradition to remain simply theoretical. For what we say to be seen as true, our students must see the concrete difference that our statements make. They must test out what we teach them. What we say to them about the value and dignity of human life must be experienced by them as making a difference in fact to someone, somewhere, somewhen. And it is certainly not enough for us to say, "Oh, well, there is the Jesuit Volunteer Corps, and there are various summer service projects in which the students can go off and do all sorts of swell things for others." We cannot allow that divorce between the lecture-hall and their concrete experience. When students return to our campuses, they must find opportunities—and not in a few isolated courses—to reflect critically and, if at all possible, in a multidisciplinary way, on their experiences in service and in other cultures. We cannot permit ourselves or them the mistake of thinking that "out there you *do*, in here we *think*." Here we think about what is done there. We must lead them into critical thinking about their experience. And we should do all in our power to make certain that engagement in service for social justice is not limited to a few students or simply to those who choose to involve themselves in it. Indeed, those who do not choose it are most often precisely those who need it most.

Why is it so important? There are many reasons, but let me offer one that matters especially to a theologian. It has to do with what, with all due respect to Saint Anselm and Saint Thomas Aquinas, is the only effective proof for the existence of God that I know. There are many proofs for an "Unmoved Mover" or an "Uncaused Cause," but that has nothing to do with the God who is least wrongly understood as pure and perfect self-gift. The proof of which I am thinking is found in Dostoevsky's *The Brothers Karamazov*. Fairly early in the novel, Dostoevsky presents us with a series of conservations with Father Zosima, the wise and holy monk whose words continue to echo in the book long after he has died. The last of these conservations is with "a woman without faith." An obviously distraught woman approaches Zosima to request his assistance with a problem that she says is destroying her. We quickly find out that she is in good health, prosperous, and seemingly untroubled in any obvious way. But she insists that something horrible has happened to her and that her whole life is being drained of meaning and purpose. She goes so far as to tell the monk that if he cannot help her, she thinks she will kill herself. She explains that, at some point—she doesn't know how, for there was no great crisis—she ceased to believe in God. It happened bit by bit, and she herself was shocked to realize that she no longer believed. Now everything is colorless, tasteless, to her. Everything has become ashes. She says, quoting Pushkin, nothing is real, save the weeds that grow on her grave. Zosima tells her that what she is experiencing is the worst thing that can happen to a human being, and that he thinks he can help her. She must go home and every day, without fail, in the most concrete and practical way possible, she must love the people around her. If she does that, Zosima says, then bit by bit she will come to the point at which she cannot but believe in God. "This way," he says, "has been tried; this way is certain."

The whole of the novel is a commentary on this scene, a huge debate about Zosima's tried and certain way. I think that Dostoevsky is right: the only workable proof for the existence of God is an experience, and that experience arises out of daily concrete and practical love for those around us.

After all, long ago, we were told by the author of the First Letter of John that anyone claiming to love God, whom he cannot see, while not loving the brother or sister whom he does see is a liar

(1 John 4:20). Not a liar in the sense of one who deliberately and knowing tells an untruth, but rather one who speaks falsely because he doesn't know what he's talking about. He cannot know what the word *God* means because God is *agape*, pure and perfect self-giving love. If that is the least wrong way to think about God, then one cannot know who God is—and therefore *that* God is—if one never knows agapic love. After all, to compare absolute Mystery to self-giving love isn't very helpful if one has no clue what self-giving love is. Comparing the Unknown to the unknown isn't very helpful. One must have the concrete experience of *agape* to understand who God is and, more importantly, to experience that God is. And if belief in the existence of God—which is, among other things, affirmation of purpose and meaning in life—is central to one's existence as a fully human being (and I cannot imagine how the question whether there is purpose and meaning in life is not), and if education is not merely vocational training but the development of a fully human being, and further, if the tried and certain way to belief in God is concrete and practical love of others, then direct engagement in social justice and service to others is crucial to our students and to our task as their teachers. Not just an important auxiliary—*crucial*. We cannot introduce others into the Catholic intellectual tradition without it.

And so there, in what I fear is absurdly too small a space, are the key issues that I suggest to you as hallmarks of education in a Catholic and more especially a Jesuit context: sacramentality, humanization as divinization, introduction into a living conversation that transcends time and space, and an insistence on social action and reflection upon the action. That is what we have to give to our students. To borrow a phrase from the greatest teacher of Christianity, "Do this and you will be perfect."

Further Reading

As people in "secular" fields of work become familiar with a particular spirituality (for instance, Ignatian), they can discover, to their chagrin, that although they have a sophisticated understanding of history or education or business or law, their level of theological understanding has hardly progressed beyond what they learned as a child from parents and/or church. If you feel inspired by Michael Himes's "Living Conversation," you may want, from time to time, to pursue some more theology.

Work on the "character" of God—Himes's first topic—has been the focus of some very creative theologians in recent decades. I recommend four books and a central chapter in a fifth:

Elizabeth Johnson, CSJ, *She Who Is: The Mystery of God in Feminist Theological Discourse* (New York: Crossroad, 1992).

Sallie McFague, *Metaphorical Theology: Models of God in Religious Language* (Phila.: Fortress, 1982).

Paul Coutinho, SJ, *How Big Is Your God? The Freedom to Experience the Divine* (Chicago: Loyola Press, 2007).

Karl Frielingsdorf, *Seek the Face of God: Discovering the Power of Your Images of God* (Notre Dame, IN: Ave Maria Press, 2006).

Marcus Borg, "God, the Heart of Reality," *The Heart of Christianity: Rediscovering a Life of Faith* (San Francisco: HarperSanFrancisco, 2004), 61–79.

Though not treated by Himes, another area worth looking into is the interpretation of scripture (the Bible). The so-called "historical-critical" method has dominated this field for a long time, but—important as it is—some scholars are beginning to question whether it goes far enough; it fails to nourish and make claims upon the life of the believer. Sandra Schneiders, IHM, following hermeneutical (that is, interpretational) presuppositions of Hans Georg Gadamer and Paul Ricoeur, and using a variety of methods, wrote "The Foot Washing (John 13:1–20): An Experiment in Hermeneutics" (*The Catholic Biblical Quarterly* 43 [1981], 76–92) and later refined and developed her ideas into a book-length study: *The Revelatory Text: Interpreting the New Testament as Sacred Scripture*, 2nd ed. (Collegeville, MN: Liturgical Press, 2005; originally published in 1991).

Another theological discipline—ethics or morals—usually progresses at a careful pace, but every once in a while gets especially exciting when some imaginative people begin to challenge hidden assumptions of the field and offer a new model of what constitutes virtue, the good life. Such a contribution is that of Anne Patrick, SNJM, "Power and Responsibility: Changing Paradigms of Virtue" (*Jesuit Education and the Cultivation of Virtue*, ed. William J. O'Brien [Washington, DC: Georgetown University Press, 1990], 33–49).

A relatively new but fast-growing area of Christian ethics is ecological theology. Peoples' new awareness of Earth is marked by "strong paradox: the more we discern how precious all life on Earth is, the more we also realize alarmingly how human actions are ravaging and exhausting the natural world," says Elizabeth Johnson, CSJ, in her beautiful, short essay "Passion for God, Passion for the Earth" (*Spiritual Questions for the 21st Century: Essays in Honor of Joan D. Chittister, OSB*, ed. Mary Sembrow [Maryknoll, NY: Orbis, 2002], 118–25).

Finally, let me recommend two recent books that offer a contemporary spirituality grounded in excellent theology: *The Holy Longing: The Search for a Christian Spirituality* (New York: Doubleday, 1999), by Canadian Ronald Rolheiser, OMI. Two of Rolheiser's chapters I find outstanding: "Consequences of the Incarnation for Spirituality" (recall Michael Himes on this subject) and "A Spirituality of the Pascal

Mystery." My Xavier University colleague Joseph Bracken, SJ, has taken his long-standing interest—now genuine expertise—in process thought (especially that of mathematician-physicist-philosopher Alfred North Whitehead) and produced a "metaphysics of universal intersubjectivity" all the way from the Three-Persons-in-God down to the field of subatomic particles (yes! intersubjectivity within the atom): *Christianity and Process Thought: Spirituality for a Changing World* (Philadelphia: Templeton Foundation Press, 2006).

Epilogue

A Parting Word

Let me bring this volume to a close with a few paragraphs from the last chapter of Margaret Silf's *Inner Compass: An Invitation to Ignatian Spirituality*:

> Most of us don't start the journey at the beginning, or even at any other sensible prescribed point. We begin, quite simply, from where we are, and for most of us that will be long after we have already missed the third hawthorn tree [a landmark in a mountain-walk guidebook that Silf had mentioned earlier] and perhaps a good few other apparently vital landmarks. I am reminded of the traveler who lost his way and asked for directions. After a long and convoluted explanation of how to reach his destination, his informant gave up, with the comment, "But if I were you, I wouldn't start from here."
>
> God knows better. With God we always start exactly where we are, and he is both the path and the compass. So it becomes possible to stop for a moment on the journey and look back at the maze of paths behind us. Like most of you, perhaps, I can now see several hawthorn trees where I took the wrong turn. In Ignatius's language, I made the wrong "election." So what can I do about it now? Stand and regret? Or go back to the bottom of the hill and try again? Or remember that God is Now and God is Here, wherever we are, in whatever unchosen places or situations, and that it is God whom we seek, not a particular path.
>
> I remember at school singing the hymn "God is working his purpose out, as year succeeds to year." At the time, I suspected that this was wishful thinking or that, if it were true, this purpose would always be a mystery to me. I know better now. I know that my own deepest desires are gradually drawing me closer to God's desire for me. I can look back now over a fair length of my own path and see some of the other paths I might have taken. Some of them may seem (from here) to

have offered an easier, more direct route home, but I can never, shall never, need never know what pitfalls they might have been concealing. All I need to know is that wherever I am is where I am with God, in the here and now, and that this journey, which is my real vocation, is unfolding itself out of all my life's choices—wise and unwise—as a skilled weaver might create his cloth out of all kinds of unlikely bits of wool. Let us share God's blessing now, free of regret for the landmarks we have missed, alert and alive with trust for all that lies ahead.

Appendices

Do You Speak Ignatian?
A Glossary of Terms Used in
Ignatian and Jesuit Circles

George W. Traub, SJ

A.M.D.G.—*Ad Majorem Dei Gloriam* (Latin)—"For the greater glory of God." Motto of the SOCIETY OF JESUS. [See MAGIS.]

Apostle/apostolate/apostolic—Apostle is the role given to the inner circle of twelve whom Jesus "sent out" (on mission) and to a few others like Saint Paul. Hence apostolate means a "mission endeavor or activity" and apostolic means "mission-like."

Arrupe, Pedro (1907–1991)—As superior general of the SOCIETY OF JESUS for nearly twenty years, he was the central figure in the renewal of the Society after VATICAN COUNCIL II, paying attention both to the spirit of IGNATIUS the founder and to the signs of our times. From the Basque country of northern Spain, he left medical school to join the JESUITS, was expelled from Spain in 1932 with all the other Jesuits, studied theology in Holland, and received further training in spirituality and psychology in the U.S. Arrupe spent twenty-seven years in Japan (where among many other things he cared for victims of the atomic bomb in Hiroshima) until his election in 1965 as superior general. He is considered the founder of the modern, post-Vatican II Society of Jesus.

Cura personalis (Latin meaning "care for the [individual] person")— A hallmark of Ignatian spirituality (where in one-on-one spiritual guidance, the guide adapts the Spiritual Exercises to the unique individual making them) and therefore of Jesuit education (where the teacher establishes a personal relationship with students, listens to them in the process of teaching, and draws them toward personal initiative and responsibility for learning [see Pedagogy, Ignatian/Jesuit]).

This attitude of respect for the dignity of each individual derives from the Judaeo-Christian vision of human beings as unique creations of God, of God's embracing of humanity in the person of Jesus, and of human destiny as ultimate communion with God and all the saints in everlasting life.

Discernment (also "Discernment of spirits")—A process for making choices, in a context of (Christian) faith, when the option is not between good and evil, but between several possible courses of action all of which are potentially good. For Ignatius the process involves prayer, reflection, and consultation with others—all with honest attention not only to the rational (reasons pro and con) but also to the realm of one's feelings, emotions, and desires (what Ignatius called "movements" of soul). A fundamental question in discernment becomes "Where is this impulse from—the good spirit (of God) or the evil spirit (leading one away from God)?" A key to answering this question, says Ignatius in his Spiritual Exercises, is that, in the case of a person leading a basically good life, the good spirit gives "consolation"—acts quietly, gently, and leads one to peace, joy, and deeds of loving service—while the bad spirit brings "desolation"—agitates, disturbs the peace, and injects fears and discouragement to keep one from doing good.

Education, Jesuit—IGNATIUS OF LOYOLA and his first companions, who founded the SOCIETY OF JESUS in 1540, did not originally intend to establish schools. But before long they were led to start colleges for the education of the young men who flocked to join their RELIGIOUS ORDER. And in 1547 Ignatius was asked to open a school for young LAY men.

By the time of his death (1556), there were thirty-five such colleges (comprising today's secondary school and the first year or two of college). By the time the order was suppressed in 1773, the number had grown to more than 800—all part of a system of integrated humanistic education that was international and brought together in a common enterprise men from various languages and cultures. These JESUITS were distinguished mathematicians, astronomers, and physicists; linguists and dramatists; painters and architects; philosophers and theologians; even what today would be called cultural anthropologists.

These developments are not surprising; the order's founders were all University of Paris graduates, and Ignatius's SPIRITUALITY taught Jesuits to search for God "in all things." After the order was restored (1814), however, Jesuit schools and scholars in Europe never regained the prominence they had had. Besides, they were largely involved in the resistance to modern thought and culture that characterized Catholic intellectual life through the nineteenth century and beyond.

In other parts of the world, especially in the United States, the nineteenth century saw a new birth of Jesuit education. Twenty-one of today's twenty-eight U.S. Jesuit colleges and universities were founded during that century. These schools served the needs of an immigrant people, enabling them to move up in the world while maintaining their Catholic belief and practice in a frequently hostile Protestant environment.

After World War II, U.S. Jesuit higher education (as American higher education generally) experienced enormous growth and democratization under the G.I. Bill. Significantly, this growth entailed a shift from a largely Jesuit faculty to one made up increasingly of lay men (and more recently women). Further, VATICAN COUNCIL II (1962–1965) released a great burst of energy in the

Catholic church and Jesuit order for engagement with the modern world, including its intellectual life. Finally, Jesuit schools in the 1970s and 1980s moved to professionalize through the hiring of new faculty with highly specialized training and terminal degrees from the best graduate schools.

These sweeping changes of the last fifty years have brought U.S. Jesuit schools to the present situation where they face crucial questions. Will so-called Jesuit institutions of higher education simply merge with mainstream American academe and thereby lose any distinctiveness and reason for existing—or will they have the creativity to become more distinctive? While taking the best from American education and culture, will they still offer an alternative in the spirit of their Jesuit heritage? Will they foster the integration of knowledge—or will specialization reign alone and the fragmentation of knowledge continue? Will they relate learning to the Transcendent, to God—or will SPIRITUAL experience be allowed to disappear from consideration except in isolated departments of theology? While developing the mind, surely, will they also develop a global, cross-cultural imagination and a compassionate heart to recognize and work for the common good, especially for bettering the lot of the poor and voiceless [see MEN AND WOMEN FOR OTHERS/ WHOLE PERSONS OF SOLIDARITY and THE SERVICE OF FAITH AND THE PROMOTION OF JUSTICE]—or will the dominant values present in them be self-interest and the "bottom line"?

Faber, Peter (1506–1546)—Latin and English version of Pierre Favre, University of Paris student from the south of France who roomed with IGNATIUS OF LOYOLA and FRANCIS XAVIER and together with them and several others founded the SOCIETY OF JESUS. In the course of seven years, he traveled some 7,000 miles and served in seven different western European countries. The largest part of his ministry was in Germany. There he drew up guidelines for ecumenical dialogue with Lutherans, but these were, sad to say, hardly put into practice. Among the early companions, he was known to be the finest guide for those making the SPIRITUAL EXERCISES.

Finding God in All Things—IGNATIAN SPIRITUALITY is summed up in this phrase. It invites a person to search for and find God in every circumstance of life, not just in explicitly religious situations or activities such as prayer in church (e.g., the Mass) or in private. It implies that God is present everywhere and, though invisible, can be "found" in any and all of the creatures which God has made. They reveal at least a little of what their Maker is like—often by arousing wonder in those who are able to look with the "eyes of faith." After a long day of work, IGNATIUS used to open the French windows in his room, step out onto a little balcony, look up at the stars, and be carried out of himself into the greatness of God.

How does one grow in this ability to find God everywhere? Howard Gray draws the following paradigm from what IGNATIUS wrote about spiritual development in the JESUIT *Constitutions*: (1) **practice attentiveness** to what is really there. "Let that person or that poem or that social injustice or that scientific experiment become (for you) as genuinely itself as it can be." (2) Then **reverence** what you see and hear and feel; appreciate it in its uniqueness. "Before you judge or assess or respond, give yourself time to esteem and accept what is there in the other." (3) If you learn to be attentive and reverent, "then you will **find devotion**, the singularly moving way in which God works in that situation, revealing goodness and fragility, beauty and truth, pain and anguish, wisdom and ingenuity."

God—Various titles or names are given to the Mystery underlying all that exists—e.g., the Divine, Supreme Being, the Absolute, the Transcendent, the All-Holy—but all of these are only "pointers" to a Reality beyond human naming and beyond our limited human comprehension. Still, some conceptions are taken to be less inadequate than others within a given tradition founded in revelation. Thus, Jews reverence "the Lord" (the name of God, *YHWH*, is holy and its vocalization unknown); and Muslims worship "Allah" (the [only] God).

Christians conceive of the one God as "Trinity," as having three "ways of being"—(1) Creator and covenant partner (from Hebrew tradition) or "Father" (the "Abba" of Jesus' experience), (2) incarnate (enfleshed) in JESUS—the "Son," and (3) present everywhere in the world through the "Spirit." IGNATIUS OF LOYOLA had a strong Trinitarian sense of God, but he was especially fond of the expression "the Divine Majesty" stressing the greatness or "godness" of God; and the twentieth-century Jesuit theologian Karl Rahner could talk of "the incomprehensible Mystery of self-giving Love."

The reluctance of some of our contemporaries to use the word God may be seen as a potential corrective to the tendency of some believers to speak of God all too easily, as if they fully understood God and God's ways.

Gospel (literally "good news")—The good news or glad tidings about JESUS.

Plural. The first four works of the Christian scriptures (Matthew, Mark, Luke, and John) that tell the story of JESUS—each with its own particular theological emphasis—and thus invite a response of faith and hope in him.

Ignatian—Adjective, from the noun IGNATIUS (OF LOYOLA). Sometimes used in distinction to JESUIT, indicating aspects of SPIRITUALITY that derive from Ignatius the LAY PERSON rather than from the later Ignatius and his RELIGIOUS ORDER, the SOCIETY OF JESUS.

Ignatian/Jesuit Vision, Characteristics of the—Drawing on a variety of contemporary sources which tend to confirm one another, one can construct a list of rather commonly accepted characteristics of the Ignatian/Jesuit vision. It . . .

- sees life and the whole universe as a gift calling forth wonder and gratefulness;
- gives ample scope to imagination and emotion as well as intellect;
- seeks to find the divine in all things—in all peoples and cultures, in all areas of study and learning, in every human experience, and (for the Christian) especially in the person of JESUS;
- cultivates critical awareness of personal and social evil, but points to God's love as more powerful than any evil;
- stresses freedom, need for DISCERNMENT, and responsible action;
- empowers people to become leaders in service, MEN AND WOMEN FOR OTHERS, WHOLE PERSONS OF SOLIDARITY, building a more just and humane world.

The relative consensus about these six characteristics should not be taken to indicate that they exhaust the meaning of the living IGNATIAN tradition. Like the living tradition of Christian faith, of which it is a part, no number of thematic statements can adequately articulate it. At the heart of both traditions stands the living person of JESUS, who cannot be reduced to a series of ideas.

No one claims that any of these characteristics are uniquely Ignatian/Jesuit. It is rather the combination of them all and the way they fit together that make the vision distinctive and so appropriate for an age in transition—whether from the medieval to the modern in Ignatius's time, or from the modern to the postmodern in ours.

Ignatius of Loyola (1491–1556)—Youngest child of a noble Basque family fiercely loyal to the Spanish crown (Ferdinand and Isabella), he was named Iñigo after a local saint. Raised to be a courtier, he was trying valiantly to defend the fortress town of Pamplona in 1521 when a French cannonball shattered his leg. During a long convalescence, he found himself drawn away from the romances of chivalry that had filled his imagination from an early age to more spiritual reading—an illustrated life of JESUS and a collection of saints' lives.

After his recovery, he set out for the Holy Land to realize a dream of "converting the infidel." On the way he stopped in the little town of MANRESA and wound up spending nearly a year there during which he experienced both the depths of despair and great times of enlightenment.

Ordered to leave Palestine after being there little more than a month, Ignatius decided that he needed an education in order to be able to "help souls." In Barcelona, he went to school with boys a quarter his age to learn the rudiments of Latin grammar, then moved on to several Spanish university cities. In each he was imprisoned and interrogated by the Inquisition, because he kept speaking to people about "SPIRITUAL things," having neither a theology degree nor priestly ordination.

Finally, turning his back on his homeland, he went to the foremost university of the time, the University of Paris, where he began his education all over again and with diligence, after five years, was finally awarded the degree "Master of Arts." It was here at Paris that he changed his Basque name to the Latin *Ignatius* and its Spanish equivalent *Ignacio.*

While at the university, he had roomed with and become good friends with a fellow Basque named FRANCIS XAVIER and a Savoyard named PETER FABER. After graduation, these three, together with several other Paris graduates, undertook a process of communal DISCERNMENT and decided to bind themselves together in an APOSTOLIC community that became the SOCIETY OF JESUS. Unanimously elected superior by his companions, Ignatius spent the last sixteen years of his life in Rome directing the fledgling order, while the others went all over Europe, to the Far East, and eventually to the New World. And wherever they went they founded schools as a means of helping people to "FIND GOD IN ALL THINGS."

IHS—The first three letters, in Greek, of the name JESUS. These letters appear as a symbol on the official seal of the SOCIETY OF JESUS or JESUITS.

Inculturation—A modern theological concept that expresses a principle of Christian mission implicit in IGNATIAN SPIRITUALITY—namely, that the GOSPEL needs to be presented to any given culture in terms intelligible to that culture and allowed to grow up in the "soil" of that culture; God is already present and active there ("God's action is antecedent to ours"—Jesuit General Congregation 34 [1995], "Our Mission and Culture").

Thus in the first century Saint Paul fought against the imposition of Jewish practices on non-Jewish Christians. And in the sixteenth and seventeenth centuries, Jesuits like Matteo Ricci (1552–1610) and Roberto de Nobili (1577–1656) fought to retain elements of Chinese and Indian culture in presenting a de-Europeanized Christianity to those peoples, only to have their approach condemned by the Church in the eighteenth.

Ideally, the GOSPEL and a culture mutually interact, and in the process the gospel embraces some elements of the culture while offering a critique of others.

Jesuit—Noun. A member of the SOCIETY OF JESUS. The term was originally coined as a putdown by people who felt there was something terribly arrogant about a group calling itself the Company or Society of Jesus, whereas previous religious orders had been content to name themselves after their founder (e.g., "Benedictines," "Franciscans," "Dominicans"). Later the title was adopted as a short-hand name by members of the Society themselves, as well as by others favorable to them.

Adjective. Pertaining to the Society of Jesus. The negative term, now that *Jesuit* has been rehabilitated, is *Jesuitical* meaning "sly" or "devious."

Jesus (also "Jesus [the] Christ," meaning Jesus "[God's] anointed one")—The historical person Jesus of Nazareth whom Christians acknowledge to be, by his life (what he taught and did) and his death and resurrection, the true revelation of God and at the same time the exemplar of what it means to be fully human. In other words, for Christians, Jesus shows what God is like and how they can live in response to this revelation: God is the compassionate giver of life who invites and empowers human beings, in freedom, together with one another, to work toward overcoming the forces of evil—meaninglessness, guilt, oppression, suffering, and death—that diminish people and keep them from growing toward ever fuller life.

In his Spiritual Exercises, Ignatius has the retreatant devote most of the time to "contemplating" (i.e., imaginatively entering into) the life, death, and resurrection of Jesus, so as to become more and more a companion of Jesus. And when Ignatius and his companions from the University of Paris decided to establish a religious order, he insisted that it be called the Company or Society of Jesus [see Jesuit—Noun].

Judaeo-Christian Vision or Story, The—Here is a version of the Judaeo-Christian vision or story, told with certain emphases from Ignatius of Loyola.

The great and mysterious Reality of personal love and self-giving that many call God is the origin and destiny of all creation, the whole universe. God is present and at work in everything, leading it to ful-filment. All things are originally good and potentially means for those creatures called human beings to find the God who made and works in them. Still, none of these things are God, and therefore they are all radically limited.

Indeed, in the case of human beings (who somehow image God in a special way), their relative freedom results in a new dimension of being whereby not just good but also evil exists in the world: selfishness, war, domination—racial, sexual, economic, environmental—of some over others. Human history, then, is marked by a struggle between the forces of good, or "life," and evil, or "death."

God has freely chosen to side with struggling, flawed humanity by participating more definitively in human life and living it "from the inside" in the historical person of Jesus of Nazareth. This irrevocable commitment of God to the human enterprise grounds and invites people's response of working with God toward building a community of justice, love, and peace—the "kingdom" or "reign" of God that Jesus preached and lived.

As with Jesus, so for his followers, it takes DISCERNMENT—a finely tuned reading of oneself and one's culture in the Spirit of God—to recognize in any given situation what helps the coming of God's reign and what hinders it. In the face of human selfishness and evil, the way ultimately entails self-giving, going through suffering and death in order to gain life—indeed, life everlasting. And along the way, because the followers of Jesus are wary of idolizing anyone or anything (that is, making a god of them), they are less likely to become disillusioned with themselves or others or human history for all its weight of personal and social evil. Rather do they continue to care about people and the human enterprise, for their hope is in God, the supreme Reality of personal love and self-giving.

Kolvenbach, Peter-Hans (1928–)—Dutch-born superior general of the SOCIETY OF JESUS from 1983, when the JESUITS were allowed to return to their own governance after a time of papal "intervention," until 2008, when he resigned at the age of eighty.

He entered the Jesuits in 1948, went to Lebanon in the mid-1950s, earned a doctorate from the famous Saint Joseph's University in Beirut, and spent much of his life there, first as a professor of linguistics and then as superior of the JESUIT vice-province of the Middle East.

By his own admission, he was relatively "ignorant of matters pertaining to justice and injustice," when he went from Beirut to Rome for Jesuit General Congregation 32 and witnessed the faith-justice emphasis emerge from the Congregation under the leadership of PEDRO ARRUPE [see THE SERVICE OF FAITH AND THE PROMOTION OF JUSTICE]. Still, as superior general, he worked tirelessly in collaboration with his advisors to implement and extend the direction in which his predecessor had been leading the Society [see MEN AND WOMEN FOR OTHERS/WHOLE PERSONS OF SOLIDARITY FOR THE REAL WORLD].

Laity (lay person/lay people)—The people of a religious faith as distinguished from its clergy; within Catholic circles, however, members of religious communities who are not ordained (i.e. "sisters" and "brothers") are often popularly associated with priests and bishops and not with lay people. (It would be more accurate to see them as neither, as having their own unique role and style of life; see RELIGIOUS ORDER/RELIGIOUS LIFE.)

Magis **(Latin for "more")**—The "Continuous Quality Improvement" term traditionally used by IGNATIUS OF LOYOLA and the JESUITS, suggesting the spirit of generous excellence in which ministry should be carried on. (See A.M.D.G.—AD MAJOREM DEI GLORIAM)

Manresa—Town in northeastern Spain where in 1522–1523 a middle-aged layman named IGNATIUS OF LOYOLA had the powerful spiritual experiences that led to his famous SPIRITUAL EXERCISES and later guided the founding and the PEDAGOGY of JESUIT schools.

Men and Women for Others/Whole Persons of Solidarity for the Real World—In a now famous address to alumni of JESUIT schools in Europe (July 31, 1973), PEDRO ARRUPE painted a profile of what a graduate should be. Admitting that JESUIT schools had not always been on target here, Arrupe called for a reeducation to justice:

> Today our prime educational objective must be to form men-and-women-for-others . . . people who cannot even conceive of love of God which does not include love for the least of their neighbors; people

convinced that love of God which does not issue in justice for human beings is a farce. . . . All of us would like to be good to others, and most of us would be relatively good in a good world. What is difficult is to be good in an evil world, where the egoism of others and the egoism built into the institutions of society attack us. . . . Evil is overcome only by good, egoism by generosity. It is thus that we must sow justice in our world, substituting love for self-interest as the driving force of society.

Following up on what Arrupe had said, the next Jesuit head, PETER-HANS KOLVENBACH, challenged the 900 JESUIT and LAY delegates from the 28 U.S. Jesuit colleges and universities gathered for "Assembly '89" to teach our students to make "no significant decision without first thinking of how it would impact the least in society" (i.e., the poor, the marginal who have no voice). And eleven years later, speaking on "the faith that does justice" to a similar national gathering at Santa Clara University (October 6, 2000), Kolvenbach was even more pointed and eloquent in laying out the goals for the twenty-first-century American Jesuit university:

> Here in Silicon Valley, some of the world's premier research universities flourish alongside struggling public schools where Afro-American and immigrant students drop out in droves. Nationwide, one child in every six is condemned to ignorance and poverty. . . . Thanks to science and technology, human society is able to solve problems such as feeding the hungry, sheltering the homeless, or developing more just conditions of life, but stubbornly fails to accomplish this.

> The real measure of our Jesuit universities, [then,] lies in who our students become. Tomorrow's "whole person" cannot be whole without a *well-educated solidarity*. We must therefore raise our Jesuit educational standard to "educate the whole person of solidarity for the real world."

> Solidarity is learned through "contact" rather than through "concepts." When the heart is touched by direct experience, the mind may be challenged to change. Our universities boast a splendid variety of in-service programs, outreach programs, insertion programs,

off-campus contacts, and hands-on courses. These should not be too optional or peripheral, but at the core of every Jesuit university's program of studies.

Faculty are at the heart of our universities. Professors, in spite of the cliché of the ivory tower, are in contact with the world. But no point of view is ever neutral or value-free. A legitimate question, even if it does not sound academic, is for each professor to ask, "When researching and teaching, where and with whom is my heart?" To make sure that the real concerns of the poor find their place, faculty members need an organic collaboration with those in the Church and in society who work among and for the poor and actively seek justice.

What is at stake is a sustained interdisciplinary dialogue of research and reflection, a continuous pooling of expertise. The purpose is to assimilate experiences and insights in "a vision of knowledge which, well aware of its limitations, is not satisfied with fragments but tries to integrate them into a true and wise synthesis" about the real world. Unfortunately, many faculty still feel academically, humanly, and, I would say, spiritually unprepared for such an exchange.

If the measure of our universities is who the students become, and if the faculty are the heart of it all, then what is there left to say? It is perhaps the third topic, the character of our universities—how they proceed internally and how they impact on society—that is the most difficult.

In the words of [Jesuit] General Congregation 34, a Jesuit university must be faithful to both the noun "university" and to the adjective "Jesuit." To be a university requires dedication "to research, teaching, and the various forms of service that correspond to its cultural mission." To be Jesuit "requires that the university act in harmony with the demands of the service of faith and the promotion of justice."

[A] telling expression of the Jesuit university's nature is found in policies concerning hiring and tenure. As a university it must respect the established academic, professional, and labor norms, but as Jesuit it is essential to go beyond them and find ways of attracting, hiring, and promoting those who actively share the mission.

Every Jesuit academy of higher learning is called to live *in* a social reality and to live *for* that social reality, to shed university intelligence upon it and to use university influence to transform it. Thus Jesuit universities have stronger and different reasons than do many other academic institutions for addressing the actual world as it unjustly exists and for helping to reshape it in the light of the Gospel.

Order—see RELIGIOUS ORDER/RELIGIOUS LIFE.

Pedagogy, Ignatian/Jesuit—Having to do with Ignatian/Jesuit teaching style or methods.

In one formulation (Robert Newton's *Reflections on the Educational Principles of the Spiritual Exercises* [1977]), **Jesuit education is instrumental** (not an end in itself, but a means to the service of God and others); **student centered** (adapted to the individual as much as possible so as to develop an independent and responsible learner); **characterized by structure** (with systematic organization of successive objectives and systematic procedures for evaluation and accountability) **and flexibility** (freedom encouraged and personal response and self-direction expected, with the teacher an experienced guide, not primarily a deliverer of ready-made knowledge); **eclectic** (drawing on a variety of the best methods and techniques available); and **personal** (whole person affected, with goal of personal appropriation, attitudinal and behavioral change).

In another formulation (*Ignatian Pedagogy: A Practical Approach* from the International Center for Jesuit Education [Rome, 1993]), Ignatian pedagogy is a model that seeks to develop men and women of competence, conscience, and compassion. Similar to the process of guiding others in the Spiritual Exercises, faculty accompany students in their intellectual, spiritual, and emotional development. They do this by following the Ignatian pedagogical paradigm. Through consideration of the **context** of students' lives, faculty create an environment where students recollect their past **experience** and assimilate information from newly-provided **experiences**. Faculty help students learn the skills and techniques of **reflection**, which shapes their consciousness, and they then challenge students to **action** in service to others. The **evaluation** process includes academic mastery as well as ongoing assessments of students' well-rounded growth as persons for others.

Both these approaches were developed in the context of secondary education, but could be adapted for higher education. [See also EDUCATION, JESUIT and RATIO STUDIORUM.]

Ratio Studiorum **(Latin for "Plan of Studies")**—A document, the definitive form of which was published in 1599 after several earlier drafts and extensive consultation among Jesuits working in schools. It was a handbook of practical directives for teachers and administrators, a collection of the most effective educational methods of the time, tested and adapted to fit the Jesuit mission of education. Since it was addressed to Jesuits, the principles behind its directives could be assumed. They came, of course, from the vision and spirit of IGNATIUS. The process that led to the *Ratio* and continued after its publication gave birth to the first real system of schools the world had ever known.

Much of what the 1599 *Ratio* contained would not be relevant to Jesuit schools today. Still, the process out of which it grew and thrived suggests that we have only just begun to tap the possibilities within the international Jesuit network for collaboration and interchange. [See also EDUCATION, JESUIT and PEDAGOGY, IGNATIAN/JESUIT.]

Religious Order/Religious Life—In Eastern Orthodox and Roman Catholic Christianity (less frequently in Anglican/Episcopal Christianity), a community of men or women bound together by the common profession, through "religious" vows, of "chastity" (better called voluntary "consecrated celibacy" [and thus not to be confused with the imposed celibacy of Roman Catholic clergy]), "poverty," and "obedience." As a way of trying to follow JESUS' example, the vows involve voluntary renunciation of things potentially good: marriage and sexual relations in the case of "consecrated celibacy," personal ownership and possessions in the case of "poverty," and one's own will and plans in the case of "obedience."

This renunciation is made, not for its own sake, but "for the sake of [God's] kingdom" (Matthew 19:12), as a prophetic witness against a culture's abuse of sex, wealth (greed), and power (domination) and toward a more available and universal love beyond family ties, personal possessions, and self-determination. As a concrete form of Christian faith and life, it emphasizes the relativity of all the goods of this earth in the face of the only absolute, God, and a life lived definitively with God beyond this world.

This way of life first appeared in the second half of the first century in the person of "virgins" (mostly women but also some men) who lived at home and, by refusing to marry and produce offspring (they claimed to be "spouses of Christ"), countered the absolutist claims of the state (Rome) and hence many of them became martyrs. After Constantine's conversion to Christianity (313) and Christianity's establishment as the state religion, "religious life" developed further as a major movement away from the "world" and the worldliness of the church. The monastic life of monks and nuns is a variation on this tradition. At the beginning of the modern Western world, various new religious orders sprang up (the largest being the JESUITS) that saw themselves not as fleeing from the world but APOSTLES sent out into the world in service. In more recent centuries, many communities of religious women were founded with a similar goal of APOSTOLIC service, often with Jesuit-inspired constitutions.

The Service of Faith and the Promotion of Justice—In 1975, Jesuits from around the world met in solemn assembly to assess their present state and to sketch plans for the future. Following the lead of a recent international assembly ("synod") of Catholic bishops, they came to see that the hallmark of any ministry deserving of the name Jesuit would be its "service of faith" of which the "promotion of justice" is an absolute requirement. In other words, Jesuit education should be noteworthy for the way it helps students—and for that matter, faculty, staff, and administrators—to move, in freedom, toward a mature and intellectually adult faith. This includes enabling them to develop a disciplined sensitivity toward the suffering of our world and a will to act for the transformation of unjust social structures that cause that suffering. The enormous challenge, to which none of us are entirely equal, nevertheless falls on all of us, not just on campus ministry and members of theology and philosophy departments.

The Society of Jesus—Catholic RELIGIOUS ORDER of men founded in 1540 by IGNATIUS OF LOYOLA and a small group of his multinational "friends in the Lord," fellow students from the University of Paris. They saw their mission as one of being available to go anywhere and do anything to "help souls," especially where the need was greatest (e.g., where a certain people or a certain kind of work were neglected).

Today, numbering about 20,000 priests and brothers, they are spread out in almost every country of the world ("more branch offices," said PEDRO ARRUPE, "than Coca-Cola")—declining in numbers markedly in Europe and North America, but growing in India, Africa, Latin America, and the Far East.

The abbreviation "SJ" after a person's name means that he is a member of the SOCIETY OF JESUS.

Spiritual/spirituality—The spiritual is often defined as that which is "nonmaterial," but this definition runs into problems when applied to human beings, who are traditionally considered "body-spirits," both bodily and spiritual. In some modern philosophies and psychologies, however, the spiritual dimension of the human is denied or disregarded. And many aspects of our contemporary American culture (e.g., the hurried sense of time and need to produce, produce) make it difficult to pay attention to this dimension.

Fundamentally, the spiritual dimension of human beings can be recognized in the orientation of our minds and hearts toward ever more than we have already reached (the never-satisfied human mind and the never-satisfied human heart). We are drawn inevitably toward the "Absolute" or the "Fullness of Being" [see GOD]. Consequently, there are depths to our being that we can only just begin to fathom.

If every human being has this spiritual dimension and hunger, then even in a culture like ours, everyone will have—at least at times—some awareness of it, even if that awareness is not explicit and not put into words. When people talk of a "spirituality," however, they usually mean, not the spirituality that human beings have by nature, but rather a set of attitudes and practices (SPIRITUAL EXERCISES) that are designed to foster a greater consciousness of this spiritual dimension and (in the case of those who can affirm belief in God) a more explicit seeking of its object—the Divine or God.

IGNATIAN spirituality with its SPIRITUAL EXERCISES is one such path among many within Christianity, to say nothing of the spiritualities within other religious traditions, or those more or less outside a religious tradition. ("Peoples' spiritual lives [today] have not died; they are simply taking place outside the church" [Jesuit General Congregation 34, "Our Mission and Culture"].)

spiritual exercises (small *s* and *e*)—Any of a variety of methods or activities for opening oneself to God's spirit and allowing one's whole being, not just the mind, to be affected. The methods—some of them more "active" and others more "passive"—might include vocal prayer (e.g., the Lord's Prayer), meditation or contemplation, journaling or other kind of writing, reading of scripture or other great works of verbal art, drawing, painting or molding with clay, looking at works of visual art, playing or listening to music, working or walking in the midst of nature. All of these activities have the same goal in mind—discontinuing one's usual productive activities and thus allowing God to "speak," listening to what God may be "saying" through the medium employed.

The Spiritual Exercises (capital *S* and *E*)—An organized series of SPIRITUAL EXERCISES put together by IGNATIUS OF LOYOLA out of his own personal spiritual experience and that of others to whom he listened. They invite the "retreatant" or "exercitant" to "meditate" on central aspects of Christian faith (e.g., creation, sin and forgiveness, calling and ministry) and especially to "contemplate" (i.e., imaginatively enter into) the life, death, and resurrection of JESUS.

Ignatius set all of this down in the book of the *Spiritual Exercises* as a handbook to help the guide who coaches a person engaged in "making the Exercises." After listening to that person and getting a sense for where he/she is, the guide selects from material and methods in the book of the *Exercises* and offers them in a way adapted to that unique individual. The goal of all this is the attainment of a kind of spiritual freedom, the power to act—not out of social pressure or personal compulsion and fear—but out of the promptings of God's spirit in the deepest, truest core of one's being—to act ultimately out of love.

As originally designed, the "full" Spiritual Exercises would occupy a person for four weeks full-time, but Ignatius realized that some people could not (today most people cannot) disengage from work and home obligations for that long a time, and so it is possible to make the "full" Exercises part-time over a period of six to nine or ten months—the "Spiritual Exercises in Daily Life." In that case, the "exercitant," without withdrawing from home or work, devotes about an hour a day to prayer (but this, like nearly everything in the Exercises, is adaptable) and sees a guide every week or two to process what has been happening in prayer and in the rest of his/her life.

Most of the time people make not the "full" Spiritual Exercises but a retreat in the Ignatian spirit that might last anywhere from a weekend to a week. Such a retreat usually includes either a daily individual conversation with a guide or several daily presentations to a group, as preparation for prayer/SPIRITUAL EXERCISES.

Ignatius had composed and revised his little book over a period of twenty-five or more years before it was finally published in 1548. Subsequent editions and translations—according to a plausible estimate—numbered some 4,500 in 1948 or about one a month over four centuries, the total number of copies printed being around 4.5 million. It is largely on his Exercises—with their implications for teaching and learning in a holistic way—that Ignatius's reputation as a major figure in the history of Western education rests.

Spiritual Guidance/Direction—People are often helped to integrate their faith and their life by talking on a regular basis (e.g., monthly) with someone they can trust. This person acts as a guide (sometimes also called a spiritual friend, companion, or director) for the journey, helping them to find the presence and call of God in the people and circumstances of their everyday lives.

The assumption is that God is already present there, and that another person, a guide, can help them to notice God's presence and also to find words for talking about that presence, because they are not used to doing so. The guide is often a specially trained listener skilled in DISCERNMENT and therefore able to help them sort out the various voices within and around them. While he/she may suggest various kinds of SPIRITUAL EXERCISES/ways of praying, the focus is much broader than that; it is upon the whole of a person's life experience as the place to meet God.

Vatican Council II (Vatican II for short)—Convoked in 1962 by Pope John XXIII to bring the Catholic Church "up to date," this twenty-first Ecumenical (i.e. worldwide) Council signaled the Catholic Church's growth from a church of cultural confinement (largely European) to a genuine world church. The Council set its seal on the work of twentieth-century theologians that earlier had often been officially considered dangerous or erroneous. Thus, the biblical movement, the liturgical renewal, and the LAY movement were incorporated into official Catholic doctrine and practice.

Here are several significant new perspectives coming from the Council: celebration of liturgy (worship) in various vernacular languages rather than Latin, to facilitate understanding and LAY participation; viewing the Church as "the whole people of God" rather than just as clergy and viewing other Christian bodies (Protestant, Orthodox) as belonging to it; recognizing non-Christian religions as containing truth; honoring freedom of conscience as a basic human right; and finally including in its mission a reaching out to people in all their human hopes, needs, sufferings as an essential part of preaching the GOSPEL.

Today, Catholics are seriously divided on the question of Vatican II, some ("conservatives") considering it to have failed by giving away essentials of tradition and others ("liberals") feeling it has been too little and too imperfectly realized.

Whole Persons of Solidarity for the Real World—See MEN AND WOMEN FOR OTHERS.

Xavier, Francis (1506–1552)—Native like IGNATIUS of the Basque territory of northern Spain, Francis became a close friend of Ignatius at the University of Paris, came to share Ignatius's vision through making the SPIRITUAL EXERCISES, and realized that vision through missionary labors in India, the Indonesian archipelago, and Japan. He was the first JESUIT to go out to people of non-European culture. And as he moved from his early missionary endeavors in India to his later ones in Japan, it seems that the implications of what we call INCULTURATION started to dawn on him.

Contents of the
Companion Volume,
A Jesuit Education Reader

Perhaps the most widespread and influential ministry to rise from Ignatian spirituality is the work of Jesuit education. The Jesuit mission in education grew out of and continues to be informed by Ignatian spirituality, so an appropriation of this work and ministry is a helpful exemplar to further illuminate the distinctive characteristics and vision of Ignatian spirituality. Thus I have edited a companion volume, *A Jesuit Education Reader* (Loyola Press, 2008). Here are the contents of that companion volume:

Appendices

Do You Speak Ignatian? A Glossary of Terms Used in Ignatian and Jesuit Circles

Contents of the Companion Volume, *An Ignatian Spirituality Reader*

Acknowledgments

Contributors

Index

About the Editor

Acknowledgments

Prologue
Ronald Modras, "The Spiritual Humanism of the Jesuits" from *America*
[1-800-627-9533; <www.americamagazine.org>] (February 4, 1995), pp.
10–16, 29–32. Copyright © 1995 by *America*. Used with permission.

Ignatius: His Life
Michael Paul Gallagher, SJ, "St. Ignatius of Loyola (1491–1556)" from *The Tablet* [London] <www.thetablet.co.uk> (27 May 2000), p. 737. Copyright © 2000 by *The Tablet*. Used with permission.

Ron Hansen, "The Pilgrim: Saint Ignatius of Loyola" from *A Stay Against Confusion: Essays on Faith and Fiction* (New York: HarperCollins, 2001), pp. 74–104. Copyright © 1994, 2001 by Ron Hansen. Used with the permission of HarperCollins Publishers.

Finding God In All Things
Monika K. Hellwig, "Finding God in All Things: A Spirituality for Today," excerpted from *Sojourners* [1-800-714-7474; <www.sojo.net>] (December 1991), pp. 12–16. Copyright © 1991 by *Sojourners*. Used with permission.

Howard Gray, SJ, "Ignatian Spirituality" from *As Leaven in the World: Catholic Perspectives on Faith, Vocation, and the Intellectual Life*, ed. Thomas M. Landy (Franklin, WI: Sheed & Ward, 2001), pp. 321–39. Copyright © 2001 by Collegium. Used with permission.

Prayer
Walter J. Burghardt, SJ, "Contemplation: A Long, Loving Look at the Real" from *Church* [published by the National Pastoral Life Center, 18 Bleecker Street, New York, NY 10012] (Winter 1989), pp. 14–18. Copyright © 1989 by *Church* magazine. Used with permission.

William A. Barry, SJ, "Prayer as Conscious Relationship" from *God and You* (NY/Mahwah, NJ: Paulist Press <www.paulistpress.com>, 1987), pp. 11–15.

Dennis Hamm, SJ, "Rummaging for God: Praying Backwards Through Your Day" from *America* [1-800-627-9533; <www.americamagazine.org>] (May 14, 1994), pp. 22–23. Copyright © 1994 by *America*. Used with permission.

The Spiritual Exercises
William A. Barry, SJ, "What Are Spiritual Exercises?" from *Finding God in All Things* (Notre Dame, IN: Ave Maria Press, 1991), pp. 11–20. Copyright © 1991 by Ave Maria Press. Used with permission.

Javier Melloni, SJ, "The Specificity of the Ignatian Exercises" from *The Exercises of St Ignatius Loyola in the Western Tradition*, trans. Michael Ivens (Leominster, UK: Gracewing, 2000), pp. 48–54. Copyright © 2000 by Gracewing Publishing and Inigo Enterprises. Used with the permission of Gracewing Publishing.

James W. Fowler, "An Experience of the Contemporary Personally Guided Spiritual Exercises" from *Life Maps: Conversations on the Journey of Faith* by Jim Fowler and Sam Keen (Waco, TX: Word Books, 1978), pp. 160–62. Copyright © 1978 by Word, Inc. Used with permission of the author.

Patrick A. Heelan, SJ, Foreword to Antonio de Nicolás's *Powers of Imagining: Ignatius de Loyola: A Philosophical Hermeneutic of Imagining through the Collected Works of Ignatius de Loyola* by Antonio T. de Nicolás, the State University of New York Press, pp. ix–xiii. Copyright © 1986, State University of New York. All rights reserved. Reprinted by permission.

Discernment
James Gaffney, Ignatian Discernment, from "Two Faces of Loyola," Loyola Day Address at Loyola University, New Orleans (Fall 1987), pp. 2–4. Used with permission of the author. A revised version was published in *America* (July 27, 1991), pp. 34–37.

William A. Barry, SJ, "Discernment of Spirits as an Act of Faith" from *Spirit, Style, Story: Essays Honoring John W. Padberg*, ed. Thomas M. Lucas (Chicago: Loyola Press, 2002), pp. 33–44. Copyright © 2002 by Thomas M. Lucas. Used with the permission of Loyola Press.

David Lonsdale, "Discernment of Spirits" from *Eyes to See, Ears to Hear* (London: Darton Longman & Todd; Maryknoll, NY: Orbis Books, 2000),

Theology to Support the Spirituality

Epilogue

Contributors

Noreen Cannon Au, PhD, is a graduate of the University of Southern California and the C. G. Jung Institute of Los Angeles. She is a practicing Jungian analyst and a faculty member of the C. G. Jung Institute of Los Angeles. She is a former member of the editorial boards of *Psychological Perspectives*, a journal of Jungian thought, and of *Human Development*, a quarterly journal featuring current knowledge from the fields of psychiatry, psychology, medicine, and spirituality. She is the coauthor of *Urgings of the Heart: A Spirituality of Integration* and *The Discerning Heart: Exploring the Christian Path*.

Wilkie Au, MDiv., PhD, a graduate of the University of California, Santa Barbara, and the Jesuit School of Theology at Berkeley, is professor of theological studies at Loyola Marymount University, where he teaches in the area of spirituality and coordinates the graduate concentration in spiritual direction. A former Jesuit, he served as director of novices in California and director of the Jesuit Collegiate Program. He is a former associate editor of *Human Development* and currently serves on the editorial review panel of *Presence: An International Journal of Spiritual Direction*. His *By Way of the Heart: Toward a Holistic Christian Spirituality* won the 1990 Book Award of the College Theology Society and his *Enduring Heart: Spirituality for the Long Haul* won an award from the Catholic Press Association of the United States and Canada in 2001.

William A. Barry, SJ, is the author or coauthor of eighteen books, has been a Jesuit for fifty-eight years, and a priest for forty-six. He earned a doctorate in clinical psychology from the University of Michigan in 1968. He has taught at Weston Jesuit School of Theology, the University of Michigan, and Boston College, and engaged in administrative work in the Society of Jesus. From 1988 to 1991 he was rector of the Jesuit Community at Boston College and on the board of trustees. From 1991 to 1997 he was provincial superior of the Jesuits of New England. At present he is codirector of a nine-month program for Jesuit priests and brothers prior to their final vows and gives retreats and spiritual direction at Campion Renewal Center, in Weston, Massachusetts. He is also editor-in-chief of the quarterly *Human Development*.

Walter J. Burghardt, SJ, (1914–2008) celebrated seventy-five years a Jesuit and sixty-five years a priest and preacher in 2006. Heralded with honorary degrees from twenty-four colleges and universities, his years of service to the Church include teaching patristic theology at Woodstock College and the Catholic University of America; forty-four years editing *Theological Studies*; serving as an original member of the papal International Theological Commission; cofounding the journal *The Living Pulpit*; creating and leading the Preaching the Just Word retreat/workshop program throughout the country; and writing twenty-four books and more than three hundred fifty articles, with an emphasis in recent years on biblical justice.

James W. Fowler is C. H. Candler Professor of Theology and Human Development (Emeritus), Emory University. Named a Candler Professor in 1987, Fowler earned his Ph.D. at Harvard University in Religion and Society in 1971, with a focus in ethics and sociology of religion. He taught at Harvard Divinity School (1969–75) and at Boston College (1975–76). He pursued postdoctoral studies at the Center for Moral Development at the Harvard Graduate School of Education (1971–72). In 1977 he joined the faculty of the Candler School of Theology. His pioneering research and the resulting theory of faith development have earned him international recognition. His best-known book, *Stages of Faith: The Psychology of Human Development and the Quest for Meaning*, is in its fortieth printing and has been translated into German, Korean, and Portugese editions. Portions of it have been translated into Danish, Dutch, Swedish, Icelandic, Japanese, and an Indonesian dialect. He has written or edited eleven other books and more than sixty articles, contributing to the fields of practical theology and theological ethics. Four volumes of critical discussion of Fowler's research and theory have emerged from national and international seminars devoted to his work. He has received the

Oskar Pfister Award from the American Psychiatric Association, "for enduring contributions to the dialogue between religion and psychiatry," and the William James Award from the American Psychological Association, "for contributions that advance the psychology of religion." Both awards came in 1994. In 1999 the University of Edinburgh awarded him a doctor of divinity degree, *honoris causa.* Dr. Fowler is a minister in the United Methodist Church.

James Gaffney, professor emeritus of ethics at Loyola University in New Orleans, is currently teaching in the Theology Department of the University of St. Thomas, in St. Paul, Minnesota. He was for many years a Jesuit and, after resuming lay status, continued to teach in Jesuit university faculties. He has held visiting professorships at a number of universities in the United States, Europe, and Africa, and has published many books and articles. His latest publication is a chapter on ethical aspects of patriotism, in *Ethics and Politics*, edited by Igor Primoratz. He is an active participant in Muslim-Christian dialogue, currently preparing a collaborative publication on moral judgments of warfare in those two traditions.

Michael Paul Gallagher, SJ, is an Irish Jesuit priest, at present professor of fundamental theology at the Gregorian University, Rome, where he is also dean of the faculty of theology. Previously he taught modern literature for nearly twenty years at Ireland's largest state university. He is the author of nine books on pastoral or theological themes.

Howard Gray, SJ, presently serves as special assistant to the president of Georgetown University. Previously, he was founding director of the Center for Ignatian Spirituality at Boston College and then rector of the Jesuit community at John Carroll University and also assistant to the president for mission and identity there. Within the Jesuit order, Father Gray has filled a number of leadership positions including that of provincial superior of the Detroit Province, rector of the Jesuit community at the Weston Jesuit School of Theology (Cambridge, MA), and tertianship director.

Dennis Hamm, SJ, is professor of theology at Creighton University, where he has taught Scripture for thirty-two years in both the undergraduate and graduate divisions. He holds the Graff Endowed Faculty Chair of Catholic Theology. His articles have appeared in *Biblica*, *The Catholic Biblical Quarterly*, *The Journal of Biblical Literature*, *The Journal for the Study of the New Testament*, *The Way*, *The Bible Today*, *Church*, *Worship*, and *America*. His most recent book is a commentary on the Acts of the Apostles in the Collegeville Bible in the New Collegeville Bible Commentary.

Ron Hansen was born and raised in Nebraska and educated at Creighton University, the University of Iowa's Writers Workshop, and at Stanford University, where he was a Wallace Stegner Creative Writing Fellow. He is the author of the novels *Desperadoes* (1979), *The Assassination of Jesse James by the Coward Robert Ford* (1983), *Mariette in Ecstasy* (1991), *Atticus* (1996), and *Hitler's Niece* (1999). He has also published a children's book, *The Shadowmaker* (1987), a book of stories, *Nebraska* (1989), and the collection of essays *A Stay Against Confusion: Essays on Faith and Fiction* (2001), and he has edited two short-story anthologies, *You Don't Know What Love Is* (1987) and *You've Got to Read This: Contemporary American Writers Introduce Stories That Held Them in Awe* (1994). His last published novel was the screwball comedy *Isn't It Romantic?* (2003). He has recently completed a novel, *Exiles*, on Gerard Manley Hopkins and his writing of "The Wreck of the Deutschland." He teaches at Santa Clara University, where he is the Gerard Manley Hopkins, SJ, Professor in the Department of English.

Patrick A. Heelan, SJ, studied geophysics, quantum field theory, and philosophy of science. He published many papers on how deeply interpretation is involved in perception and in the natural sciences through the human bodily engagement with things and measuring instruments. He taught at University College (Dublin), Fordham University, State University of New York at Stony Brook, and presently teaches courses on the philosophy of science, and science and religion at Georgetown University. A Festschrift in his honor was edited by Babette Babich-Strong: *Hermeneutics of Natural Science, Van Gogh's Eyes, and God: Essays in Honor of Patrick A. Heelan, SJ* (Dordrecht/Boston: Kluwer, 2002).

Monika Hellwig (1929-2005) was born in Breslau, Silesia, which was then part of Germany. Her Catholic father and mother of Dutch Jewish background and an adult convert to Catholicism moved the family to Berlin in 1935, and then, to flee Hitler, to Limburg in the southern Netherlands. After the war, Hellwig earned a law degree from the University of Liverpool and at twenty-two joined the Medical Mission sisters. After her novitiate, she studied in the United States at the Catholic University of America, studied linguistics at the University of Oklahoma, and was then sent to Rome to be a ghostwriter for a Vatican official during Vatican Council II. When she returned to the States, she left her congregation and completed a doctorate in theology at Catholic University in 1968. She taught at Georgetown for twenty-eight years, becoming the Landegger Distinguished Professor of Theology. Early in her years at Georgetown, she adopted three children. Writing and lecturing extensively, nationally and internationally, she received thirty-two honorary degrees and fifteen named awards, and served as president of the Catholic Theological Society of America. Her published works include: *Understanding Catholicism, Jesus the Compassion of God, The Eucharist and the Hunger of the World, A Case for Peace in Reason and Faith* and *Guests of God: Stewards of Divine Creation*. In 1996, she left Georgetown to become the executive director and then president of the Association of Catholic Colleges and Universities, which she led until 2005. Just a month before her death of a cerebral hemorrhage, she had become a senior fellow at the Woodstock Theological Center at Georgetown University.

Michael J. Himes, a Catholic diocesan priest, is professor of theology at Boston College. His books include *Fullness of Faith: The Public Significance of Theology* (with Kenneth R. Himes, OFM), *Doing the Truth in Love: Conversations about God, Relationships, and Service*, and *Ongoing Incarnation: Johann Adam Möhler and the Beginnings of Modern Ecclesiology*. He is the coeditor of *Finding God in All Things* and *The Legacy of the Tübingen School* and the translator of J. S. Drey's *Introduction to the Study of Theology*. He has taught and lectured widely in the United States, Canada, Europe, and Australia.

David Lonsdale teaches Christian spirituality in graduate programs at Heythrop College, University of London. He is a former editor of

The Way, a review of Christian spirituality, and author of two books on Ignatian spirituality and discernment as well as numerous articles. In 2006–7 he held the Veale Chair in Christian Spirituality at the Milltown Institute, Dublin, Ireland. He has been involved in adult Christian education and formation for more than twenty years and his books have been translated into several languages.

Javier Melloni Ribas, SJ, was born in Barcelona, Spain, in 1962. He has a doctorate in theology and a master's degree in cultural anthropology. He is a member of *Cristianisme i Justicia* and professor of spiritual theology in the Faculty of Theology of Cataluña. A specialist in interfaith spirituality and dialogue, he has had several extended stays in India. His publications include *Los caminos del corazón: Una aproximación a la Filocalia* (Sal Terrae, 1995); "Los ciegos y el elefante: El diálogo interreligioso" (*Cuadernos de Cristianisme i Justicia* 97 [1999]); *La mistagogía de los Ejercicios Espirituales de San Ignacio* (Mensajero-Sal Terrae, 2001); *El Uno en lo multiple: Aproximación a la diversidad y unidad de las religiones* (Sal Terrae, 2003). He lives at the Jesuit retreat house in Manresa.

Ronald Modras is professor of theological studies at St. Louis University, where he has taught since 1979. He received his doctorate in theology at the University of Tübingen, Germany. He has written and lectured widely on Ignatian spirituality and Jesuit education. He initiated and wrote scripts for *Shared Vision*, a three-part video series on the Ignatian mission of Jesuit education and is the author of *Ignatian Humanism: A Dynamic Spirituality for the 21st Century* (Loyola Press).

Suzanne Zuercher, OSB, is a member of the Benedictine Sisters of Chicago. She is a licensed clinical psychologist with a master's degree from Loyola University Chicago. She served as a campus minister at Loyola and staff member and codirector of its Institute for Spiritual Leadership. For twelve years she was president of St. Scholastica Academy in Chicago. She is a pioneer in the spirituality of the enneagram and has lectured in North America, Europe, and throughout Asia, and has authored *Enneagram Spirituality, Enneagram Companions,* and *Merton, An Enneagram Profile.* She works with Wright Directions, a consulting firm serving faith-based organizations.

Index

About the Editor

George W. Traub, SJ, has spent more than two decades fostering a greater understanding of the Jesuit mission and nurturing Ignatian identity in higher education.

A Jesuit for more than fifty years, his passion has always been Ignatian spirituality—studying it, teaching it, writing about it, practicing it, and guiding others in this spiritual pathway. He is trained to lead the Ignatian Spiritual Exercises, having interned under Walter Farrell, SJ, at Colombiere Center, Clarkston, MI, and has since directed and trained others in directing the Exercises. In the first half of the 1980s, he served as director of early and continuing formation for Chicago Province Jesuits. He received his graduate degree in theology and spirituality from Loyola University Chicago and his PhD in English literature from Cornell University. He is Jesuit professor of theology and executive director of Ignatian Programs/Mission and Identity at Xavier University.

Traub is the author of *Do You Speak Ignatian? A Glossary of Terms Used in Ignatian and Jesuit Circles* (Xavier University, 1997), now in its tenth edition; is the coauthor of *The Desert and the City: An Interpretation of the History of Christian Spirituality* (Macmillan, 1969; Loyola University Press, 1984); and has edited *A Jesuit Education Reader* (Loyola Press, 2008), which is a companion volume to his reader on Ignatian spirituality.